Christ, Stress and Glory

Cover: *Cornerstone* by Leigh Hurlock.

You are built upon the foundations of the apostles and prophets, and Christ Jesus himself is the cornerstone. Every structure knit together in him grows into a holy temple in the Lord.

Ephesians 20–1

May I see God's face
And gaze to my fill on his likeness.

Psalm 17:16 (trans Flood)

For the Lord hath pleasure in his people . . .
Let the saints be joyful with glory:
Let them rejoice in their beds.

Psalm 149:4–5
The Book of Common Prayer

It is the purpose of God that we should 'share the likeness of
his Son' – here and now.
Glory to the Father for such a plan
Glory to the Son for such a pattern
Glory to the Spirit for such empowering
Glory be to God on high

Donald Coggan, *The Servant-Son*, p. 106

Christ, Stress and Glory

The Foundation Guide to Overload

WANDA NASH

DARTON · LONGMAN + TODD

First published in 1997 by
Darton, Longman and Todd Ltd
1 Spencer Court
140–142 Wandsworth High Street
London SW18 4JJ

ISBN 0–232–52178–6

A catalogue record for this book is available
from the British Library.

Unless otherwise stated, the biblical references in
this book are taken from the New Jerusalem Bible, published and
copyright 1985 by Darton, Longman & Todd Ltd and
Doubleday & Co. Inc.

Designed by Sandie Boccacci.
Set in 10.5/12.5 pt Bembo by Intype London Ltd.
Printed and bound in Great Britain by
Redwood Books, Trowbridge, Wiltshire.

I should like to dedicate this book to the many officers and members of the International Stress Management Association of which, until recently, I was UK Chair. The generosity and optimism with which people from around sixty disciplines have shared their experience and expertise underpins everything presented here. They all work for a better world. Thank you to each of them.

Contents

PART 2: SKILLS OF THE MIND

PART 3: SKILLS OF THE EMOTIONS

Foreword

The author of this book has had very considerable experience in meeting with people as individuals and in groups. In doing so, she has brought relief and health (in its deepest sense) to many. She has also looked long and hard into the documents which go to make up the Christian Scriptures, and especially into the four Gospels. In this book she seeks to bring the two together – people with their needs, Scriptures with their bearing on those needs.

One of the greatest gifts that Christianity has to make to society at the end of our second millennium is the gift of silence and the understanding of it – silence in public worship, silence in our houses, silence in our lives as individuals. Ours is a noisy age – traffic, television and radio, social intercourse. We seem to be afraid of silence. So we grow a society frenetic and shallow; it needs, perhaps more than anything else, to stop talking, to relax, to withdraw, to listen, and so to be renewed.

This is a down-to-earth book, with many illustrations drawn from life to help us see what the author is getting at and to aid us in getting there. 'Down-to-earth' – so it should be, for it directs us to him who 'came down' to meet our human needs. I wish the book well.

DONALD COGGAN
Archbishop of Canterbury 1974–80

Introduction

Jesus Christ never fudged things. Take suffering, for instance: he took it on board, looked it squarely in the face, and did something about it. The evidence in the four Gospels is that he did something like that with stress. This book concentrates on the *Hows* of taking stress on board and making sense of it, and it focuses on how Jesus himself managed it. There are any number of books that examine the theology and teaching of Jesus; this one is concerned simply with his behavioural responses.

Today the subject of 'stress' has a high profile. It is almost always associated with images that weigh one down, like a heavy weight, a steamroller, a trap; something to avoid, to get out from under, to get away from. Stress is so much a part of our lives – some say an essential component of our strategy for survival – that if we were to dispose of it altogether we would be living vegetables. Maybe there is a *usefulness* to stress. Maybe if we take it on board, look it squarely in the face, we can find out something about turning it into glory, the glory of the Kingdom of God.

Something else emerges from this book. Maybe 'stress' is a modern equivalent for the term 'suffering' as it applied to many lives before we had our sophisticated means of dealing with ill health. Suffering used to be seen as a pivotal experience, one that led directly to bitterness and despair, or opened a doorway to God. Does stress always put barriers in our way? Or can stress be a doorway which opens up towards God?

The writers of each of the four Gospels approach stress quite differently. Matthew shows us his keen awareness of the stresses that came at Jesus. He notes with considerable detail the prophecies and expectations which are ranged around him.

Mark records the responses of Jesus to these stresses. The decisions and actions of Jesus are carefully recorded, and in particular his efficient use of energy, and the aptitude of his chosen responses.

Luke pictures for us the towering persona, the awesome presence, of Jesus the Christ; it leaps out at us from each event. Luke makes us feel we are there, right in the presence of someone who is physically powerful, totally single-minded, and who has a personality that is purposeful and in control.

In John the text carries more of the metaphor, the meanings within the stories and the way these underlie the coping strategies of Jesus. The continual confrontations with the Pharisees are highlighted, and their spiritual testing of Jesus. The fourth Gospel describes how he turns everything around into the glory of God. John lifts us up.

Nowhere do we find any hint that Jesus was cowed by stress, although it can be argued that he had the most stress-provoking task the world has ever known. What can we learn from his management of stress in his day, which will inform our management of stress in our day? As this book progresses, we will be looking at how he dealt with the stresses coming at him in his daily life, and at how we more commonly deal with the stresses coming at us in our daily lives. Overall the stories of Jesus' passion are too momentous to be discussed in terms of 'stress'; they are too full of awe and mystery for this sort of everyday scrutiny.

The Main Content

In Mark 12:28–34 there is an incident where a lawyer listens totally absorbed on the edge of a group of learned religious leaders while they try to catch Jesus out. Let's call this man Levi. Twice the priests pose trick questions, involving queries which have been contrived to press Jesus into a corner. Levi is enthralled by the way Jesus handles the situation, and with the calm logic he uses to straighten out their verbal twisting.[1] Levi appreciates these answers; not only their cleverness, but the way they demonstrate Jesus' undeflected grip on the truth. In addition, they are very practical. Levi is a literalist and a perfectionist, and all his life he has yearned to know which is the absolute *best* way to live. Now is his chance, and after a pause while he summons his courage he asks, 'Which is the very first of all the commandments?' Jesus turns and looks at him; he sees the integrity and insight of Levi, the directness of the question which is unlike the others. He knows that Levi wants the whole truth, it doesn't have to fit in with his covert agenda. So Jesus calls out firmly:

'The Lord our God is the one, only, Lord, and
you must love the Lord your God with all your heart,
with all your soul,
with all your mind
and with all your strength.'

Levi could have jumped for joy, but the moment is too solemn for
that. He is a leader of theological students himself and he knows Jesus
is right – 'Well spoken, Sir!' he says. 'This is far more important than
any burnt offering or sacrifice!' Never before in the Scriptures have
those four categories been put together in just this way.[2] The four
areas of the personality, woven into a whole, have never previously
been recognised so acutely:

- the heart, signifying all emotions, dedicated to the glory of God;
- the soul, implying the things to do with values and vision, directed
  to the service of the one God;
- the mind, and all the mental activities gifted to us, used to further
  the advance of the purposes of God; and
- the strength (or might), which involves every physical faculty we
  have care of, tuned to advance His Kingdom.

Jesus recognised how close to the Kingdom of God Levi had come,
and the wisdom which had clothed his reply.

We, too, shall be looking at each of these categories, in a different
order, and we will find that each level has its own startlement.

Things to do with the body are the easiest to observe, and they
have grown in priority as we become more concerned with the
environment and how we behave. The tools with which we have
been supplied on the physical level can be misused, and stress may
result. The surprise here is the way in which Jesus re-tuned stress and
suffering into glory; but in the Gospels there is never a glorification
of suffering. Jesus' use of his physical skills gives us permission to use
ours as effectively.

Things to do with the mind will follow. In our age mental skills are
highly developed and highly rewarded. The startling thing is that
even when these tools are fully stretched they are inadequate to deal
with stress on their own. A person cannot be reduced to, nor confined
by, their thinking. To 'define' something is to 'determine the limits
of'[3] it; and it has been said[4] that cogitation is another way of spelling

'co-agitation'. Jesus' use of his keen mentality shows us how to sharpen ours, as tools; but not to be limited by them as controllers.

Things to do with the heart are less definable. How I act depends on what I think, and how I think is coloured by what I feel. The tools of strong feelings and emotions are often covered and held back; we know they are so powerful that they can lead to hurt and damage just as much as to healing and glory. The surprise is the extent to which Jesus used his strong emotions to express where he was, but without loading them on to others. His wise use of the tools of the emotions leads us to be more courageous with ours.

Things to do with the spirit are deepest of all, and in connection with stress management they are the least discussed today. While they remain hidden and little identified, their power to balance remains untapped. It can be said that our present world is full of beings, but it is remarkably short of Being. The astonishment is the way in which Jesus demonstrates this with his feet, rather than with his words.

The synthesis of these four categories, body, mind, feelings and spirit, is represented by a Celtic knot in Appendix 1 of this book.

We are each left with the responsibility of recognising and maintaining our own tools: where someone has been given much, much will be expected of him, and the more he has had entrusted to him, the more will be demanded of him.[5] The Gospels are shot through with this concern with personal responsibility. Have you noticed? *Everyone mentioned in the Gospels is an individual*! Except for the threesome at Bethany, no one person is attended to by Jesus simply because they belong to a social unit; in the Gospels there is not even a 'normal' family! We are *all* treated as individual entities, each with our unique supply of tools, skills, and circumstances.

To counterbalance this somewhat frightening responsibility, God responds with profligate provision and – to us – a crazy extravagance of love. Just look at a few of the stories of this astonishing outpouring of generosity:

- the super-abundant wine released towards the end of the party at Cana;
- the baskets of pieces left over at the mammoth picnics – none of the fragments were left to rot but were *all collected in*, every scrap was valued and gathered into baskets for further use;

- the welcome given to the prodigal son – his elderly and respected father looking out for him and breaking into a run to hug him with joy; the carefully nurtured calf which was food for hundreds, not just the welcoming party of the extended family;
- the reward of the labourers who, through no fault of their own, arrived at work late in the day but who were paid for a full day;
- the worthfulness of any chosen sacrifice, when Jesus tells us that what we leave for the sake of him or the good news or the Kingdom of God will be replaced many times over in this life as well as receiving the gift of infinite life in the next.[6]

With such generosity, all things are possible: over and over again we see that God is the inexhaustible source of ingenuity and the unfathomable wellspring of initiative and love and generosity.

This is to God's glory. It is not a matter of triumphalism; nor is it about being intransigently positive. Positive thinking is all very well at the right time and in the right place, but this book is about facing up to what *is*, without any self-protective tunnel vision. All the elements of our highly sophisticated personal skills are in the Gospels, but often they pass unrecognised for what they are. These very same tools are the ones our Lord took hold of and used, not only to deal with the stresses that came at him, but to turn those stresses to the glory of God.

Following Jesus Christ through the four Gospels with this in mind is a fascinating activity. There is such a huge variety of incidents and stories recorded there, and to watch the very human choices in behaviour with which he responds to them is totally absorbing. Jesus himself turns out to be the stress manager par excellence of all time, and he role-models (in total accuracy!) the optimum way of acknowledging and processing the demands made upon us today.

Perhaps even more important are those things we can learn from Jesus' human behaviour about turning the problems and sufferings of our world to the glory of God. Is that possible today? Is it taking it a bit too far? *Or is it essential* in order to avoid being driven by our present cultural climate to race over the edge like the Gadarene swine?

The 'Whys' of This Book

These are threefold.

Firstly, my own intense interest in the subject. During the many years that I have been involved with presenting stress management courses and conferences to a wide variety of people I have observed a double hang-up. Groups which are largely made up of professional or business people are reluctant to discuss the area of meanings, directions, purposes, and the spiritual values of their lives. Those groups which are made up of people who express their interest in things of the spirit, have suggested that all they have to do is pray and they will have all the resources of the Holy Spirit to call upon, so why should they consider the needs of the body? My own concern is to claim God's provision in every area, and His[7] expectation that all the tools He provides should be well maintained and well used.

Secondly, I have been asked to put the fruit of this experience into a book for the use of anyone who may be interested in it either for themselves or for encouraging those with whom they come into contact.

And thirdly, this book will be the foundation text of a training course for leaders who want to present the material themselves. For this purpose, the charts in the Appendices can be enlarged and photocopied to make tutorial handouts.[8]

The 'Hows' of This Book

The use of Bibles

Since I am not a biblical scholar, in preparing this material I have relied heavily on comparing various translations of the Bible which are readily available to the public. The versions I have most used are:

> The King James Authorised Version, OUP (AV)
> The Revised English Bible, OUP and CUP, 1989 (REB)
> The New Revised Standard Version, Geoffrey Chapman, 1993 (NRSV)
> The New Jerusalem Bible, DLT, 1990 (NJB)
> The Good News Edition, Bible Society, 1976 (GNB)
> The Living Bible, as paraphrased by Kenneth Taylor, Hodder & Stoughton, 1965 (LB)
> The New Testament in Modern English, paraphrased by J.B. Phillips, Geoffrey Bles, 1960 (JB)
>
> and, The New Living Translation, Tyndale Publishers, 1996 (NLT), published three weeks before the final draft of this manuscript was handed to the publisher.

Comparison of the text from all these presentations of the four Gospels has contributed significantly to my thinking; for easy reading of texts lifted out of their context, and for ease of copyright, the New Jerusalem Bible has been the most used for all Gospel quotations. Attribution to another rendering has been specifically noted.

The arrangement of text references has been somewhat arbitrary. On the whole, single references have been left in the body of the page, while multiple references have been put into the notes of each chapter at the end of the book. Where words in quoted texts have been emphasised with italics, this choice of emphasis is mine.

As you embark on the journey of discovery, I hope (with some trepidation) that some of the things that have enthralled me will also be of use to you, and that something in these pages will spark even more joy in you. As Dame Julian says: 'Jesus our courteous lord waits to solace and mirth his dearworthy friends with marvellous melody of endless love.'[9] That promise is for each and every one of us.

Jesus Christ as Human Being

– a Model of Human Response to Stress?

•••

It's up to you. You may want to leave this discussion to the end, it rather depends upon what has prompted you to read the book. If you are primarily interested in how Jesus Christ as a human being dealt with the stresses that came at him, start here. If you are more gripped by ideas of how to tackle the stresses that we, today, have to deal with, and how we can do so in a way that follows Christ, then start at chapter 1.

The following pages are an invitation to explore the peculiar circumstances of the life that Jesus lived, and the tactics that he devised to tackle them. In particular, we will be looking at the behaviour of his responses, rather than at the themes of his teaching. Overall, the argument is this:

- twenty centuries ago there was one human being who – in perfect communion with his Father – met the extraordinary stresses which were coming at him with efficiency and effectiveness;
- not only this, but he managed to re-tune them to the glory of God. This being so, are there ways of behaving that we could shadow in our century,
- to the benefit of ourselves and our environment,
- and also to the greater advance of the Kingdom of God?

Stress itself is an enormously complex subject. As soon as you think you've got hold of it, whether for yourself or for others, it slips away and takes up another shape. In trying to describe it, there are three basic components to identify: stressors, stress-signs, and stress-skills.

xx   *Christ, Stress and Glory*

Stressors

The things that we perceive as causing us stress are often defined in terms of demands and expectations. These demands and expectations may come across to us from others (or at least we *think* they are demands and expectations coming across from others, and this is something very different but it has similar effects); or from ourselves. As we shall see, these differentiations are important, but it calls for a high degree of self-awareness to discriminate between them.

If these stressors seem to demand more of ourselves or our resources than we feel we have available to us, or they seem to demand more of ourselves than we are willing to expend, then we will experience negative stress.

If these stressors demand resources that we feel we can and want to expend, then the stress we experience will be positive. Many people say of themselves that they 'thrive under pressure', they actually enjoy responding to challenge.[1]

The ideal is for each of us to recognise the stressors for what they are, and then to choose methods of dealing with them that neither deny their pressure, nor drain us of the power to use them constructively. The crucial point is whether I am aware of the range of tools I could use in the situation, and whether I can deliberately *choose* to apply whichever is the most apt for *this* specific circumstance *now*.

Stress-signs

These are the effects in each of the areas of body, mind, feelings and spirit which reveal the destructive nature of over-stress. Levels of unacceptable stress differ from person to person, and the way in which this distress is shown varies from one individual to another. There is no one stressor that will produce the same stress-signs in every person. The definition and measurement of causation and effects are notoriously elusive in the field of stress management.

Stress-signs may be *of the body*, such as muscular tension, fatigue, lowered resistance to disease, insomnia, difficulties with the functioning of any of the major systems of the body – breathing, circulation, digestion, sensing, skin, reproduction; or *of the mind*, such as confusion, blankness, difficulties with decision-making, bewilderment with priorities, anxiety, inability to say 'no'; or *of the feelings*, such as irritability, intolerance, becoming overwhelmed, isolation, low self-worth; or *of the spirit*, such as aridity, lack of purpose, and that particular threat of our times, meaninglessness.

Stress-skills

This is a useful term which includes the responses, behaviours and attitudes that form adaptive responses to stress. It covers the tools and talents that are natural to any particular personality, and also those that are consciously developed. Sometimes an attitude or response may appear to be contrived, but if the result enlarges that person's ability to cope with stress, and makes them easier to live with, and to contribute better to God's Kingdom, then it is more than worth the necessary effort.

The Experience of Jesus Christ as Human Being

The *expectations and demands* that assaulted Jesus as he lived on this earth came at him from all levels. They are unparalleled in history. It's worth taking a little time over the following list, and stepping aside from the usual way we think of Jesus. He was a man with flesh such as ours, nerves such as ours, and the full gamut of emotions such as we have. With some imagination, it is staggering to think that that was the equipment he had to deal with the following:

- He was born into a nation which, having been through the oppression of a series of political occupiers, lived on the expectation of release. This expectation also included release from the oppression of sin. The phenomenal double task was to be undertaken by a single idealised man. Never before or since has a people built up such an expectation over centuries of prophecy. The concept of the Messiah was unique. It pervaded every aspect of life.
- In the immediate months *before* Jesus was born, those who were to care for him experienced dreams and visions; announcements came from angels to those who were to be closest to him; and supranormal happenings changed the physical bodies of women who were to nurture him. In whatever spiritual context these events were interpreted, they could do nothing but raise to an exceptional level the expectations put upon this singular and precious new child.
- In the immediate months *after* Jesus was born, those around him

experienced the excitement of the shepherds, the ones who witnessed the angels and heard about the glory that was to follow the birth of this young baby. The adults caring for Jesus – who included Mary and Joseph, his grandmother Anna, and his aunt Elizabeth – experienced the surprise of the welcome of Simeon and Anna the prophetess when Jesus was presented at the Temple. In stark contrast, they also experienced the horror and bewilderment of an uncontainable consequence: his birth had panicked their temporal king into ordering the slaughter of all the baby's boy peers. This was followed by the divine command to undergo self-imposed exile in a foreign land for the safety of this one child. And added to all this was the unforeseeable homage of wise men gathering at their door from unknown lands. The compound effect of this series of events bringing unprecedented attention could not fail to raise their expectations of the child Jesus.

- As Jesus grew, these vast expectations were tempered by an ordinary life lived in an ordinary town in an ordinary way. The only unordinary record during the thirty hidden years of his life is marked by an overdeveloped expectation that Jesus had towards his own parents. The fact that he held this idea at all tells us volumes about the way he had been brought up. Jesus, as a young lad of twelve, expected of his parents that, when he 'disappeared' for three days, they would necessarily know he was safe in the great golden Temple of Jerusalem, seeking the company of the most learned theologians in the land.

- The time came for Jesus to launch into his own public ministry, leaving the carpenter's shop and the home of his mother to begin his peripatetic career. The first thing he met was the acclamation of his strange cousin John, wildly asserting that he was the Lamb of God. The singular effect that he, Jesus, had on this popular, sensational, roaring prophet was obeisance ('I am not fit . . .'), and the impulse of John's own disciples to leave him and join Jesus. This situation was galvanised by the expectations of the longing crowds and their political and spiritual frustrations, and it is difficult to underplay. The psychodynamics of a scene that engaged such a criss-cross of projections, needs and demands is hard to absorb for us today. And Jesus Christ, as yet inexperienced in the control of mass emotion, found himself in the thick of it. In our human understanding, the stresses and temptations of this scene are colossal; the risks to Jesus as a man, and to the mission of God as carried by him, were beyond ordinary management.

What did he do, how did he respond? *He walked away into the desert. He disappeared from public view.*

• When Jesus reappeared in public the demands and expectations put upon him increased. References to just a few will do to signify some of them. They came at him both from the crowds who watched him ceaselessly, and from those close to him, who knew him well.[2]

Luke 3:15–16 Everyone was expecting the Messiah to come soon. This was the question of the hour, and was being discussed everywhere.

Mark 2:13 And he went forth again by the seaside; and all the multitude resorted unto him (AV).

John 6:2 A huge crowd were following him wherever he went, to watch him heal the sick.

Luke 5:17 It seemed that men turned up from every village in all Galilee and Judea, as well as from Jerusalem.

John 2:23 Many people were convinced that he was indeed the Messiah.

John 3:1 A Jewish leader said, 'We all know that God has sent you to teach us'.

John 2:5 'Do whatever he tells you to do . . .'

Luke 8:4 A large crowd was gathering to hear him – many others were still on their way, coming from other towns.

Luke 4:36 'Even the demons obey him'/'he gets his power from Satan'/'even the winds and storms obey him'.

Matt. 9:18 The rabbi of the local synagogue worshipped him and said: 'My little daughter has just died; you can bring her back to life again'!

Matt. 12:18–21 Jesus quotes God speaking to Isaiah: 'See my Chosen One! He is my Beloved, in whom my soul delights. I will put my Spirit upon him, and he will judge the nations. He does not fight or shout; he does not raise his voice! He does not crush the weak, or quench the smallest hope; he will end all conflict with his final victory, and his name shall be the hope of all the world.'

Luke 19:38 'Hosannah to the King!' an expression of the high expectations in the crowd and among the children as Jesus approached Jerusalem riding on the back of a young donkey.

All these expectant masses were in effect demanding of Jesus:
Save us! Answer us! Heal us! Feed us! Deliver us! Give us a sign!

• There was also that strange phenomenon of people falling down

in front of Jesus. Jairus, the eminent citizen, 'came . . .and fell at
Jesus' feet and pleaded with him' (Luke 8:41); the suffering woman
who had bled for twelve years 'came forward trembling and falling
at his feet explained . . .' (Luke 8:47); Legion, the man tormented
of demons, as soon as he saw Jesus, 'gave a shout, fell at his feet
and cried out at the top of his voice . . .' (Luke 8:28); on the
mountain when God spoke from the cloud, the disciples 'fell on
their faces . . .' (Matt. 17:6); and even at the final chapter of Jesus'
life, the soldiers coming to arrest him in the Garden of Gethsemane
'all fell backwards to the ground' (John 18:6). These incidents by
their very nature would be alarming and stress-engendering.

- Besides the yearnings among the masses for redemption from their
  personal cares, there were various other forms of expectation which
  Jesus had to meet, some of them tried extravagantly to put him
  down. There were the suspicions and deviousness of the community leaders. For instance, the Pharisees and Jewish leaders who
  were waiting to trap him:
  Luke 19:47 The chief priests and other religious leaders and the
    business community were trying to find some way to get rid of
    him . . .
  Luke 11:53 The Pharisees and legal experts were furious . . .trying
    to trap him.

- Perhaps even worse was the disbelief which came from those from
  whom Jesus could expect proper support. This disbelief meant he
  could not work miracles in his own home town. Even members
  of his close family are reported to have wanted to take him away
  from the people because they thought he was out of his mind
  (Mark 3:21).

  Three times during his ministry the fickle crowd which cheered
  him at one moment, turned upon him and tried to drive him out
  or stone him. Once in his home town of Nazareth (Luke 4:29),
  again outside the Temple in Jerusalem (John 8:59), and also following his discourse at the feast of Dedication (John 10:31). These
  incidents were of course capped by the crowd shrieking for his
  eventual crucifixion during the passion which led to his death.

- Perhaps the thing with the greatest pull of all upon Jesus was when
  he came in touch with the mystical hopes and yearnings of this
  great spiritual nation:
  John 1:10 Although he made the world, when he came into it the
    world didn't recognise him.

These many and conflicting reactions to his ministry would in themselves be a cause of infinite stress in the ordinary way. How did Jesus, the man, cope?

Jesus' Human Response – and His Use of Stress-skills

There can be no doubt about the stressors that were levelled at Jesus Christ as he lived his human life on earth. Our task is to so examine his response to these human stressors, that we can learn from him how we can apply similar responses to the stressors that come at us in our lives. There is no one who can claim they have more cause for human stress than he did. In his earthly life Jesus Christ was a Master Exemplar of the craft of Stress Management. He chose his tools with accuracy, and applied them with care and precision – he was, after all, a carpenter. In him we have a model which makes use of all the same tools with which we are supplied; the four Gospels are full of hints about how he engineered them, but some of this description is so encrusted with the piety of the ages that their everyday, every-hour relevance has been lost. Nevertheless, his economy of energy, his total present-mindedness, and his continual communication with his Father are remarkable. These things would have enabled him to recognise the imminence of stress-signs. But there is no record of Jesus being affected by dysfunction in his body, mind, feelings or spirit. Such was the skill he used, that he was able to deflect them; this he did with the appropriate use of stress-skills.

It's as if the Creator has laid out specific tools on the workbench with which we ourselves can deal with stress, and then He leaves it to us to pick them up and test them out. We, as humans, each have to decide which of the range of tools is more appropriate to develop for our particular situation. Jesus Christ used them all, as we shall see in detail in the following pages, and we only need some of them. He needed to apply the whole range of tools in order to cope with the huge expectations with which he was faced.

In this preliminary section of the book, we shall look at some of the principles which guided Jesus in the use of these tools and skills. The major part of the book discusses specific situations. These main principles include:

– the way in which, from the very beginning, Jesus taught and practised self-awareness;

- the ways in which Jesus handled the expectations coming at him; and
- the way in which Jesus turned these demands and projections to the glory of God.

Jesus and Self-awareness

Jesus' knowledge of his own mission is indisputable. Whether he knew it in full as a twelve-year-old boy when he discussed major issues with the doctors of the Temple, or whether it grew gradually from then and through the trials in the desert, faced by Satan, we cannot know. But from the time that he is recorded as re-entering the public world and starting his ministry, Jesus always exercised acute awareness of the present moment and his personal role within it. As we shall see, he is constantly urging this ability on others. Textual evidence for this self-awareness includes the following.

(i) Personal self-assessment
The Gospels bear witness to constantly reiterated phrases coming as short bursts from Jesus. Verbal explosions such as 'Watch; be alert!'; 'He who has ears to hear, let him hear!'; 'Look to yourselves: be on your guard!'; 'Hold yourself in readiness!'[3] These are imperatives, and speak of his own attitude of continuous self-assessment, something that was important to him and which he wanted each one of us to develop. Jesus' knowledge of himself extended beyond this sharp sense of the present-moment, to the deep comprehension of his own mission and its consequences. For all his emphasis on humility, he accepted about himself that 'something greater than Solomon is here' (Luke 11:31); for all his yearning for unity, he knew that the immediate effect of his teaching would be one of division (Matt. 10:34 and Mark 13:8–10); and for all his unconditional loving, he foresaw that his own end would be one of excruciating suffering.

(ii) Personal decision
In the very first public exposure of his own ministry, Jesus demonstrated the basic principle on which he ran his own life. When his mother considered it was time to force his hand and make him demonstrate publicly his miraculous power of helping other people, he didn't deny this longing of hers, but he decided for himself when he should do what he did. He never denied the expectations of others; he very seldom reproved people for having them;[4] he was

fully aware of their implications both for those who held them and for himself. None the less he consistently kept for himself the responsibility of how he should act in *this* present moment, without ever allowing that decision to be taken over by others. Perhaps uniquely, perhaps to an extent it had never been done before, *Jesus resisted being hooked into the expectations of others*. With one exception: he would fulfil the expectation if, and only if, it contributed to the glory of God.

(iii) Personal truth

It is astonishing that, in the face of so much adulation – and condemnation,

- *Jesus did not collude with others in their desire to glorify him*. Time and time again Jesus judged that the only result of spreading the news of his accomplishments would be self-publicity. Perhaps he was also wary of the power of human exaggeration and lust for sensation. There are many references to the way he instructed recipients of his healing powers 'not to tell anyone'.[5]

    This contrasts sharply with the occasion when Jesus specifically tells someone to spread abroad the experience of the power of God. To the man formerly called Legion, Jesus said, 'Go back home and report all that God has done for you' (Luke 8:39).[6] The rarity with which Jesus asked others to promote his work verbally calls for two further comments which reflect on our behaviour:

- It is of great significance to us that Jesus went out of his way to *avoid increasing the expectations with which he was surrounded*; we ourselves are often in danger of actively courting high expectations from others. We take pride in extending our good reputation. Self-promotion is the name of the game. Image is all important. I belabour myself with trying to be more than I am, and simultaneously I look for confirmation of it from outside. We burden ourselves with possessions, qualifications and material crutches to give ourselves credibility, and then complain too much is asked of us. We get caught up in this double trap. Jesus was so sure of his own authority he didn't use these things in order to bolster himself.

- Jesus understood full well the difference between believing by report, and *believing through his own personal experience*. Much of our own stress is due to reliance on knowledge that is second- or third-hand. It takes too long to check it all out, and in our information-overloaded culture we are forced to take on the opinions and investigations of others. There is a vast difference between what I know, and what I think I know, but the two can be easily confused. At all times Jesus stayed with what he knew from his own personal experience. Others' experience, observed experience, he put into stories.

(iv) Personal response

The way Jesus behaved in any particular situation was governed by the issues of that situation alone. He responded, rather than reacted, to whatever happened. His ability to respond (response-ability) was strong and accorded with the real demand of the moment, it was not automatic – according to habit or custom. His answer to the irate religious leaders wanting condemnation of the woman caught in the act of adultery was full of originality and surprise to everyone (John 8:2–11); as were his responses to the paralytic let down through the roof (Mark 2:3–12) and his reply to the behaviour of Zacchaeus (Luke 19:2–10).

(v) Personal authority

Jesus was the author of his own authenticity. He was noted for his personal authority.[7] His own sense of 'I Am . . .' was markedly strong.[8] Just as he based his own knowledge on what he experienced for himself rather than hearsay, he allowed others to come and watch what went on, but not to re-interpret it. His self-knowing was rooted in what God his Father communicated to him.

> John 5:19 'In all truth I tell you, by himself the Son can do nothing; he can only do what he sees the Father doing.'
>
> John 6:38,40 'I have come from heaven not to do my will, but to do the will of him who sent me . . . It is my Father's will that whoever sees the Son and believes in him should have eternal life.'
>
> John 7:16 'My teaching is not from myself: it comes from the one who sent me; anyone who is prepared to do his will, will know whether my teaching is from God or whether I speak on my own account.'
>
> John 8:26 ' . . .the one who sent me is true, and what I declare to the world I have learnt from him.'
>
> John 8:28–9 'What I say is what the Father has taught me; he who sent me is with me, and has not left me to myself, for I always do what pleases him.'

> John 12:49 'For I have not spoken of my own accord; but the
> Father who sent me commanded me what to say and what
> to speak.'

(vi) Personal channelling

When others wanted to praise Jesus, such attempt to 'glorify' him
was *always* deflected away from himself and back onto the Father.

> Matt. 19:17 (LB) 'Why do you call me good? There is no-one
> good but one, that is, the Father.'
>
> Luke 11:28 A woman cried out, 'Blessed the womb that bore
> you!' Jesus replied, 'More blessed still are those who hear the
> word of God and keep it!'
>
> John 5:17 'My Father still goes on working, and I am at work
> too.'
>
> John 12:27–8 'Now my soul is troubled . . . it is for this very
> reason that I have come to this hour. Father, glorify your
> name!'
>
> John 13:20 'Whoever welcomes me, welcomes the one who
> sent me.'
>
> John 13:31 'Now has the Son of man been glorified . . . and
> God will in turn glorify him in himself.'

Jesus Christ's self-awareness undergirded his response to the
innumerable stresses that came at him. The things that were, for him,
'everyday' stressors. The ways with which he coped with the *worst*
stressors he met are even more noteworthy. The time he spent on his
own in the desert, assaulted by temptations of extreme hunger, the
prospect of easy power, and the lure of using divine grace to his own
ends; the time when his dearest friend was dying; the time when he
knew that all his disciples would be put under extreme public testing
for his sake; and the time when he foresaw them running away,
isolating him with the tormenting imperial guards: on all these
occasions he could have bewailed his fate and succumbed to feeling
a victim; what he did in fact was that he pointed to the *opportunities
they offered to glorify his Father.*

- In answer to the devil's invitations, he referred each time to the
  furthering of God's will (Luke 4:3–14);
- in answer to the call to see Lazarus, Jesus exclaimed, 'This sickness
  is to God's glory' (John 11:4);
- referring to their inevitable future trials, Jesus encouraged his dis-

ciples by calling them opportunities to publish the coming of God's Kingdom (Matt. 10:18; Mark 13:9);

- even with the prospect of his terrible desertion, Jesus allayed the guilt of his disciples by implying it was written in the Word of God, and that he would meet them again in Galilee after his resurrection (Mark 14:27–8).

'Giving the Glory to God' – Can *We*?

What does this term, 'glorifying God', mean in practical terms when we ourselves are under high levels of stress?

- It means to expand our awareness, in ourselves and others, of the presence of God in the midst of the trouble; to allow His purposes in our world, His peace, His power into the centre of our being, whatever the odds are against actually feeling it.
- It means to draw back the curtains a little, loosen the self-obsession, let God's own light flood in. To lift the masks and defences behind which we protect ourselves, even from the reality of God. To let go and let God.
- Then things can happen when, and as a result of experiencing stress, we can lay ourselves open to His way a bit more. A bit more like Jesus Christ did.

Compared with modern biography, the Gospels are very scrappy. In reading them closely we long for more detail, more information. We can't help being aware of how little we are actually told about Jesus. We are left to infer and deduce. One thing does shine clearly and constantly. Jesus the man took charge of his own responses, his own choices in answer to each and every incident, comment, happening in his life. He never simply reacted automatically, according to expectation or emotional reflex. That's what makes him so surprising, so endlessly full of invention, so commanding of our imitation and desire to follow him. He is the ultimate model for our response to stress. He is the stress manager par excellence.

In earlier times, theologians pointed up suffering as a doorway to God. Maybe today – when we have the technology to prevent or remove so much physical deformity and disease – stress itself can be seen in a similar light. Not the trouble and difficulty as such; but when we are aware of our own stress, the manner in which we choose to respond can become for us a doorway to God.

As Jesus Christ himself said:

'Look up! Lift up your heads! your [liberation (REB)] draweth nigh! Take heed to yourselves, lest at any time your hearts be overcharged with . . . the cares of this life.' (Luke 21:28,34 AV)

'Be on the alert! Praying at all times for strength . . . to stand in the presence of the Son of Man.' (Luke 21:35–6 REB)

Part 1

Skills of the Body

Responsibility for My Body Is Mine

Exercise, diet, fluids, relaxation

TO COUNTERACT:

Physical muscular tension
Tiredness, fatigue
Diet, and drink, imbalance
'There's nothing I can do . . . '
Being trapped, de-powered

••••••••••••••••••••••••••

Anne Other was tight. Not tight as in inebriated – she was quite the opposite of letting things go. Her lips were tight, her skirts were tight, she held her elbows tightly against her body, she crossed her arms, and crossed her knees. Perhaps, subconsciously, she was protecting herself.

Anne's shoulders were hard under her padded-shoulder jacket; she was armoured, and she was In The Right. It was too risky to see life from the other person's point of view, so she fixed her own horizons and then she wasn't frightened by them.

But – people didn't like her very much; she didn't have many friends. Anne knew that she talked little, ate little, slept little, and played never. That way she could be sure she was In Control.

Anne Other would say, quite often, 'I can't relax, I can't give in; I've got to hold myself together, so where's the point?' And she would tighten her belt another notch.

You must have met Anne; she is very near to most of us, even inside each of us somewhere.

Stress is such a funny thing. With some people – from the very best of motives – it brings out a pattern of responses like Anne's, they just tighten their control. Yet with others, it makes them 'go all to pieces', to break open too far. The same demands, the same threats, can affect different people in quite opposite ways.

Each of us is a bag of tools for God. He has supplied each of us (who are 'ordinary') with all the tools we need, and then He left us with the responsibility of developing the skills of how to use them. The trouble is that some of the tools may have been damaged along the way; some may have got neglected, or misused, or been inappropriately applied; some may still be lying in their original package, unopened, with the service manual still unread. Sometimes it needs someone else to help us to understand the instructions left with us by the maker. In the Gospels Jesus Christ puts the responsibility for choosing how to use these tools very firmly into our own hands, just as he himself took on the responsibility of caring for his own tools. We don't have to wait around until someone else points out that we should take more exercise, or eat more wisely, or make sure we get enough sleep – as if we needed permission from outside ourselves to look after ourselves. Jesus did everything that was necessary to make sure he was in proper condition to work for the glory of God. The first and most obvious layer of these tools is in the area of our physical selves.

When we feel that the demands being made upon us are too great we protect ourselves and stiffen up. Perhaps we feel we can't find the time to look after ourselves; we gobble our food; we drink too little – or too much; we don't exercise; we don't sleep well for worry. Particularly when we are trying really hard, we can convince ourselves that giving time to our own needs is 'selfish'; that the claims made on us by our relatives or the job or our commitment to others always have to take priority; and that looking after our own bodily tools is the last thing to be given attention. Ignoring myself can seem positively meritorious.

The things to do with the body are on the most obvious, tangible, pinchable, knowable level of our experience. Our bones, muscles, tendons and nerves are the very stuff of our here and now. Perhaps it is just *because* we think of them as so obvious that we override the signals they send us. It is easy to feel superior, that the mind is more important than the body, and that the things of the body are somehow connected with 'self-indulgence'. The dangers of greed, laziness and selfishness seem to overshadow our genuine need to service the tools in our bodies, and sometimes it seems that to deny our own appetites becomes a glorifying task. We can convince ourselves that in denying the regular needs of the body we will gain credit from somewhere. We may even become quite martyrish about it.

This is not the record of Jesus in the Gospels. Asceticism indeed does have its place, together with self-denial and fasting; bodily mortification has a long Christian tradition. But in these days of peculiarly high stress levels, when change and challenge and speed and information overload have reached degrees never experienced since the world began, it is crucial to keep all the tools that God has provided for us in good shape, in working order, in optimum performance, specifically to advance His Kingdom. That is the model of Jesus Christ in the four Gospels.

If we look at the record of how Jesus Christ used his bodily tools when he lived as a human being on this earth we come across some startling surprises.

Social drinking: Jesus' first public sign was to do with bodily things – social drinking. It wasn't a miracle to do with supplying the drought-ridden desert people with enough spring water to keep them healthy, although that would have sat well with our own standards of what is 'worthy'. It wasn't a pious act of transforming dangerous alcohol, or dirty sewage water, into something purer to drink. Jesus' first public sign was to do with providing a superfluity of wine towards the end of a dancing party. It was about enjoyment, enrichment, encouraging people to 'let go', lowering the barriers between people, so that those who had all sorts of financial and family worries in ordinary life could get away from them for a time. No doubt a good sleep would follow, and then they could return to their normal daily relationships with a greater sense of 'flow' and well-being.[1]

Water: Water was a significant symbol to Jesus: when he was thirsty he asked for it; he urged people to ask him for it when they were spiritually thirsty; he noticed when it wasn't offered to him to wash before a meal; he used it to wash the hot and dusty feet of his friends.[2]

Water is becoming better recognised for the amazing gift that it is, but some studies are still under-publicised. It has been shown that nearly everything we use to flavour water has a dehydrating effect. In addition to our usual intake of coffee, tea, alcohol, bottled waters, and canned mineral drinks, we should be giving our body-cells ordinary tap water with which to refurbish themselves. This is more essential than all the things we drink. Heated or chilled, it makes no difference, but in countries where public water is purified, tap water is better for our cellular fluid than any commercialised preparation. Several pints a day of straightforward tap water supplies us with calcium, iron and other minerals in addition to washing impurities out of our system and resaturating our cells. Since over three-quarters of our normal body-weight is made up of water, this is an issue to be taken seriously.

Eating together: Jesus also enjoyed the social activity of eating together. He invited himself to other people's houses for a meal, especially when he wanted to make friends of those who were hostile to him, or when he wanted to get to know the problems of those who were eager to meet him. He frequently used the image of feasting in the stories he created to wrap around his teaching. In everyday life he noticed the children who played at partying, and he defended his hungry disciples for picking corn that wasn't theirs. Jesus knew of the hunger of others, and took steps to more than satisfy it when the crowds listening to him were far away from home. The first thing he asked others to do for the little girl whom he brought back from death was to bring her some food. When he wanted to convince his disciples that he was 'real' after he returned from the dead he asked for food. And before he left this world he left his friends the remembrance of his presence in the form of bread.[3]

In spite of the importance of food, Jesus didn't spare worry and energy on what there was to eat, because he knew that God who created us understood our need and would provide for it, if only we would co-operate properly.[4]

Our popular media is crammed with ideas about 'good' eating, and material on this subject is available elsewhere. Obviously, any obsessional imbalance in the way we use our food needs professional help, but the following guidelines may help someone who has difficulty dealing with food to enjoy their body better. For instance, imagine the body using its own voice to say:

– please don't lumber me with more than satisfies my natural hunger;
– try re-educating my taste buds, so that flavours can get through to them without being smothered first by sweetness or grease;
– give my digestive system a treat by supplying it with food that is unprocessed (unless the digestion is delicate), so that the crunchiness and juiciness of raw fruit, barely-cooked vegetables, and fresh nuts can be properly appreciated;
– get into the habit of listening to my stomach, rather than my brain,

about what would please it. If only you would listen, they will soon tell you when they are too distended, or too shrivelled, or working too hard on heavy food, or needing something lighter for a change;

- interestingly, in a social gathering people tend to eat less, rather than more. If you enjoy the conversation and relationships, your satisfaction is less dependent on being physically over-filled;
- at times my digestive system positively wants a rest from all that churning, and it welcomes a bit of a break. Occasional fasting has had a good record down the centuries.

Exercise: Jesus exercised a great deal. In all his travels we are told only once that he used a donkey, although this was the usual form of transport for respected leaders. He travelled the length and breadth of his country, and neighbouring areas, on foot.[5]

The exercise popularised in the media can be expensive both in time and money. The need to release our muscles from the tension that everyday life locks into them can be met in ways that are easier and less expensive. For instance:

- Building frequent 'micro-breaks' of stretching, into every hour or so of whatever task I am doing. This has been shown to avoid the pile-up of tension in the muscles which results in strain.
- When I have to stay sitting, because I am in a meeting or on public transport for instance, without even moving my position I can deliberately tense groups of muscles and then let them go totally limp. In this way I can clear my head and let out the accumulating stress in my body at the same time.
- It costs nothing but a bit of effort to use the stairs in my house to get myself breathless two or three times a week; even running on the spot for a few minutes every day is a healthy, cheap way to exercise. It can be less boring if I use a cassette or listen to the radio while I am at it. It is not wise to push your body too far.
- Positively 'striding', in contrast to ambling sociably, for around twenty minutes every other day releases stress, improves the immune system, builds up my endorphins so I enjoy life better, reduces the risk of being attacked by depression, heart disease, and cancer, and adds years to my life. With claims like that, what is stopping me?

Sleep: Sleep, also, was important to Jesus. There were times when he went up into the mountains to spend the whole night in prayer, but when he really needed to sleep he did so, whatever the circumstances around him. When his nearest and dearest were at their wits' end struggling in the storm, and actually fearing that their boat would capsize and they would die – even then, Jesus needed to sleep so he found a cushion and slept. The despair of his friends did not keep him awake; he slept soundly until they told him of their terror.[6]

It is a bad habit of our times that we allow ourselves to be stimulated right up to the last minute of the day. We are so keen to make the most use of our time that we work, plan, study, care for others, and watch exciting TV programmes (often late night TV viewing is made up of horror and violence), and then expect a sudden switch-off of all our nervous energy when we want to sleep. It is hardly surprising that we have to battle in the morning to get up and throw off the exhaustion of the night. There are some simple things to help strengthen the pre-sleep pattern:

– Allow at least an hour to wind down before getting into bed. Get into a regular routine of turning off the TV and chatting; clearing the kitchen and putting the cat out; taking a stroll under the stars; having a warm relaxed bath with a good (but unchallenging) book; using time to pray gently rather than fervently; being receiving and loving, rather than demanding and competing.

– In wakeful times during the night, take the chance to enjoy the quiet, comfort and privacy of being in bed; it is the striving to get to sleep that stops sleep.

– Let your mind rest on one word or phrase or image, without struggling with it; this will help to keep other concerns and worries out of the picture.

– Have paper and pencil at hand to write down dreams, or any issue that keeps your mind busy; that means it can be sorted out in the morning, but not right now.

– If you really get into a spiralling thought pattern, it is more use to get up and move, make a warm drink, listen to the radio, and break into the spiral rather than remain in bed fretting that it won't go away.

– Some people find listening to their own breathing is very calming. It can be even more effective deliberately to rest the chest muscles and instead use the belly muscles to breathe with, allowing the soft abdominal wall to swell gently out and back. This low, slow breathing is further described in chapter 4.

Physicality: Jesus' deep understanding of physicality, and his deliberate use of it, is mentioned constantly in the Gospels. He used spit to heal a deaf man's dumbness, and made mud out of spittle to heal a man's blindness; he advised oil to fill up wounds in order to heal them; he wrote in sand when he made a judgement; he asked Thomas to push his fingers into his wounds to enable him to believe.[7]

Anne Other likes keeping clean. Mess, to her, means chaos. Wetness has to be dried; surfaces must be cleared and spotless; appearance and image is all important. Indeed it is, in its place. Order is all very well, but control and rule can be very sterile. Disorder can allow me to see new possibilities. There is something about coming to terms with the very messiness of physicality that increases the give and take between people, that enables me to put up with the ambiguities of other people's habits and opinions better; it can even help me become less resistant to the wide openness of God. Maybe Anne Other could allow a bit of mess now and again, and find herself bending a little, even put on some looser clothing sometimes. Then not only would there be less tension about her but she might turn out to be more likeable. We all need to have gaps in our borders.

Touch: Following on from physicality was Jesus' use of touch. Touch is an enormously powerful tool; it is in the first experience of a newborn baby of its own separateness, and the first intimation of care and love in the world it is entering. Touch can solace or harm, heal or hurt. Jesus often took people who came to him by the hand, or he laid his hand on them to heal them. Jesus put his arms around children, pulled up those who were supposed dead by his hands, used his hands to wash the disciples' feet. Jesus received touch, with great feeling as we shall see later, from Mary, Judas and John among others, as well as cruel touch from the soldiers.[8]

Anne Other backs away from touch because she knows it can be invasive, it breaks into her own personal space and she is suspicious of intimacy. But in not risking intrusive touch, she is depriving herself of rewarding touch. Even those who live on their own can be comforted by the presence of an animal to stroke. Terminally ill patients have been encouraged to 'feel better' by making contact with the warm soft fur of a pet. Concentration in prayer can be greatly helped by getting to know a small article of creation through touching it and feeling it. There is a growing understanding of the benefits of massage, both for the physical body and spirituality.

Rest: Perhaps most surprising of all is the extent to which Jesus made use of – rest. We in our sophisticated preoccupation with busyness put 'rest' at the bottom of the pile, to be fitted into our lives only if and when everything else has been done. Mental, emotional and spiritual withdrawal will be looked at in later chapters; here it is useful to note the continual use made by Jesus, who had the most urgent and demanding commission ever taken on board by any living human being, of retiring to a quiet, friendly environment to rest, to recharge, to refill.[9]

Some of the best-known texts in the New Testament can lose their potency simply because they are so overused. On the whole, what we most crave for when we feel unskilled, tired, at our wits' end, is empowerment, strength, new energy, determination: alternatively for the whole situation to be changed or removed. But what Jesus says is that when we go to him with our feelings of being burdened he will supply us with – rest![10]

To us, today, somehow 'rest' has come to mean something that is suitable for those who cannot quite manage without it. It is for those who are less capable, less busy, less indispensable than I am myself. At best, it has become an optional extra. We forget that in the blueprint of creation 'rest' is a totally inescapable place for renewal. Not the noisy and exciting renewal of highly-charged activities that leave us exhausted, but the relaxed, chosen, single-pointed calm of emptying ourselves of all hassles. In our greedy and grabbing society a very basic principle has got lost. It is this: *in order to be refilled, a bucket first has to become empty.*

Proper recognition

It is important to discern to what extent I am keeping the tools which God has provided me with in good order. This is for the sake of advancing His Kingdom, but there is a further point at which this becomes a self-indulgent exercise, and is at the expense of others' needs. The evidence of the Gospels is that always and always it was the potential for the glory of God that ruled the choices of Jesus, the perfect human being. When deprivation reduced the extent to which he could demonstrate the glory of his Father, he took steps to fill out his own bodily needs. Self-indulgence scarcely comes into the picture: keeping his skills at optimal service level for the glory of God emphatically does.

There is a wonderful technical term to describe the condition of being unable to recognise or express what is happening to your own body. It is called alexithymia. In some people the neural pathways between the sensory nerve endings in the body and the receptors in the brain are so overridden by the will that they actually atrophy – they become dumb. The conversation and exchange that is taking place continually between the various hormones and chemicals employed in our physical make-up is seriously inhibited. We fail to recognise what we need, when we need it. The tools of our bodies get rusty and unserviced.

There is nothing in the Gospels that suggests our Lord Jesus Christ ever allowed this to happen. Sometimes he *chose* to override the pain that his body was registering, as when he chose to remain silent at times during his trials; but the general evidence of the records of his earthly behaviour are that he used all the bodily tools he possessed, and he used them to their optimum, in order that they could serve his desire to fill his life bringing glory to God.

Use of the Senses

Observation, enjoyment, celebration

TO COUNTERACT:

Compassion saturation
Dullness, flatness
Misplaced stoicism
Assumed martyrdom

● ●

There are many circumstances that trigger stress. It may be a collection of hassles which pressurise, a series of acute challenges, or something to do with a personality difficulty. Wherever it starts, a common trait is that the sufferer feels too trapped to enjoy life. Vivacity and vigour drain away, and we hear phrases like 'I feel shattered'; 'I'm at the end of my tether'; 'No one is listening to me'; 'I can't cope'. There is no energy left for pleasure.

'Pleasure' . . . ! It is a word that spins out circles of different connotations, from the simple right up to shades of obscenity. In our own country we have special difficulty with the word, and we still bear the marks of the Puritan influence which has been sealed into our history. It seems that the English are less adept at expressing pleasure and delight than any of those in tropical or Mediterranean countries; and some say that the Celtic and Gaelic people know how to express their enjoyment of life better than the Anglo-Saxon. It is to do with a certain earnestness, and a perhaps laudable reserve. To give ourselves permission to demonstrate pleasure is a skill that has to be relearnt, and sometimes it has to be developed quite deliberately.

We have inherited a great weight of Christian literature warning us against 'the pleasures of the world'. By implication, it demotes any pleasure as suspect. The classical seven deadly sins are all about the consequences of totally self-centred and obsessively extended physical pleasure, which is seen as a yawning hole that is totally insatiable. This is in strong contrast to our modern emphasis on the gladness that God offers us. The verve and impetus of delight and joy speak of pleasure which is celebrated through the senses, through our eyes and ears and touch and taste and sexuality: all these can be used to different ends, one of self-indulgence or the opposite pole – the end of a dazzling and reciprocal enlargement of our experience of God.

There are four occasions recorded in the Gospels when a 'voice from God' was *heard* with physical ears, by at least several people simultaneously. It is extraordinarily significant that these four messages were all to do with goodwill and delight. On the first occasion, shepherds heard with their ears angels glorying in the birth at Bethlehem. They were rapt by: 'Peace to all in whom God *delights*', 'with whom He is *pleased*', 'for those who *enjoy* His favour'.[1]

The second event was when Jesus was baptised, and the crowd at the River Jordan heard, 'This is my beloved Son, in whom I take *delight*'.[2]

The third time the voice sounded out loud was heard was up on the Mount of Transfiguration; the three disciples heard, 'This is my Son, the Beloved; he *enjoys* my favour'.[3]

Perhaps the most moving of all, just as Jesus is facing the agony he is about to tackle and, in spite of his despair, he cries out, 'Father, glorify your name', the crowd hears the response from heaven 'I have *glorified* it, and I will *again glorify* it.'[4] To be pleased, to enjoy, to take delight in, to glorify – this is an exchange beyond words.

It can be difficult to persuade worthily-motivated people that sensing pleasure is in itself healing and therapeutic – it is not only a matter of distraction from stress. The subject of the pleasure in relationships needs considerable exploration, and it will be looked at again later. That pleasure lifts the pressing darkness of felt stress, and that enjoyment adds to the ability to handle stress, has been shown in objective measurements in physiology and psychology. These are benefits not only to one's own life, they also add to the capacity of helping others in theirs. Pleasure is a buffer against becoming bogged down, and it builds up a sense of affirmation. Sometimes 'pleasure' has to be actually timetabled into life, made a top priority, against all 'good sense'. Demands will be met more creatively and effectively having had a dose of *hedonia* – try thinking of it as a prescription! *Hedonia* describes quality rather than quantity: pausing to feel a breeze on the skin, to absorb the colours in the sky, to take in the sound of water, can be as restoring as an organised trip to the theatre. Both have to be allowed, in a busy, challenging life.

Maybe it is simply a question of giving ourselves permission. The importance of making time and place for delight is greatly raised if we follow the model given to us by Christ.

Jesus and Eyes and Ears

Jesus made full use of his delight in using his eyes. This is clear from his many references to the natural world. The obvious ones include birds, lilies, fruits, corn, wind, rain, storms, stones, even hairs. Evidence of Jesus' acute use of his ears includes his tales of children playing the pipes in the market place; the call of a single appealing voice above the hubbub of the crowd; the bleat of the distant lost lamb; his love of the stillness of quiet places.

Jesus was very aware of the different levels of using eyes and ears. He knew well the capacity of some of his hearers to 'look without seeing and hear without hearing or understanding' (Matt. 13:15). He explained to his close friends why he wrapped the point he wanted to make around with a story, instead of giving it straight with didactic teaching. He quoted Isaiah:

> This people's heart has grown coarse,
> their ears dulled,
> they have shut their eyes tight
> to avoid using their eyes to see,
> their ears to hear,
> their heart to understand,
> *changing their ways*
> *to be healed by me.*[5]

Jesus knew how very selective we are in our seeing and hearing, and how we can refuse to take in anything we don't at that moment feel like seeing or hearing. Using the eyes and ears openly and honestly is healing. He repeatedly cried out to the crowd, 'Anyone who has ears should *listen!*'[6] And again, later on, he says to those closest to him, 'Blessed are your eyes because they see, your ears because they hear!' (Matt. 13:16)

Jesus and Taste

Jesus took delight in tasting, eating, feasting, drinking, and this has already been noted in the previous chapter. In the ordinary way of things it is people who enjoy hospitality who are offered it the most often. In this way, Jesus must have been a very rewarding guest since he was so constantly invited by people into their own homes.

Jesus and Touch

Touch was perhaps the most powerful of all the senses in the hands of Jesus. It must be, I suppose, one of the deepest pleasures of all to know that one has the capacity to change dramatically the life of someone else for good, and then actually doing it. Jesus Christ, as a total human, had this capacity. But he didn't keep to himself the triumph that it brought with it – he handed all the glory over to God. This is important: partly because it was in this way that he avoided building up the stress of 'having to perform'; and he side-stepped the drive 'to go one better' each time. He knew of the traps we constantly succumb to, of taking glory to ourselves when something has come off well. With Jesus, the deep, deep pleasure of giving healing was unalloyed, unspoilt, because he lived the fact that the delight came from God, passed through his hands, and returned to God.

The touch of Jesus was profound; it even spread to the clothes he was wearing. People in the crowds tried to touch the edge of his cloak, because then they were healed.[7] We have one particular incident when, in spite of the crush of bodies around him, Jesus felt the power of healing leaving him and demanded to know who had received it. So this was no merely casual brush against his clothes, no automatic dispensing of some spiritual aura. The touch extracted something from him, it was gift – asked for, given and received. Such is the quality of favour, pleasure, exchange.

It is a strange reflection that today we use the phrase in anger 'Don't you lay your hands on me!' or 'If I catch you laying a hand on her!' . . . In the way in which the same phrase is used with reference to Jesus it *always* implies healing.[8]

He took so much delight in children. Even when, perhaps, the children had been scrabbling for his attention, squabbling in their attempts to reach him, and then were overawed by the disciples' repulsion of them. Jesus himself put his arms round them, laid his hands on them and gave them his blessing.[9] The contact of the skin of Jesus' hands, and the bodiliness of the children, were powerful and to God's glory.

There was another profound factor in this touch of Jesus. With the special sense of authority for which he was noted, Jesus Christ defied the rigorous and respected laws of religious people about uncleanness. With his ungloved fingers he touched things that were untouchable – lepers in particular, organs that were congenitally malfunctioning or misshapen such as eyes and tongue, the freshly raw and bleeding ears of the servant, and a ceremonially unclean stretcher carrying a dead boy.[10] To go against such strong conventions in such a spectacular way meant that these were matters of great importance to Jesus himself.

As we have seen, after his return from the dead, and in order to convince Thomas of this reality, Jesus invited his friends to 'touch me and see for yourselves; a ghost has no flesh and bones as you can see I have' (Luke 24:39).

These contacts of touch were non-possessive. When he presented himself to Mary after his resurrection, Jesus was very definite. 'Don't cling to me,' he said. For him, touch was contact and exchange; it was not a matter of grabbing and holding and containing. Touch was not about invasion, or possession. And his touch was never used to inflict pain.

Jesus and Sexuality

In another important use of the senses, how can we interpret Jesus' use of sexuality? As far as we know, Jesus reached the mature age of thirty unmarried – very unusually for his culture. It is singular that in the records of his life Jesus is equally open and friendly with

- those who were single, such as the trio of Mary, Martha and Lazarus at Bethany; or
- those who were married, as were the vast majority of the Jewish nation; or
- those who were same-sex orientated, as in all probability were the Roman centurian and his special servant; or
- those who were on their own through bereavement, such as the widow of Nain, and Peter's mother.

He chose for his travelling companions a male group; but he was not put out that the group knew he had a different relationship with each of them. It was not just that he had a communal love for them and there was a general liking between them, but Jesus himself put value on having a particular affinity with individuals as well. He fostered a separate relationship with Peter, Judas, Thomas, James and of course John.

Women, in first-century Palestine, were particularly associated with things to do with the senses; they were seen as being primarily responsible for cooking and cleaning – and indeed a group of them looked after Jesus and his disciples in Galilee (Mark 15:41; Luke 23:49) – and they prepared the spices to wrap around Jesus' dead body. But his associations with women were remarkable for those times in which he lived: in spite of the surrounding cultural strictures, Jesus showed no defensiveness when he was alone with a woman. Some of the most detailed accounts of long conversations recorded in the Gospels are those with women on their own. Each of these, incidentally, was outside his home country; one was at the well in Samaria, and the other was with a woman from Syrophoenicia. It was a woman who washed Jesus' feet with her tears, broke a phial of luxurious perfume over them, and dried them with her hair – all at a public dinner! None of these acts of the senses did Jesus, the supreme exponent of love, reject.[11]

Negative, painful stimuli of the senses were not rejected either. Jesus experienced acute hunger, scourging, being spat at in the face, having thorns pushed down into his skin, in their full impact – all in addition to the total physical torture and confinement of the crucifixion.

How Does our Use of the Senses under Stress Compare?

Physiologically, the initial response to acute stress is that our senses are sharpened. We see things more brightly, hear things more acutely, and our nerve-endings become unusually sensitive. We take in all the signals that are coming at us, in order to inform the decision we have to make in answer to the challenge. Such arousal is necessary and appropriate if we are to scan all the circumstances instantly and make a vital decision. If, in the split second as the bus rounds the corner, we have to decide whether to continue crossing the road or to draw back, we need all the data we can get from our senses to make an accurate judgement. This biological process was in Jesus also. However, if we remain super-sensitised for too long, we become irritable at the constant arousal. Try slamming a door behind someone who is in such a state and fur flies; do the same behind someone who is relaxed and there is no big deal. If this heightened degree of sensitivity continues, we cope with it by shutting our senses down, cutting out the signals. As a result, we become bored and apathetic, unapproachable, glum, unamused and unentertained. In order to be reactivated the stimuli have to be increased. We see this today in the competing heights of visual violence which attack our dulled senses. The problem is that with us, the more we are sensitised the more we run the risk of sensitivity saturation. The signals coming through our senses may be either affronting or pleasant, but their message gets crowded out.

So pleasure gets blocked. Ordinary appreciation dries up. Spontaneous enjoyment leaves us cold. Normal sexual responsiveness turns either towards the states of frigidity and impotence, or it may give way to a craving for the acting-out of fantasy.

High stress levels can bring sensual aridity. In their search to get out of this cul-de-sac, some people turn to overcompensation; natural delight is replaced by patterns of comfort eating, or reliance on alcohol or nicotine or drugs, and/or superficial sex.

This gloomy down-spiral can be arrested early if we resist closing down on the here-and-now appreciation of what our senses are giving us, whether the stimuli are those of pleasure or pain. Whichever is present to us as individuals, we may be able to let ourselves feel it, and stay with it, as Jesus did. He neither disguised nor ran away from anything his senses told him.

In order to do this, we as fallible and scarred humans have to come to terms with a paradox. If we are to retain a genuine use of our senses, we have to guard against oversaturation in whatever they register, especially when it is observed second hand. Sometimes we have to take care we don't become so sated that we can no longer experience genuine response. Perhaps we should protect ourselves from too-frequent exposure to images of horror, for instance, putting a ration on our daily allowance of visual violence so we don't become immunised by it. Then we could give a bit more time and energy to building up our appreciation of ordinary delight and gladness. The common giving of thanks for whatever is good and full of celebration; allowing pleasure and enjoyment to be spontaneous, and shared and expressed – to others and to God. Giving it away, not hanging on to it.

Our basic senses are treasure houses of delight in split-second moments as well as in cultivated occasions. Many of us have to relearn how to make the most of them, without either squandering or smothering the gifts they bring us. The exchange of touch; the breathtaking holiness of sexual tenderness; the flow of smiles and laughter; a child's delight in discovery. And many of us have to allow ourselves to include in our lives the principle that in expressing pleasure we give pleasure; that enjoyment is one of the basic reward systems in all our relationships; and that this applies to our relationship with God just as much as it applied to the relationship Jesus delighted in with his Father.

On the level of our physical senses Jesus rejoiced at the simplest things: a single coin lost and found; a widow – who was poor – placing her small coin in the charity box; the sparrows that God knew and numbered. And he put the art of celebration in a nutshell: 'Do friends of the bridegroom refuse to eat at the wedding feast? Should they be sad while he is with them?'[12]

As Robert Bridges put it:

> Daily doth th'Almighty Giver
> Bounteous gifts on us bestow;
> His desire our soul delighteth,
> Pleasure leads us where we go,
>   Love doth stand
>   At His hand;
> Joy doth wait on His command.

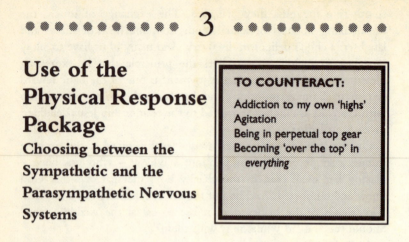

●●●●●●●●●●● *3* ●●●●●●●●●●●

Use of the Physical Response Package

Choosing between the Sympathetic and the Parasympathetic Nervous Systems

●●●●●●●●●●●●●●●●●●●●●●●●●●●

This is one of the primary skills of stress management. Once again, it involves raising my awareness of how I am going to choose to behave at any one instant. It means developing my own ability to swop between one of two systems supplied by the Creator to carry messages within my body. The blueprint of our physical make-up includes a package of automatic nervous responses that lead us into the *highs* of life, and also a package of automatic nervous responses that lead us into the *deeps* of life. Although these two systems are embedded in our bodies and will work without any consciousness on my part – as happens with animals – when I can be aware of choosing between them, it greatly increases the range of tools I have with which to tackle overstress. When I can decide whether it is appropriate for me, at this particular moment, and in these particular circumstances, to be on the route which leads to the 'highs' of life, or alternately on the route that leads to the 'deeps'[1] of life, then I hold an important key. With this key I can turn into the mode in which I generate and spend energy, or instead I can turn into the mode in which I conserve and rebuild it.

The basic theory goes like this: at any time I might be challenged. This challenge may consist of

- a physical nature, such as having to jump in and rescue a child from a situation of danger; or it may be of

- a mental nature, such as when I have to find the solution to this problem before an imminent deadline; or it may be of
- an emotional nature, such as when I am asked to listen to the problems of yet another troubled person; or it may be of
- a spiritual nature, such as being called upon to offer holy consolation.

The puzzle is this. If I am full of fitness and fettle, I will make the most of any of these challenges. Of its own accord my body will automatically pump out hormones and enzymes which get instructions to my nerves, muscles and bones via the *sympathetic nervous system*: a package of connected responses will tell them to generate as much energy as is needed to accomplish the task in hand with utmost efficiency. These messages will result in my heart beating faster, my pulse rate quickening, my blood pressure going up and the speed of my breathing increasing; all this will ensure that more oxygen is pushed to my furthermost muscles and they are primed to move. The speed of my mental activity goes up too. My mind will race at taking in ideas, and this will process the data I receive. Other messages will close my digestive system down, temporarily, so eating and absorbing food doesn't distract from the urgent action to be taken. The liver releases more glucose into the bloodstream to boost the supply of energy further, and perspiration escapes in order to cool the outside of the body. A whole team of interconnecting functions are put at 'action!' stations, and the entire organic structure is on top alert. In this way, the sympathetic nervous system makes sure that I will rise to the challenge with zest, and feel good about the 'high' it gives me. No problem. The child will be rescued safely (if speedily!), the deadline will be met, the troubled person will be helped, and the soul consoled.

But all the time I am getting myself worked *up*, the stores of resources on which I rely for future activities are breaking *down*. I am generating energy, but liable to be spending it at a greater rate than I am generating it. The stores of blood sugar in my body are lowered, and the extent to which I can continue to respond with maximum efficiency reduces; my immune system becomes less reliable, and things like my sense of humour, my openness to others, the sense of my own 'centre', are all weakened.

If I go on piling challenge upon challenge, I may well be building up my own ideas of being on top and competant, but I will be risking the breakdown of my mental and emotional resources, and the wasting away of my spiritual health. Adrenalin gives me a satisfying 'buzz', but if I continue to live off this buzz and become addicted to it, the point will come when I start to dither. At some time I may hesitate just too long and the child gets hurt; or my mental processes 'freeze' and the deadline arrives without a solution; or I am too drained to listen to yet another trouble, and someone is left feeling unheard; or I am too dried up and full of dreading doubts to cope with solacing another. At this point it is highly likely that I get ill.

There is a superb alternative to this over-alerted situation, one that is already provided in the blueprint for creation and is in my own hands. Instead of obstinately insisting that I can thrive on pressure endlessly, I can choose to become refilled by switching into the *parasympathetic* nervous system.

The whole of the animal kingdom makes full use of this alternative package of responses – except the highly developed Western cultures of humankind. We consider ourselves too wise and sophisticated to need it, and we wilfully override all the time-honoured means of activating it. If I choose to give it a chance, the parasympathetic nervous system will produce hormones and enzymes that almost exactly counteract the stressing functions of the sympathetic system. These will automatically bring down my heart rate, my pulse rate, my blood pressure, my breathing rate, the entire metabolic rate of the whole physical system. While these speeds come down, all my stored resources are built *up*. When I can allow myself to rest in the place of the 'deeps', healing is speeded, my immune system is strengthened, and my sense of humour, and of direction, and self-worth all improve; I find I can listen better, receive and empathise, relax, ponder and meditate more fully, and contact some of the things in me that are immeasurable. Things such as intuition, play, laughter, and mystery;[2] these take on a greater authority.

I can choose to go to this deep place, and when I go there I go to be resourced, to be built up and renewed, not simply as an opt-out when I can cope no longer. Scientific studies have shown that becoming familiar with that deep place on a regular basis actually enables me to *function better* when I am on the alert, than if I never visited it.

Today, in our frenetic society, deep relaxation and meditation have become skills that have to be deliberately re-learned. Young babies, as well as all animals, know well how to be in the place where the parasympathetic is ordering their responses, and they experience the total acceptance, tolerance and contentment of their inner world.

If they are allowed to stay there for a while, without being disturbed by well-meant 'stimulation', they relate better to the outer world when they return to it. It is the overwrought older and more educated people who try to live without this daily experience.

When it comes to a discussion of prayer, the two complementary physical orders of the sympathetic and parasympathetic nervous systems are particularly relevant: the earnest, verbal, wordy lists and intentions of praying in the 'alert' mode are very different from the wordless, receptive, waiting, basking states of prayer in the contemplative mode.

It is a fascinating exercise to read the Gospels with the specific aim of discovering if and how the reported behaviour of Jesus Christ includes the chosen use of each mode. Things are *done* in the sympathetic nervous system, and the bulk of the Gospel writing is concerned with recording what Jesus *did*. He travelled and taught and healed and fed and suffered. He upheld all the liturgical Jewish requirements – reading the Scriptures and attending the word-filled synagogue services, being present at the Temple festivals and being part of the debates with the religious leaders. But slipped in here and there are small references to his *not-doing* habits – things so regular and regularly accepted that they didn't need 'preaching' about. The Hebrew spiritual masters wrote of an ancient tradition of wordless prayer, and the use of a silent Godward mantra; Jesus, as a man educated in the Jewish religion, would have been totally familiar with this less-recognised teaching.[3]

The evidence of the way Jesus used the parasympathetic nervous response in order to recharge his energy is revealing. There are at least four different ways in which Our Lord resisted the expectations with which he was surrounded. Over and over again in the following pages we shall come across the astonishing ability of Jesus to *resist overload*.

(a) His habit of withdrawing from the crowds into the warmth and intimacy of his chosen support group will be highlighted in chapter 7.

(b) His method of extracting a single person from the waiting and watching group surrounding them in order to take them to be healed in privacy will be noted in chapter 9.

(c) His powerful, and astonishing, ability to say 'no' to the demands of needy people constantly coming at him will be discussed in chapter 11. Just for now, two incidents are interesting. In Luke

4:42 the crowds caught Jesus up and begged him to stay with them. But 'No,' he said, 'I must go'. And again in Matthew 16:4 when the Pharisees and Sadducees were arguing with him to test him, 'he left them and went off'.

(d) In the face of all the above pressures on him, Jesus still made it a *first priority* to find time and space to get away from everything and everybody and be alone with his Father, praying for long hours by himself. These were the times above all when he would simply absorb the presence and purpose of God; when he would receive and be refilled with the power and peace of his Father.[4]

So, when it comes to us, what can we do about getting in touch with the functions of the parasympathetic nervous system?

1. First and foremost we can acknowledge our need of using *all* of the tools with which God has provided us, not just those ones we perceive as being exciting. Being in the 'highs' is excellent and rewarding; but those highs are maintained by visits to the 'deeps'.

2. We must choose, deliberately, to make the time and space to get to recognise how the parasympathetic response feels and works. Making a habit of doing this daily, or at least several times a week, enables us to build up such a familiarity with this different physiological state, that we can dip into it for a few seconds at any moment.

   Jesus himself took time out to get into the remote places, but he told us to 'come apart and rest awhile', or to 'go into your secret room'. Maybe he was resonating with Isaiah, 'Go to your private room, shut yourselves in. Hide yourselves a little while' (Isa. 26:20). In a busy household this will need organising:

   – telling the rest of the family that I will be unavailable for a short time, but they can count on me being a better partner/parent/person when I return (they'll soon discover the practical reality of this!);

   – where necessary, unplugging the phone or putting it on ansaphone;

   – dampening the doorbell;

   – finding a place where I can be by myself whether it is in the bedroom or the garden shed or the attic or in a warm bath or even in a lay-by in the car;

   – having with me something to remind me what I am about,

such as a picture, a book, a smooth stone to hold, a crucifix or a rosary;

- deciding on a physical position where I can forget my body and the pressures on it; it is good to loosen tight bands, and either to lie down fairly flat or sit upright in a supportive chair; many people use a meditation stool, or sit cross-legged on a raised cushion;
- and most of all, welcoming total silence.

Even those who are at work can find a few minutes to be on their own: if they are absent in the toilet for ten minutes rather than two it will seldom be noticed.

3. We may want to take classes in relaxation or meditation, or join a group who practise it regularly, or find books and tapes that appeal to us individually.[5]

4. Incorporating micro-breaks into our daily lives is a natural follow-on from this recognition of the need to use the parasympathetic at frequent intervals. These micro-breaks involve simple things like

- changing activity for a few moments; if I am perpetually too active, I should sit down; if I am sitting at a desk or machine or computer, I should stand up, stretch, and walk a few steps
- squeezing up the fists, eyes, and buttocks and being aware of the increased tension for a few seconds; then letting it go and enjoying the release from constriction. This is known as isometric exercise
- closing the eyelids and using the muscles of the eyeballs to extend them from side to side, up and down; this will reconnect the functions of the left and right lobes of the brain
- take a social break; chat for a few moments, have something to drink, drop your concentration so it will return with greater clarity

Avoiding monotony by having tiny breaks of variety has been shown to reduce the risk of repetitive strain syndrome, headache, and irritability.

5. The use of breathing appropriately is described in chapter 4.

6. Making use of laughter and play more often – see chapter 18.

7. Letting go with some form of general relaxation, bringing in enjoyable activities – sport, art, music, walking, gardening, hobbies, socialising; but these things must be uncompetitive or we are back in the sympathetic mode.

8. Maybe it sounds a nonsense, but we have to take *rest* seriously!

This is a word that has been considerably devalued in recent years. It has become something that I do when everything else is finished, if and when I have time. Or something that others resort to when they are unable to cope any longer; I don't need it. Yet it is a word constantly used in the Old Testament as something God has given us as a command: 'In returning and rest shall you be saved' (Isa. 30:15[6]); 'Yahweh says, "Look . . . ask . . . which was the good way? Take it and you will find rest . . . " ' (Jer. 6:16). Both of these commands were refused: 'you would have none of it. "No," you said,' and 'But they have said, "We will not take it" '. Rest is also offered by God as a resource: ' "Here you can rest! Here you can let the weary rest! Here all is quiet." But they refused to listen' (Isa. 28:12,13). In the New Testament we tend to take many favourite sayings for granted, they can become overfamiliar. When I am exhausted, overladen, bewildered, I want to pray for courage, discernment, power. Our Lord offers us – *rest* (Matt. 11:28). Hebrews 4 is a eulogy about rest, and our salvation.

The word 'rest' is sometimes translated in modern versions in different ways. Synonyms such as 'refuge in the desert' have been used, or 'abstinence from striving'. Even stronger is '*restoration of the soul*'; now, that is the parasympathetic nervous response in a nutshell.

●●●●●●●●●●●● 4 ●●●●●●●●●●●●

Appropriate
Breathing
Head, heart, belly

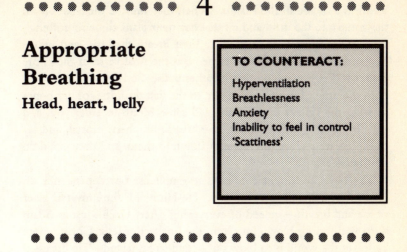

TO COUNTERACT:

Hyperventilation
Breathlessness
Anxiety
Inability to feel in control
'Scattiness'

●●●●●●●●●●●●●●●●●●●●●●●●●●●●

It's a good idea to keep on breathing. To take air in and let it out. But *how* to do it, and how to *choose* how to do it, is another matter. The Bible is peppered with words which allude to breathing.

- The very first thing that God did to Adam was to *breathe into his nostrils the breath of life* – and man became a living soul (Gen. 2:7).
- At Noah's time, every living thing *having the breath of life under heaven* was threatened (Gen. 6:17); but God decreed that one pair of all that was alive and *had the breath of life was preserved* to start a new generation afresh (Gen. 7:15).

Throughout the Bible there are two types of God's breathing, and each mention of it belongs to one distinct polarity or the other. There is nothing 'mild' about any of the allusions to breath or breathing, they are always of the utmost significance. In the Old Testament, whenever God is described as using His breath, it accomplishes either the greatest good or ultimate destruction. The result is according to God's choice and as He sees fit. We hear that Job declares that 'in His hand is the soul of every living thing and the breath of every human being' and Job's friend talks of equality and says, 'God's was the breath that gave me life'; but in the same book we are told that 'under the breath of God, they perish: a blast of his anger and they are destroyed.'[1]

Total dependency on God and the way He chooses to use His breath is a theme in the Psalms: 'When they breathe their last breath they return to the dust, and on that day their plans come to nothing', and again 'When God takes away their breath they die, and return to the dust from which they came.' But the final verse in the entire psalter is 'Let everything that breathes praise God.'[2]

In the time of Ezekiel, God said to the vast quantities of dry bones littering the valley's floor, 'I am will cause breath to enter you, and you shall live' . . . 'Prophesy to the breath; prophesy, mortal, and say to the breath . . . and the breath came into them, and they stood up on their feet'![3] [4]

The New Testament continues to emphasise our dependence on God for breath and life. Paul says, 'He Himself is the universal giver of life and breath – indeed of everything' (Acts 17:25). Just as Adam starts with breath blown into him, the final act of Jesus Christ before he leaves the world is to blow out breath to his friends. 'He breathed on them and said, "Receive . . . " ' (John 20:22).

Scriptural words like breathe, breath, wind, and spirit are often interchangeable. The analogy of the wind of the Holy Spirit, and the wind that preceded the revelation of the still small voice[5] are outstanding examples of how 'inspire' – the intake of bodily breath – and 'inspiration' – the intake of the Holy Spirit – become intermingled.

The running theme that cries out to be extrapolated from this material is that of *choosing* **how** to make use of this totally essential vital force. And also how, characteristically, left to ourselves we have misused it.

Animals and small babies use their breath as it was designed to be used. Watching them as they lie on their backs, relaxed and totally contented to be who they are, we can observe the way the soft muscle of the abdominal wall rises and falls in a gentle, unhurried, slow rhythm. Minimal effort, no striving. They are lying there, relaxing in the parasympathetic mode. As we have seen in the previous chapter the parasympathetic has been likened to a capital account in the bank, where resources are accrued from which energy can be drawn whenever it is needed. By relaxing, their bodies and minds will in fact function still more efficiently later. The sympathetic nervous system has been likened to a current account in the bank; getting and spending energy, but carrying a high risk of overspending. If we can persuade ourselves that we can choose which way to breathe so we can be in charge of these two alternatives – whether, at any time, we want to be 'building up' or 'spending out' energy – we will have a powerful tool at our command.

This is a strong analogy concerning our present culture. On the whole we are getters and collectors. We gather, or grab, and hold on to, anything we can get hold of. Information and talents and possessions and qualifications. We are in constant danger of overload. When confronted with a challenge, we take a quick breath in; then realising what it means, we take in another; 'I've got to get . . . ' and another short intake; 'Oh I forgot . . . ' and yet another. Metaphorically and physically, one short gasp after another, until we build up our store of already-used air to such an extent that the space left to take in fresh useful air is squeezed into the top third of our lungs. Just because we forget that basic principle of Thomas Traherne, that in order to refill a bucket it first has to be *emptied*.

The physiological result of this very common type of breathing is that the balance between the held-in, exhausted carbon dioxide and new, refreshing oxygen is so distorted that we become hyperventilated. Hyperventilation on all counts is a Bad Thing. It carries a long list of bad effects. An inadequate supply of oxygen to the muscles makes them tense and tired; too little oxygen to the brain leads to mental confusion and anxiety; my digestive system becomes upset; the vessels in my body which carry blood and air become constricted so my circulation and respiration are impaired; I get cramp; the supply of blood to my heart becomes unstable; I can't sleep; my immune system and reproductive systems lose efficiency; I get emotional and intolerant; all this leads into a down-spiral of despair. I feel unable to cope; and put the blame onto other people. Hyperventilation can also lead to panic, and be the result of panic. A really bad picture.[6]

Not only am I using my normal breathing apparatus incorrectly, but I am breathing solely with my chest muscles. We are taught to take deep breaths in by expanding the rib-cage: in order to do this we heave up the bucket-handles of our ribs, we push up the heavy bones in our shoulders and backs, we articulate something like 180 tiny joints and boney interfaces with the breast-bone and with the vertebrae of the spine[7], and all this *against gravity*. Chest breathing is very active breathing; it is run by the sympathetic nervous system. It is entirely appropriate when we want to be active, or when we feel emotional and need to breathe great sighs of emotion. But it is very exhausting to use it the whole time, and it risks hyperventilation.

God has provided us with an alternative, and with the power to choose this alternative. Once again, it is controlled by the parasympathetic nervous system.

Many people think of the alternative as 'diaphragmatic' breathing. The difficulty with this term is that the diaphragm can neither be seen from the exterior of the body, nor can it be felt, since it has no sensory nerve endings. It is a large flat muscle forming a floor to the chest cavity (in which lie the stomach, heart and lungs) and a ceiling to the abdominal cavity (in which lie the rest of the digestive tract and the reproductive system). An easier way to get in touch with parasympathetic breathing is this:*

- Lie comfortably on a bed or on the floor on your back, with a pillow under your head and another under your knees. Loosen your belt and anything that is tight around your waist. Now take a deep breath in, so your lungs are filled to capacity.
- Slowly and gently start to blow your breath out, being aware of the lobes of your lungs under your shoulders emptying and flattening; the lobes of your lungs in the centre of your chest emptying and flattening; and the part of your lungs that lies right under your midriff emptying and flattening. This may take 8–18 seconds.
- Go on emptying your lungs until there is nothing left to empty. Then stop emptying. Don't let your brain tell you to breathe in quickly; just leave it to your body to do whatever it wants to, and watch it.
- When your body is under such pressure to take in more air urgently, it can't be bothered with all that articulation of joints and heaving up of muscles against gravity, and so it will use the quickest and easiest way available to it to refresh itself with good incoming air. You will notice the soft, pliable muscle below your belt swelling out – no bones to move, no gravity to defy, no joints to articulate. Then the muscle will subside, rest, and rise again, softly and gently. No gasping or overreaching or panicking. The body will fill the lungs *from the bottom*, not the top, and just to the extent it needs to take in oxygen, no more and no less, with great efficiency.
- What has happened, is that because the abdominal cavity is vacuum-packed and hermetically sealed, when the abdominal muscle swells out it automatically pulls down the upward curve of the diaphragm so air is drawn in, mechanically, to the lungs. This

* Those with a tendency towards asthma may have to modify this exercise of extended expelling of breath. Their own doctor or clinic staff will advise them.

movement starts a very small repositioning of all the organs in the abdominal cavity, and the efferent nerves coming through from the inside of the lower spine are minutely massaged. These are parasympathetic nerves, and the whole parasympathetic system is stimulated. You may notice your hands start to tingle as the blood circulation is re-distributed from the internal organs to the periphery, and your fingers become warm and full. People describe them as 'fat sausages', and the palms of the hands become speckled. You may experience a feeling of light-headedness as the blood to the brain is temporarily reduced, and the lower part of the body feels heavy and leaden. People speak about feeling relaxed, centred, grounded. If you choose deliberately to continue to breathe using the gentle rise and fall of your belly muscles (but not repeating the long blowing out as if that was an exercise), this state of deep relaxation can be extended. You will notice that nothing else in your body is moving, that your chest, shoulder and back muscles are perfectly still. It is of great practical value to become familiar with the use of the lower muscles with which to breathe, in place of the complex chest system.

The occasional *chosen* use of a long out-breath and the consequent use of 'belly-breathing' has many advantages. For instance:

– when I hear the telephone ring and I know it is from a difficult caller
– when I am aware I am tightening up in the face of some conflict
– when I am becoming bored and depleted of energy
– when there is a row or expressed dissention among the people I am with
– when I am interrupted by something trivial, and I don't want to flare back
– *before* I resort to a gasp of exasperation.

If I can catch my mental reaction in time and tell myself to *breathe out* – I can instantly contact a state where I am less disturbed and fragmented. I can become more receptive, listen more positively while using less energy, and become less emotional. Belly-breathing is useful too, if I want to lower my own pulse rate, myself; and when I want to get to sleep, but my mind is racing. I can be in charge of any incidence of inappropriate over-arousal, if I simply remember to use my abdominal muscles to breathe with, instead of the upper thoracic ones.

In the Gospels, when Jesus Christ refrained from overreacting but remained responsive and open, it is likely he was using the physical gifts of his Father in the parasympathetic mode.

It is up to each of us to learn to choose when it is appropriate to be active and aroused, and when it is appropriate to be receptive and relaxed. This choice can apply to our physical behaviour, our mental and emotional response, and to our prayer-life. It all depends on how we choose to use the tools God has provided for us.

5

Finding Like-minded Support
Choosing group support

It can be so easy, getting into the 'poor little me' mode. Becoming lock-ed into the idea that no one else quite understands my difficulties, and no one else has similar problems, or even that no one else really cares.

There was a man named Tom. He was known as the life and soul of the party. More than anything, he wanted to keep up his good image at work; in secret he was without close friends. He told nobody about his difficulty in communicating with his wife; or his other difficulty about not being able to get down on the floor and play with his children (he could fool others but not his own kids); or his difficulty with always coming up with the right flip answer (he might dry up next time); and certainly not about his terror (suppressed of course) that one day his boss would find him out. One day someone might realise that it was all a hoax; they might actually see through his struggle to look as though he never had to struggle at all.

One evening Tom was down at the pub, hoping to get forgetfulness from his troubles. His defences came down a bit and he heard Bill saying he hadn't spoken to his wife for two weeks, and his b★★★ children had noticed the frosty mood and kept out of his way, and if his secretary knew she'd soon take advantage of his misery, so what could he do? Just have an affair and ruin his family? Bill pricked up his ears and suggested they both went to the football match the following day.

They both blew out their emotions in yelling at the football match. Then, both relieved and exhausted, they walked towards home. On the way they discovered their similarities – not identical identities, but bits that were similarly hurting. It made all the difference that there was someone else on the same emotional pitch.

Very many of us are brought up to believe that it is strong to resist 'feelings'. Feelings make me vulnerable, and expressing them to others lays me wide open to attack. The goal for many people is to be self-sufficient, self-reliant and self-contained. Those who get on with their work without asking too many questions are admired, they can manage on their own. Often they are the people to whom others will turn for advice, and they enjoy the reputation of being a pillar of strength. To express their own feelings seems like weakness, and they mustn't 'give in' to it; that would be to risk being classed amongst the chatterers and gossipers. Or letting out their own difficulties seems a low priority in view of all the problems of other people around them. Those who try to get through their lives without opening up their feelings tend to barricade themselves. They want to appear to be invulnerable, but they get caught up behind their own defence works. When they really need to turn to someone else there is no one around. The storms burst in when they are on their own, and they start to flounder, losing their familiar foothold.

Getting together in a like-minded group provides a platform of support when a person on their own feels they are drowning. Two things happen when a trouble is shared. Just by talking about it, it seems to become less insoluble; putting the problem into words, words to be understood by someone else, enables me to map it out, to find my own way through it. As often as not, just laying it out in sentences, helps me to discover a pathway through the tangle. In addition, however much I think I know what the other person will say, they always say something different, and that 'something different' will put a new angle onto the situation. We will find triggers of ideas that lead towards ways of coping that hadn't previously been thought about.

The network system of self-help groups has had wide publicity. Whether it is a daily domestic concern such as losing weight, stopping smoking, or protecting the neighbourhood, or something even more pressing, it has been shown that tackling it in a group is far more effective than battling with it alone. The advantages of looking at severe difficulties, such as post-traumatic syndrome, addiction, or survival of sexual abuse, within the context of a supportive group are being increasingly acknowledged. Since the extended family has become so mobile, and ordinary social groupings provided by the church or the street have lost their place, the levels of stress among ordinary people have risen dramatically. The nuclear family has been expected to contain within its boundaries *all* the varied needs, relationships and feelings of two adults and two children, to the exclusion of others, and as it becomes overheated so it implodes. It is urgent that we re-discover the importance of supportive friends alongside us, but outside our close family groupings. It is a strange fact that often ordinary friendship seems to be too low a priority to give space and time and place to today. It is expected just to happen. When it doesn't, I have a puzzled sense of having missed out on something, but I am confused as to how it got left out. I always thought it was such a good thing to be strong and do things my way.

Feeling I am on my own is extremely stressful. Whether the loneliness is physically real or simply imagined, it can make me tense or hyperactive. When I am lonely – which is different from being alone – I may become withdrawn, or conversely I may need to throw my weight about; I may overcompensate madly or appear to be superior to others. These sorts of behaviour make it difficult for others to get near me, so I become habituated to the idea that it is they who don't want to get near me.

If having a group of friends to support me is so important, what do I do that is so different from the way Jesus set about it?

> – *Sometimes I think that if I have taken on the Lord's work it is only me that can do it and others will simply get in the way. I don't need others.*

• Jesus' calling was his, alone, so he could easily have presumed that his Father would look after him and the work that he had to do, in His own way. But he didn't. He went out of his way to find people to work alongside him. He took time to do this, selecting one individual at a time, not simply joining up with a ready-made grouping.

> – *When I think I have an understanding of a problem that is superior to others' I get on and deal with it by myself. It is too much bother explaining all the detail to those who are less 'with it' than I am.*

• Jesus was intellectually superior to most of his fellow human beings. Why should he bother with those more stupid than him? Yet the friends he searched out were not the educationalists of the day;

they were not those with superior philosophical qualifications. Jesus found people he could share his vision with who had their feet on the ground among the everyday concerns, mishaps, and affairs of daily life. He wanted very basic ingredients against which he could try out his own methods of communication, and out of which he could fashion the Kingdom of God.

> — *When I am in love with someone, or with a project, I want to bury myself entirely in the object of my love, I want to leave everyone and everything else outside.*

• Jesus had a closer relationship with the Father than anyone who has ever lived. He could have easily assumed that this relationship was the only thing to be fostered in his life, that he had to give every hour and every possible minute to communicating in prayer to God, and in so doing bypass all other human relationships. Instead, *in addition* to this absorbing communion with his Father and extending *out of* it, he opened wide his ability to accept others as they were and showed them how to build up their own relationship with God themselves.

Jesus Christ was unique; he was different in every way it was possible to be different. He had every reason to stand apart, to be able to cope on his own, yet he looked for other humans around him, just like the rest of us. Jesus knew that constantly doing things on your own was very stress-engendering. Humans are built to be in groups. He not only knew this in the very heart of his being, but he also knew that with all the hundreds of people seeking him out for help, he himself had to set about finding his own closest continuing friends. In order to be not on his own he had to take on practical, physical, bodily behaviour to build a physical, social, emotional buffer around him. He knew that the greater the demands that were to be laid upon him, the greater the need to have this human buffer towards the outside world.

So Jesus gathered around him a bunch of people who could stay with him. These were people whom he could teach to carry on his work after he had returned to the Father, but they were also travelling companions, friends who shared his meals and living quarters; who were with him day and night whatever he did and wherever he decided to go. But they were astonishingly unlikely colleagues. They proved to be inadequate and slow to understand, they clung to misguided demands and they mishandled situations, they were rivals haggling and competing for his approval. Yet for all this, and even in spite of the risk of betrayal, Jesus remained loyal to them. In some extraordinary way he himself drew strength from their very human company.

Sometimes it becomes important that we ourselves go out to find friends, to construct a personal support group of our own. It is a fantasy that such a support network just grows and hey bingo! when I am in trouble there they will be, all my friends to share the burden with me. Many of us live our lives as if this was the case, particularly when we are overburdened with stress pressing upon us. We neglect our own need for friends, and we forget their needs too.

Maybe there are patterns in the way Jesus gathered his disciples that we can learn from.

- Jesus didn't simply take on board those in whose company he found himself in his family. Some of his closest friends were two cousins of his, but he specifically states that families may be divided over their commitment to him, that the Kingdom of God may set one part of a family against another. He himself turned aside from his own family when they came looking for him (Luke 8:19).
- So he deliberately set out to put himself in the way of gathering friends. He went to places where people were – such as the crowd attracted to John the Baptist, the market-place, and the centres of local work – and was prepared to discover friendship even while he looked for it.
- Jesus was selective, he didn't welcome just anyone who fancied travelling around with him (Mark 3:13–15). There is no evidence that he included among his disciples those men who had previously left John to join him.
- Jesus possessed a very special charisma that drew people to him, but in spite of this there was nothing 'automatic' about this attraction. In the stories about the calling of the first disciples, it appears that this charisma was irresistible: one was concentrating on his fishing and suddenly left his nets; another was busy at his job counting money he had extracted from others for tax purposes; but quite instantaneously left all his accounting and up and went after Jesus; and yet someone else was simply daydreaming under a tree but when he was noticed he got up in the most determined fashion to follow Jesus. But it is significant that in spite of these and other stories of instant attraction, there were some who resisted (Luke 9:57–9).

- Jesus never used coercion. When the rich young man decided against following him he didn't try to over-persuade him. Jesus always respected other people's choices (Mark 10:21–3).
- Jesus chose a group of mixed gender for his friends (Luke 8:3).

In all these things, Jesus was *proactive*. He didn't just wait around until friends turned up out of the air.

> – *When I feel friendless, I'm apt to blame all those other people who apparently don't want to be friends with me. Often we have to choose, quite deliberately, to make the time and space to get to know people. To put ourselves actively in the way of gaining friends.*

Jesus would turn to his small group to mull over his daily experience, and sometimes to expand upon it. At other times he would simply get away from the eyes of the public to rest with them.[1]

> – *Sometimes I feel I can only lay claim to my friends' time and attention when there is something specific to say, to bemoan, or to celebrate. Someone said to me, 'I wanted to get in touch with you but I didn't have anything special to say.' Just wanting to be together, to share time together without a 'purpose' is a priceless gift.*

When we want to find friends, there is so much on the purely practical and physical level that we can set out to do. And on this level alone, there is a model for our behaviour in Jesus Christ. Managing the emotional level, and the spiritual development of 'soul-friending', comes later.

Diminished by Pain?

The stress of continuing pain

> **TO COUNTERACT:**
>
> The 'trapped'ness of ongoing pain
>
> The 'guilt' expressed by those 'not healed'
>
> Feeling unattended to, unloved, disregarded

•••••••••••••••••••••••••••••••

What to do with the stress of continuing pain?

So much has been studied, written, and preached about the meaning of pain, this is not the place to add to that theory.[1] But are there skills of the body that relate to those times when I feel far from whole, when I am ill, uncertain, damaged, incapacitated?

Whatever the condition behind the pain, the primary task is to alleviate or correct it. If self-help is insufficient, then professional help must be sought. When all that has been done, some are still left with physical pain, sometimes without any reachable cause. Painkillers and appropriate medication can help, as can warmth, comfort and correct diet. But what about what is left after all the obvious relief has been offered?

Many pain centres today do something more than prescribe painkillers. This is a brief introduction to the other side of pain.

One of the chief reinforcers of any sort of pain is resistance to it.[2] While my muscles, sinues and nerves are shrieking, they tighten up. My mind is geared into 'for God's sake, take it away, get rid of it, let me out of it'. Most of us stay in that state until something outside of us comes to relieve us. Do we have to rely wholly on help from outside? What about what is inside us?

It is my own approach to the pain-that-remains which is the prime mover. Resentment and bitterness, or brave denial, may be modes of coping that I have witnessed and adopted for myself, but there are other approaches.

For instance, resistance to pain can be lessened by learnt deep relaxation, and pain arousal can be reduced by parasympathetic breathing. When it is relaxed the body can get on with its own deep healing, and breathing in the parasympathetic mode reduces the natural but noisome complaints of the mind. Many pain clinics run courses in deep relaxation.

There is an additional course which requires particular sensitivity. It is where sufferers are taught to avoid avoiding the pain, and to lower their resistance to it by, paradoxically, doing the opposite. They are taught to sink deeply right into the heart of the pain; to accept that it is there, almost as if it has a right (or purpose) to be there. Not exactly making friends with it, but it's a sort of 'let's get on with this together, mind and body', so the internal warfare can lessen. If the struggle between resisting the pain, and granting it permission to be there, can calm down a bit, a stage can be reached from which something more positive can develop.

Is there anything more?

Yes, a whole world more, and it is difficult to capture in words; it can't be reached until the physical body is relaxed, receptive and willing. There are various routes to this state. Sometimes God takes over and gives a dramatic episode of healing; or sometimes a person has to suffer extremes, as if it is a last resort that they are persuaded to give over control; and sometimes the continuing route is voluntary. There are a few very special people who deal with pain as if it were a colleague, and they manage it quite differently. Let me tell you about three stories. The first concerns someone of great intelligence and great ability. Let's call her Pat.

Pat is highly trained in the understanding of other people. She has suffered for years with a disintegrating spine, and the more it hurts and incapacitates her, the more she struggles to overcome the pain and spend her energy on other people's troubles. Those with problems queue up to see her, while her back gets worse and worse. For years she has lived from one crisis of spinal collapse to another, insisting she can't relax. She most certainly never gives up. Finally her consultants admit there is something there they do not understand and they tell her they can do little about it. It is a watershed in her medical history: the temptation to give way to despair is horrendous. This is an extract from her letter:

'I don't know if others will stay with me or not, but it's not up to me

now. I really can't sort, control, or do, anything. Truly I have no other choice but to "rest from my own works and cling to God". I know it sounds crazy. But now it is such a burden gone. It is in one way the best thing that has happened – God is glorious and I've been able to see how crazy and out of touch with His purposes for my life I've become over the last years. How I've lung to my own plans and built my own life. Not all of it has been terrible because God is the God of redemption. But it's like the prodigal – I've been in a far country and wasted many resources. I have "spoilt" my inheritance and what has God done? Come running out to meet me – in a big hug. I suppose saying "At last! Now I can begin to start something! May I have this dance?" '

Pat ends her letter by saying: 'Please keep faith with me and remind me of these things when I need someone to keep holding my hands up, and I forget.'

The next person is someone who has been confined to her chair for years. Let's call her Valerie.

Valerie's diagnosis was unclear; there appeared to be no major dysfunction of her skeletal or muscular system, but any attempt to walk or stand resulted in extreme nervous agony, and unbearable pain. Valerie's family got used to the inconvenience of the wheelchair, and arranged their lives around ways of making the best use of it. One day the whole family went to a healing convention, more out of curiosity to see what would happen to others than with any great expectation for themselves. They were amazed when, halfway through the evening, they saw their mother uncharacteristically respond to the call from the platform to go up and receive the ministry of healing. Valerie wheeled herself down the aisle to the ascending steps at the far end. They watched open-mouthed as she received the laying-on-of-hands. That was nothing to their amazement as they saw her walk – albeit unsteadily – up the steps to the platform by herself. They joined in the jubilation of the crowd; the roar of thanksgiving was unforgettable. Valerie's cure held up, and the lives of all the family were changed from that moment. For the entire family the giving of glory to God became the first motive of all their behaviour from then on. Their God reigned, they were triumphant with their visible proof, they told the whole world about it.

The other story is quite different. It is of a man who was a priest in a downtown parish, called Pete.

Pete worked quietly and unreservedly among the poor, the homeless, the addicts, and their children. The hierarchy knew of his work, but he got no special attention or extra resources, perhaps he didn't even ask for them. As he got older he developed diabetes, so he had to take on a very strict diet and to merge his daily programme around the times for his injections. The years advanced and he developed ulcers on his feet which lamed him; eczema on his body which interfered with his sleep; deterioration of his eyes which all but blinded him. He recognised his disabilities and did all there was to do in the way of getting physical help. He prayed a great deal, for other people. His physical condition took its natural worsening course, but his love and understanding of his people grew. His patience and compassion multiplied, it passed through him to those he met and on to the others that met those whom he met. This man shone with the love of God – for Him and by Him. It was totally transparent that he was precious to God; and that the love and generosity with which he responded was all the more remarkable because it was transmitted through the pain, never in spite of the pain.

People like these are rare, but all the more to be listened to. It's a bit like this: in such circumstances I, being crammed with self-pity, might say '*I want out*'. But in their love of God these rare people are saying, 'Lord, I know I hurt, but I'm prepared to *stay with it*, if You can make use of it.' There are very few of us who are asked to love God in this way; perhaps there are more than we are prepared to recognise in our achievement-oriented culture. They are the ones who are saints.

> Almighty God,
> whose most dear Son went not up to joy
> but first he suffered pain,
> and entered not into glory before he was crucified:
> mercifully grant that we, walking in the way of the cross,
> may find it none other than the way of life and peace;
> through Jesus Christ our Lord.
>
> Collect for Lent 3
> *The Alternative Service Book*

Jesus, as far as we know, experienced very little personal illness. Hardship, discomfort, hunger, blisters, no doubt. But he lived pain. He knew the pain of disappointment, grief, rejection; and at the last the torture of the soldiers. He himself relieved the pain of others throughout his life, but we can never underestimate the fact that he chose, at the end of his life, to accept pain for himself. The inescapable *fact* is that Jesus, God's only Son, did not call upon the twelve legions of angels he himself said he had at his disposal,[3] but that, although he prayed with blood and sweat not to do so, he discovered that he was expected by God to experience the extremes of pain. God expected of His Best Beloved the act of accepting pain.[4] Since that act of Jesus, the philosophical framework of Christianity is the only one of all the world religions that positively *makes use of pain*.

Pain is never to be looked for; it is not 'sent'; it is never to be not relieved; but when it is still there in spite of all our efforts, our response to it opens new possibilities, and these do not diminish us. Can hurting be useful?

So, for the rest of us, the ones who are not saints, is there something about the acknowledgement and offering of our own pain, doing our best to lessen it but when some of it remains doing our best not to resist it but to *offer* it? To use it how God Himself would like us to use it? The immensity of such generosity is beyond the understanding of those who have not yet been asked to do it, but the evidence of those who are in that place is one of the most telling sources of love and grace that we can possibly witness.

Picture–story of Zacchaeus

Luke 19:1–10

Jesus already knew what was going to be expected of him. He told the disciples – with no mincing of his words – about his determination to go up to the festival in Jerusalem. He already foresaw that there he would be betrayed, arrested, tried, rejected and killed. None the less, as he strode ahead leading the way he was far from gloomy.

He had had a lot to resolve lately. The journey leading to Jerusalem via Jericho was a time to prepare for the transition from straightforward mission to his final agony; he had to face an event that would be intensely personal, a private transaction between himself and cosmic powers, in which he would need every last drop of his deepest soul, and yet it would all be entirely public. Jesus knew the stresses of any transition, the uncertainty, instability, apprehension that are part and parcel of the process. He knew, too, the urgent desire of the disciples to protect him. They had tried to protect him from the 'nuisance' of the children, the 'inconvenience' of the beggars, the 'unworthiness' of the destitute. They projected their need – *their* need – that he should be seen to be only in the company of the respectable and the religious. Jesus wasn't at all sure that they had taken on board his new principles to live by – that the last shall be first, and the first last; that muchness didn't count for much; that God did the doing, not us; that God wasn't a being that simply reacted to our pleas, but He was the subject and He was proactive. There was a lot going on inside Jesus as he strode ahead, trailing behind him the crowd with the disciples. As the breeze caught his hair and beard, and the blood pumped through his muscles and joints as he stretched his stride, his sense of well-being and resolution heightened; the adrenalin helped him to clear his thoughts and to put his priorities in order. All the time, God the Father was walking by his side.

44

★

Zacchaeus had a lot to consider too. He had always been small, small even among his own compact race. As a child he was put down, belittled, squashed. But he soon learnt – to get what you wanted you had to push; since his school-days he'd been a pusher. No one would get anything for him. But bit by bit he worked his way up – he'd show them. He wanted passionately to be taken seriously, to 'get to the top'. And now he had. He still didn't get much respect from others though, he was still lonely and isolated, without close friends. The way he had taken to gain influence had perhaps been predictably unpopular, but at least people did now notice him. He had got rich by squeezing people of money for taxes (a good proportion of which he had kept for his own services); he had got so good at it that now he supervised others doing it too. He was 'big' at last. But although his public stature was obvious, he didn't feel all that great inside. A bit lost really.

Something interesting was happening in the road at Jericho, Zacchaeus' home town. 'What's in it for me?' he thought. 'Shucks, these blasted crowds, dense enough to stop me knowing. Some sort of major goings-on; they're not going to take note of me, for all my fine robes. How to get around this one?' Then Zacchaeus remembered the tree at the head of the town, where he had climbed as a young boy to reach over people's heads. Small as he was he was agile. He dropped his great cloak and skirted the crowds through the back streets, arriving at the sycamore tree ahead of them. He always liked being ahead. Forgetting his honour and feeling the return of his childhood skills he skimmed up the tree. Now he could oversee everything. He wasn't going to be kept down, not he, Zacchaeus!

★

One of the disciples was feeling decidedly put down. He was feeling marginalised, insignificant. He was fuming. Here he was, having left his job and his family to wander around the country with Jesus, but always with dozens of others! He didn't get a look in! What really hurt was the way Jesus had disregarded his efforts to protect him from all these disreputable and demanding people. He realised that Jesus liked his peace and quiet occasionally. But when he had shouted at the beseeching blind beggars to shut up Jesus had walked in front of him and healed them! Somehow he had to find a way of showing Jesus his good intentions.

Then he saw his opportunity. 'That nasty little man who makes everyone suspicious – he's so keen to draw Jesus' attention he's even made a fool of himself and climbed a tree! A gold-digger up a tree! Jesus hates ostentation, this time he'll be grateful to me for getting rid of him. 'Go away you worm!

Keep out! You're not the one Jesus wants near him, like me! Get down I tell you, stop yelling!'

★

But Jesus was master of his own decisions, Jesus took responsibility for himself. He laughs out loud at the unexpectedness of seeing proud Zacchaeus up a tree. Zacchaeus laughs back, full of childish glee. Jesus responds to his lack of dignity, and calls to him, 'Come down here, Zacchaeus, I want to be with you! I saw you scramble up there, but I can only talk to you if you are by my side. I'll come home with you now, if you want me, so come soon.'

And Zacchaeus dropped down from the tree throwing his hat in the air. Even little people could be the friend of Jesus, he didn't have to strive any more. All the things he'd struggled for he could give away; there was a better way of being beside people. No longer striving, achieving, grabbing and trying to impress people, he would let everything go and just love them. He didn't have to be high always, he could come down, and reach into the deeps with Jesus. He was better.

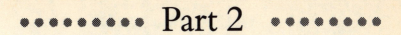

Part 2

Skills of the Mind

●●●●●●●●●●● 7 ●●●●●●●●●●●

The Use of Reason, Logic and Control

Jesus as 'manager'

> **TO COUNTERACT:**
>
> Confusion, indecision, mental fog
> Misinterpretation, spiralling worry
> Emotionalism
> Transferring blame to others

●●●●●●●●●●●●●●●●●●●●●●●●●●●

Joe and Joanne Universe know all about the body. They attend the gym several times a week; they eat all the right foods and drink only what is good for them. They know their anatomy and physiology, and they can choose to breathe correctly at appropriate times. But they are not so good at the tools given to them in their minds. Joe discovers that when he has too many decisions to make about his career he gets confused, and then he physically can't achieve what he wants to achieve. Joanne knows that when she is worrying about the children and the neighbours it affects the concentration she needs for her body-building. They both have come to realise that there is a direct link between the way they use their minds and the way their bodies work. If they allow their energy to leak, or to be dissipated, due to inefficient thinking, they won't be able to reach their physical targets. The strange thing is, that even if one of them becomes mentally unfocused, it will affect the performance of the other. So they decide to employ someone else to manage their engagements, administer their timing, and to decide upon their priorities.

Jesus Christ had no manager or mission administrator. According to the observations of the crowds he was unlearned. ' "How did he learn to read? He has not been educated" ', they said (John 7:15). His management skills came from daily observation and from the Scriptures.

For instance, he found a synopsis of how to manage people in Jeremiah 24:

49

God says: ' . . . I mean to concern myself with the welfare of [my people] . . . My eyes will watch over them for their good, to bring them back . . . , to build them up and not to break them down, to plant them and not to uproot them.' (vv. 5–6 NJB)

'I shall give them the wit to know me, for I am the Lord; they will be my people and I shall be their God, for they will come back to me wholeheartedly.' (v. 7 REB)

As a brief statement of management skills, this is a pretty accurate outline, one that would have been well known to Jesus. The main literary vehicle of knowledge in his time was the Torah, and he had the ability to use passage after passage to point up his own argument, always to great effect. He must have spent hours and hours with the handwritten scrolls in the village synagogue – there wouldn't have been copies at school or at home.[1]

Skills of the mind are about sorting out the ceaseless activity of the conscious intellect, and regulating the chaos that could sit there into some sort of constructive output. Instead of allowing the constant movement of my mind to dart anywhere with no purpose, or even worse, watching it circle round and round in a descending vortex of worry, I can harness its activity and put it to good use. When I have discovered how to do this for myself, I will be better equipped to enable others to manage theirs. Unfortunately, none of the Gospels are autobiographical, so we have no direct account of *how* Jesus developed his mental skills. None the less we have plenty of material describing the ways in which he used them to manage others.

The basis for his observation of how people 'tick' must have been the interchange of traders and travellers in Jesus' home town as he grew up. Both the good and the not-so-good drivers of caravans would have to come to Joseph's shop to get their trailers, carts and yokes repaired. As a growing lad Jesus would have overheard stories of deceit and ribaldry, sharp dealing and disappointment, square honesty and crooked contriving. There are frequent comments made by his biographers on his intimate knowledge of what goes on inside people's minds, for better or worse. He knew humankind to the core. 'Jesus knew all people . . . he never needed evidence about anyone; he could tell what someone had within.'[2] He had developed acute mental skills in order to apply this wide range of understanding to the variety of people and situations he came across in his three years of public life.

Logic and Spirituality

Jesus had a powerful command of 'left brain' logic. The left-brain functions are sharp, exact and pointed, quite different from the rounded, metaphoric functions of the right brain. Jesus used the legalism of logic with artistry and subtlety to counter the criticisms that came at him. The religious scholars and lawyers of his time spent their entire professional lives dissecting the nuances of phrases in the Torah, the Jewish scriptures. Yet each time they accosted him with their knowledge, and tried to trap him into their hostility,[3] he came out on top. He met them on their own ground, and then out-manoeuvred them with his intellect and humour. In stating his own position he was neither mealy-mouthed nor aggressive, he simply stayed with the facts.[4] The stress that the learned scholars hoped to heap on him was defused by being answered with straightforward logic.

Two examples will be enough here:

(i) 'If I am not doing my Father's work, there is no need to believe me; but if I am doing it, . . . at least believe in the work I do; then you will know for certain . . . that the Father is in me and I in the Father' (John 10:37–9).

(ii) When the Pharisees came to him in pretence of being on his side, they smarmingly affirmed that Jesus taught the truth without fear or favour; but was it right, they queried, to pay taxes to the detested Romans? Jesus' response was to point to the image minted on the coin, and make them agree to give Caesar what properly belonged to Caesar, and to God what belonged to God.[5] So he outwitted their underhand snares with pure logic. And they fell silent.

Jesus developed this skill of returning the question put to him as a technique to deal with falsely contrived argument. Sometimes he used verbal acrobatics to disprove the hypothesis of those who wanted to cut him down, and to push their question to its logical conclusion.[6] When the Jewish leaders confronted Jesus concerning his authority in driving out demons, and later questioned his authority in driving out the traders from the courtyard of the Temple, Jesus put a question back to them. How, he asks, can the authority of Beelzebub stand if it is divided against itself? (Matt. 12:25–9) And, he further asks, under whose authority was John, the preacher beloved of the people, acting? (Luke 20:4) 'And the great crowd listened to him with delight' (Mark 12:37).

Jesus possessed a wit that was rapier sharp. A good example of this lies in his reply to the tricky question about the fate of the unfortunate woman who had to marry seven brothers in succession: he said, 'Your trouble is that you don't know the scriptures, nor know the power of God. For when these seven brothers and the woman rise from the dead, they won't be married – they will be like the angels!'[7] Further exploration of Jesus' wit as it carries over into humour is to be found in chapter 18.

'Reason' and Spirituality

Repartee, logic, reversing questions were all ways in which Jesus made use of his sense of reason. He also made use of reason in communicating his unusually wide knowledge. He well understood the affairs of common daily life; how people dealt with significant life events and transitions; how they managed financial affairs; the natural history of seasons, the weather, birds and plants; but there was something else as well.

In his astute management of human understanding Jesus did not stay behind in the safety of religious insights. He was not a separated-out mystic. His profound convictions in things of the spirit also included a knowledge of worldliness. Jesus used stories which were about the questionable tactics of people with large financial responsibilities, and sometimes he commended their ingenuity. The unjust accountant whose wiliness was set up as an example to those others living 'purer' lives is significant. There he remarks, 'For the children of this world are more astute in dealing with their own kind than are the children of light.' He told his followers to be 'wise as serpents, gentle as doves'; and when considering taking up any large project for God he warned 'but don't begin until you count the cost'.[8] Jesus' spirituality was grounded in reason drawn from practical experience.

The Gospels record the strong arguments Jesus used against worry. What is the use of it? What good does it do?[9] With all the strains and stresses that Jesus Christ was subjected to, it was crucial that early in life he learnt how to focus his mental energy constructively – that is, he learnt mind control. He clearly understands the destructive effect of worry – that is, how vital mental power can drain away and get nowhere. He uses his intellectual energy to plan and organise and work through a problem, but this is different to squandering it on spiralling thought patterns that end up where they first started. Many of us get caught up in habits of worrying. Jesus is compassionate with those who find themselves in such a state, he calls them 'my friends' and 'little flock'; but he is convinced from his own personal experience that it is of no usefulness. He tells us what *is* worth being concerned about – that we should not fall into the ways of the devil, but rather seek the Kingdom of God – and warns us to be always on guard. And then Jesus points out the difference between three sorts of mental preoccupation: ordinary carefulness; pointless worry; and a deep longing.

- Carefulness is common sense;
- anxious worry drains energy; but a
- persistent, ongoing desire fuels one's determination to see something through. Jesus expressed this yearning frequently throughout the Gospels; for instance he said, 'I have come to bring fire to the earth, and how I wish it were blazing already! There is a baptism I must still receive, and what constraint I am under until it is completed!' (Luke 12:49) With discipline and purpose, we *can* control how we use our minds, just as we can improve our practice with any tool, but some people are insufficiently exposed to the teaching of how to use this tool. Concentrating on reason is a useful first step.

Control and Spirituality

This level-headedness also shows itself in the way Jesus used his mind for the skill of organisation in specific situations. He was skilled in making order out of the confabulation of stresses that came at him by using forward planning, putting aside sessions for teaching, adjusting circumstances to suit his own ends – always keeping the further glory of his Father as his aim.[10] At various times, when Jesus noticed the large crowd growing, he organised his space by getting into a boat, or walking up a slope, or putting the crowd into groups. Jesus made careful arrangements – the details of how he did this are left undocumented – before some of the major events of his life. These include his sending out of the first evangelistic mission of the disciples, his entry into Jerusalem, and the preparations for the last Passover supper he ate with his disciples.[11]

In general, Jesus preferred to clothe his teaching in stories that were easily memorable, or metaphors that could be unwrapped on several layers. And yet he also made full use of bold imperatives: for all Jesus' empathy and concern for how other people were thinking, he used directive measures wherever he needed to make the most impact. For instance, at the rabbi's home, when his daughter was apparently dead, he commanded the wailing crowd to get out (Matt. 9:23). As Jesus was walking along the road and he saw Matthew sitting at his normal task of collecting taxes, 'Come', he said, 'and follow me, *now*' (Matt. 9:9 LB). In dealing with devils who were in possession of people's minds, Jesus was sternly imperative: 'Be quiet! *come out!*' (Mark 1:25)

And finally, in this section looking at how Jesus made use of his mental control, there is something that seems to us extraordinary. Today, a great deal of emphasis is laid on non-directional counselling; individuals who are highly experienced in managing people go on intense courses to learn how *not* to tell others what to do. Sometimes, Jesus not only told people what to do, but did it in a way that we should call 'over the top'. He was unequivocal in his commitment to the glory of God, and at times he was commanding in the way he transferred this goal onto his hearers. His adherence to the purposes of God was total: he would cut through to the marrow of any matter with his sharp rationality and acute logic, but this was often expressed in what seems to us as overstatement. Hyperbole was the medium of Jesus' culture: ' "If your right eye should be your downfall, tear it out and throw it away . . . And if your right hand should be your downfall, cut it off and throw it away; for it will do you less harm to lose one part of yourself than to have your whole body go to hell." '[12]

In all these general mental strategies of management Jesus had the approval of his hearers. 'Well spoken, Master; what you have said is true,' said one of the scribes who had listened, appreciating that Jesus had given a good answer. 'Well said, sir!' remarked some of the experts in the Jewish law. And that ended their questions, for they dared ask no more.[13]

It seems a rather ridiculous exercise, trying to single out particular strategies in the working of the mind of the Son of God, Redeemer of the world, Creator of all things. But just because he was all that, it is all the more important that we should learn from him the 'hows' of making the best use of our mental energy.

How do I use my *reason* to make sense of stress?

Rationalisation is a powerful tool in bringing order to the tumbling confusion of thoughts and emotions that commonly are a sign of too much stress. The art of finding a reason to explain the state I am in will help to focus on what immediately needs attention. I can then move on to other ways of handling the tool of reason, to be described in the following chapters. But there is a warning too. Reason can be a two-edged sword:

- if I continually insist on having an over-legalistic attitude towards others, it plays havoc with easy communication;
- if I rely over much on exact measurement, it can uproot the growing confidence of another;
- if I am derisive of someone else's inaccuracy with language, it can destroy their attempts to put things into picture language.

And even Jesus Christ found that picture language can carry far more meaning than bare facts.

Joe and Joanne Universe discovered their need to employ management skills. However, like the rest of us, they would soon find out that logic, reason, and control were not enough on their own to make their lives fulfilled.

8

The Use of Choice

TO COUNTERACT:

Fatalistic attitudes
Helplessness
Monotony
Repetitive strain syndrome

We tend to think of *choice* as an ability that is used on comparatively rare occasions. It is something to do with a new job, or finding a new home, or choosing a new spring outfit. Most of the time, most of us feel we are running on automatic pilot. 'I couldn't help myself', we say; 'He didn't know any better', 'What else could I do?', 'There was no other way out'. *There is always another way.* Most of the time we just don't bother to see it.

Ever since the seventeenth century and the search for the 'enlightened man', we have been encouraged to see things through the eyes of scientific method. A question is right or wrong, true or false, black or white. So even when we are aware of choice, we find the options are fairly limited. Jesus lived seventeen centuries before the onslaught of scientific method, and for him the choices of each separate moment were as multicoloured as the rainbow God revealed to Noah. They are for us, too, when we can get into the habit of looking for them and making use of their variety. Here we'll be looking at what we can learn from the behaviour of Jesus as he faced stress; it is not the place for an extended discussion of the doctrine of free will.

It is small wonder that for some people the concept of choice has a hollow ring about it. There are those who are severely limited by poverty, or by the lack of physical mobility, or by having to look after a dependent relative; there are those who have mental problems,

56

or who are severely disadvantaged by their social conditioning, or who are stuck in a constricting, monotone job. These situations are quite different to those where people are hampered by a narrow way of thinking and a lack of imagination or flexibility. Yet even in the most severely restricted situation it is possible to find something of choice. I can choose how I breathe, how I move, whether I tackle my task in a way that is constructive or defeatist, the tone of my voice – all these things that are in my own internal control.

Choice is about how I perceive the authority I have over my own actions:

- Is that authority based within me, or do I prefer to rely on getting it from outside of myself?[1]
- To what extent am I free to use that authority, while I am still concerned for the needs of others? Do I always have to choose between their needs and mine, or is there a way by which both are merged?
- If I feel I am a doormat, I will find choosing for myself very difficult to do. Is it 'good' and 'humble' and 'Christian' to be walked over? Was Jesus the Christ so filled with love for others that he was put upon?
- Is it reasonable to submit my power of choice totally to other people?

There are times when Jesus handed over his authority to others, but his biographers make it very clear that this was as a result of his *choice*. For instance: in John 10:18 he says, 'No one takes [my life] from me; I lay it down of my own free will, and as I have power to lay it down, so I have power to take it up again.'

When we are under great stress, it is vital that we somehow find a point where we can influence the situation by making choices for ourselves. Jesus defused stress by taking charge of the choices available to him. In the Gospels there are incidents when he chooses for himself, and others where he offers choice to those around him.

Jesus making choices for himself. Read these accounts with your imagination; picture the likely stress rampant in the event, and what could have happened if Jesus had reacted with docile passivity.

1. A series of huge pressures forced upon Jesus by the devil; they are each rebuffed by Jesus *choosing* the Word of God over and against the word of Satan.[2]
2. A man with a visible and virulent skin-disease came up to Jesus

and said, 'Lord, if you want to, you can cleanse me.' The crowd is agog and watching – is the preacher going to touch the repugnant skin? Jesus replied, '*I want to*': he stretched out his arm to the sores and 'Be clean', he said.[3]

3. On the way up to Jerusalem, some Pharisees came up to Jesus and said, 'Go away! Leave this place because Herod means to kill you!' Jesus was unperturbed and *chose* to go on in his own way. He replied, 'You may go and give that fox this message: Look! Today and tomorrow I drive out devils and heal ... For today and tomorrow and the next day I must go on ... ' – whatever the end result would be at the hands of Herod.[4]

4. As Jesus travelled extensively around Galilee, he learned that the Jews were seeking to kill him, so he *chose* not to travel round Judea.[5]

5. The disciples were arguing about the preferential treatment they thought John was in for; they were jealous and competitive. There was ugly conflict around.[6] Jesus put an end to the conflict by saying, 'If *I want* him to stay behind till I come, what does it matter to you?'[7]

6. The entire narrative of the passion of Jesus Christ is a succession of stupendous personal choices deliberately taken by him. Maybe they are typified by one short example: Jesus tasted the wine, but *chose* not to drink it.[8]

The other group is where *Jesus hands choice over to others*:

1. When the blind man (or men) of Jericho called to Jesus he said, 'What do you want me to do for you?'[9] Jesus was asking for the intention or purpose or desire to be openly expressed.

2. When the mother of Zebedee's sons pleaded with him, Jesus said, 'What is it you want?'[10] What did she most really will for?

3. At the pool of Bethesda, Jesus asked the paralysed man: 'What would you have me do? Do you want to be well again?'[11] What a strange question! Perhaps Jesus knew this man had to be galvanised into making a choice – he doesn't even reply with a 'Yes!' He has become so habituated into the state of being an invalid, feeling invalidated, that he responds with a further complaint.

4. 'After this, many of his disciples went away and accompanied him no more. Then Jesus said to the Twelve, "What about you, do you want to go away too?" '[12] It's as if Jesus really needs us to choose what we want before he can act. But he doesn't prejudge how we will respond.

The proactive use of choice underlies many of the skills of the mind that will be looked at in the following chapters – time management, adjusting priorities, delegating tasks and so on; it is fundamental to our self-responsibility. Acknowledging the range of the choices open to me, and taking responsibility for the one I choose, is the bottom line of all stress management. Jesus Christ acted on this principle all his recorded life. He was called by God, the '*Chosen One*'; and Jesus calls his twelve special friends 'the Chosen'. He says, 'You didn't choose me. I chose you.'[13] And yet he takes full responsibility that one of those he has chosen is 'a devil'.

The consequence of managing my own choice is that I am no longer able to '*blame*' another for what happens. This makes the use of choice difficult for many people. But it also brings with it a sense of self-ownership – why should I hand such a strong core of myself over to anyone else? Responsibility is something about power and ownership, and taken together with choice it means I am not afraid to be myself – which, after all, is what God intends that I should be. Let's take a very small common example.

Linda comes home from a hard day's work to find that the day's washing-up is still piled into the sink. Her two adult sons have been at home all day, and her husband arrived home half an hour before she did. Linda's immediate impulse is to storm into the living room in a rage and vent her frustration all over the family.

Surely she would be totally justified in doing this. What other choices can she possibly have?

– She can act on her first impulse and fume at the family: this is risky, because they might all react by going out, leaving her isolated; she, the injured one, will be made to feel the aggressor. Is that what she really wants?
– She can leave it in the sink and announce she won't start getting the meal until they have cleared it: that too is risky. She won't get it done because they'll opt to finish their television programme, and perhaps the football item that follows, and everybody will be so hungry by the time the meal is on the table they won't even be speaking to each other.
– She could roll up her sleeves and do it herself: risky, because she will turn into a martyr and spend the rest of the evening snapping at the others.

- She could turn around and leave the house herself and go and grouse with a neighbour: too risky – the molehill will turn into a mountain in the gossip stakes and she'll still be hungry.
- She could choose to get on with it because she wants the cleared space, and then ask the family for a self-help conference; then lists of chores can be made and allocated to each member to develop mutual responsibility: still risky; this is a good idea but it needs to be handled with care and good humour, not the qualities Linda has right now, in *this* setting.
- She could go into the living room, greet the family, explain the position as she sees it, and ask them to do something about it. *They* choose how to handle it, the problem is shared, no one is depleted.

The important thing is that Linda acknowledges all the options – and there are others too – and chooses between them. She is not bound by her usual habit of flying into a rage, but she surprises her family (and herself?) by the constructive use she makes of her stress.

Choice isn't about right and wrong, good and bad, though there might be times of better or best. Choice is about *acknowledging the options*, weighing up the possible consequences, and deciding what option is the most appropriate for this situation, this time, here and now. This is rightly an exercise of the will. Very often our choices are controlled by our feelings of the moment. They could be feelings of fear or anger, jealousy or injustice, or love and care; and it is often appropriate to bring my gut-feeling into the process. But in that split-second in which I decide how to respond, it is by bringing in the powers of reason and will that affects the potential stress.

'*Choice*' is about approaching the task ahead with an 'I want to', 'I will to', 'I intend to', 'I purpose to', 'I desire to', 'I decide to', and all these words have a common root in the scriptural Greek word. When we look at some of the examples in the Gospels where Jesus hands the act of choosing over to us, we find any of these variations could apply. There are times when he actually suggests we break free from our expected, habitual responses to a familiar situation, and discover different ways of looking at it. He invites us to be aware of present appropriateness on various occasions. For instance:

• When people who complained that his disciples didn't display fasting as a habit, in the way their reputable 'religious' leaders and the disciples of John did.[14] Jesus replies that this choice is open to all at any time, and surely while the bridegroom is actually present people should celebrate? There are times for fasting and times for feasting, and it is up to us to choose which is which.

• When he heard the complaint that money shouldn't be spent on extravagant gifts for him, but instead should be given to the poor.[15] Jesus replies that the poor are always there and worthy of our care, but that there is also a time for expressing our love richly. We are free to choose when and what to give.

• Sometimes Martha busied herself preparing interesting meals for Jesus and complained that her sister was lazy and unco-operative, just sitting listening to him.[16] There are other occasions when Jesus spoke first and longest to Martha, but on this one he chides her gently that sometimes being passive is more appropriate than being active. The choice is ours, when to be busy, and when to be still.

• The account of Jesus taking off his outer robe and stooping to wash the disciples' feet at the last supper is a familiar one. It is interesting to compare this event with his story of the landlord who returns to his house unexpectedly, to find whether those he left to care for his property had been fulfilling their responsibility or not. Jesus ends this story in a most surprising way. He says, 'How happy are those servants whose master finds them awake and ready when he returns! I tell you, he will take off his coat, ask them to sit down, and will wait on them . . . even if he should come at midnight or even later!'[17] That there is a time to serve, and a time to be served, underlines the need for choice in the lives even of those totally committed to caring for others.

Some of those who have difficulty in making full use of their gift of choice, those who insist that 'I have always done it that way' and resist change in their own behaviour, do so by trusting in theories of inherited personality types. It has been shown that any personality, whether the traits of that personality are due to genes or to conditioning, and whether that personality prefers to be a go-getter or an opt-outer, can be modified if that person wills it sufficiently strongly. The key is to take charge of my choice. If I really want to, I can even resist the expectations that I insist on carrying around about myself, and those that I think others are expecting of me. How Jesus avoided being sucked into such expectations will be expanded in chapter 11. All situations of choice require a real and sober assessment of the possibilities before a choice is made.

There are those who find that boredom and monotony are a relief, and some who like to know that someone else is in charge and making all the decisions. But, for most people, the less choice we have the greater is the stress we experience. When I feel I am trapped in a situation where there is no choice, and I can make no contribution, I tend to feel worthless. On these occasions I try to bring to mind the following story.

> One of the hostages from the Iranian activity a few years ago was being de-briefed on his return. He had been in total darkness, shackled by his ankles, and in isolation. The investigator asked him, 'In those conditions, how on earth did you keep your sanity?'
>
> 'Oh,' the ex-hostage replied, 'I kept my sanity by holding onto my sense of choice.'
>
> 'Choice!' exclaimed the investigator. 'Where was the choice in those conditions?'
>
> The answer came immediately. 'Whenever the guard arrived with my ration of bread for the day, I would break a piece off and hide it, so that I could act as host to the next person to come.' (Anon)

This carries with it the risk that I can choose mistakenly. Once I admit the full extent of the choices open to me, I have to let in the undigestible fact that, out of His immense generosity, God has handed over to us the opportunity – and the feasibility – of defying Him. It is crucial to acknowledge that I mishandle my use of choice. This may involve contrition and repentance, forgiveness and restoration. But when we doubt, yet again, we can learn from the behaviour of Jesus himself. For him, his overriding desire, will, intention, choice, was to align his human will with the purpose of God his Father. 'Father! For you everything is possible . . . But let it be as you, not I would have it.'[18]

As for us, perhaps we cannot be as confident of interpreting the will of God correctly as his own Son was. But he has told us, 'I know the ones I have chosen' (John 13:18), and '*the Son gives life to anyone he chooses*' (John 5:21). What more assurance can we need?

9

What About the Other Person's Point of View?

TO COUNTERACT:

Always being In The Right
Self-centredness
Intolerance
'Why don't they understand
    me?'
'I'm on my own'

Jesus was Right; of course he was always Right, he was the Son of God. But there is something quite extraordinary about the Rightness of Jesus Christ, Son of God. *Jesus never pushed his Rightness, his Righteousness, onto other people.*

In spite of his total conviction concerning his mission and his purpose as the mouthpiece of the Godhead, of the Creator of all things, Jesus never allowed his sense of ego to get in the way of other people's responsibility for their own beliefs. He never imposed his strong personality on the individualism of others. The mental 'set' of Jesus Christ was so tuned into the love of God both for him, and of Him, and also for others, that he never belittled anyone in order to prove his own superiority. But I do.

It is something we do all the time. Whenever our own sense of having-the-edge-over-the-other slips, we become stressed. We feel Out of Control.

Our sense of worthfulness so much depends on being *more* than the next person. Particularly in this day and age, when we are infused with competitiveness at every possible level: intellectual, professional, social, personal, spiritual. We have to convince ourselves that somehow, somewhere, we are *better* than our fellows. Cleverer or kinder or richer (or poorer) or more beautiful or more creative or more understanding or more streetwise. We have to convince others – those we come into contact with – that we are owed something a bit extra; a little bit more respect or attention or approval, because we have 'deserved' it. Nowadays, the way in which we focus on our 'rights' has taught us how much is due to us; when we don't get it we want to sue for compensation, and this can be through the legal process or by using our own innate sense of emotional contrivance and mental bullying. Did Jesus?

Something interesting happens to us when we make full use of our reason, logic, and choice. Especially if we are also in full use of the tools in our bodies, and therefore we feel fit and well. When we are on top of our form, we tend to feel In Control. A great deal of business management skills and stress management skills are geared towards this psychological state of feeling In Control. And as soon as I convince myself I have all the answers right, and I am in control, I can start letting everybody else know how right I am and they should all take their answers from me, because I've cracked it. The more I am in control, the less I will need to, or want to, listen to others. This is a tricky position to be in.

If it was possible to construct a chart of the difference between being In Control and being In Charge it might go something like this:

IN CONTROL	IN CHARGE
'That which serves to check, restrain, or hinder; power of authority to check' 'to exercise restraint or sway over'	'Care, cargo, custody; the person or thing entrusted to the keeping of another' 'the exercise of care; trust'[1]
When 'I am in control', I limit the other's opportunity to be in control or to be right	When I am 'in charge' of the tools I carry, I can choose which to use, when to use them, and when to hand them over to others
I am attempting to eliminate risk	Some risk adds to life's variety and interest
I can't risk relaxing, being	I don't mind being wrong and

wrong, letting go, being 'shown up' – I have to demonstrate I'm 'best'	making mistakes I am not threatened by being unskilled – others can often do it better
Extract from the promotion of a business stress management course: 'Take Control: Once and For All'	When I don't know, it gives others space to tell me what they know
In Control of myself, often means I am controlling of others	Being In Charge of my own responses, ideally means freeing others up to express theirs

Where does Jesus Christ fit into all this?

There is a very fundamental difference between being in control of oneself and the ability to be in charge of one's responses. The one in control is powerfully protected and defended, even armed. This can easily turn into a situation of 'me' against 'others'. Jesus had no need to be protected, defended or armed about his rightness, it just was. Jesus wanted above everything else to draw others in. It was said of him, 'Look! . . . my beloved, in whom my soul delights . . . he will not brawl or cry out . . . he will not break the crushed reed, or snuff the faltering wick' (Matt. 12:18–20). When his disciples wanted to confront certain unrepentant villagers with a reprimand, Jesus simply advised that the situation should be allowed to fade away (Luke 9:55).

When I am in charge of my responses, I can choose – if I want – to give away my sense of control. I can hand it over, let someone else have a go, acknowledge that others have just as much room to be right as I have, that their truth is as valid for them as mine is for me. Even though Jesus knew he was Right, his antennae were always out to pick up the signals that told him where the other person was coming from, to read where their experience had led them. For instance, there were various occasions on which Jesus discussed with his disciples what sort of understanding they, and other people, had of his role. 'Who do people say I am?' he asked them, and 'who do you say I am?'[2] It was a question that concerned him deeply; he asked it as they were travelling along their way, again as they approached the inevitable hassles of a large town, and after he had been praying on his own. This concern for what others said of him was as important as his desire that his closest friends should not spread around their conviction that he was indeed the Son of God. Jesus was not seeking for reported praise or approval, but he was listening with sensitivity to the feelings of others and how they were reacting to the message he brought.

This acute awareness of the position of others was demonstrated as he was at the height of his own suffering – at a time when he might have been expected to be totally absorbed in his own predicament. As he struggled under the weight of his own cross, starved and weary and beaten, he said to the wayside watching women, 'Do not weep for me; weep rather for yourselves and your children' (Luke 23:28). This knowledge of how other people were feeling (Luke 9:47) was with him even as he was dying. Tormented by his agony, he looked to the two who were still by his side through all the long hours and discerned their need even at the centre of his own – 'This is your son', he said to his bereft mother, and 'This is your mother' to his grieving friend (John 19:26–7).

The whole imprecise area of being in charge of one's own responses, and on occasion choosing to give something of one's own sense of control away, is fundamental to the way Jesus Christ re-tuned the stresses that came at him in his human life. It is very different to the common daily admonitions we hear around us, to 'get back into control of yourself'. It means riding the way in double harness. In one hand I hold the responsibility of acknowledging and owning where I am, myself; and in the other I need to hold the story of a different person. They are both valid, both of interest and concern to God the Father. Neither one should be imposed upon the other. I also have to curb my desire to superimpose my version of another's story on anyone else. It is important that I should be in charge of my own responses, yet leave that same responsibility of others to them. Controlling others is not part of Jesus' story.

Jesus reminds us of *choice* constantly. He also tells us that primarily he chooses us, we don't choose him. He chooses us – as he chose his disciples – not to become people who simply serve him, or people who only learn from him. He chooses people to be around him not as slaves or students. He treats them as guests.[3]

Tom Pierce admits he is a bit of a perfectionist. He works hard at being in control of his job, his finances, his property. He exercises hard every weekend to keep physically in trim, and he likes going on management courses that keep him mentally agile. Tom is a computer buff, and his work doesn't work unless each move, each tap on the keyboard, is right. So he knows the importance of being right. However he has noticed something odd lately. The more he comes home with the right answers, and the more he tells his wife and daughter they don't need to worry because everything is under control, the less they seem to talk to him. So he works at being even more efficient: more short-cut tips to save more time and energy, and he tells his family about these too so they can improve as much as he does, but they just turn away from him and shut off. He knows he is right and in full control and totally unstressed; so his sense of growing isolation is puzzling.

Then, one weekend, there was the incident of the garage door. Tom had been planning to repaint his double garage door for some time. He made a date in his diary, discussed materials with the decorator, and bought the best paint. It would take him all Saturday and part of Sunday to strip, prepare, undercoat, and apply two top coats of green paint properly, but it would be a perfect job when finished. He didn't know what his wife and daughter would be doing that weekend.

Tom put on his overalls and began. Just then his wife and daughter came out of the house saying their plans had been cancelled. Tom was never quite sure how it happened, but, unaccountably, there they were, each with a brush in hand, each loading the brush with green paint, and the entire door was finished by late coffee-time. It hadn't been stripped properly, and it wasn't a perfect job, but they had talked and laughed and shared news. So they all went out for a pub lunch.

Who had been 'right', and where was the 'control' in that? This incident gives Tom cause to ponder. Is it, after all, helpful to others that he is so sure of everything all the time? Is it too late to change?

Organisational Skills

Selecting priorities
Time management
Task delegation
Setting goals realistically

> **TO COUNTERACT:**
>
> Disorder
> Confusion
> Spiralling worry
> Becoming overwhelmed
> Being at others' beck and call

•••••••••••••••••••••••••••

Like the warp and the weft of weaving cloth, the subtle difference between being in control and being in charge of my responses underlies all the tasks of getting organised. Whether my primary desire is to boost my own ego and display my competence in competition with others, or whether it is to live more nearly according to the model of Jesus Christ, this basic pattern will show through. The present chapter lists classic office skills; let's see briefly what Jesus made of them.

Selecting Priorities

Whether the matter in hand is trivial or life-changing, the way we select our priorities will depend on whatever is our overriding purpose, intent, desire, motive, and will. In Jesus, that was always to align his behaviour to the purposes of God. His decisions were consistently made in the light of the eternal glory of the Kingdom of God. For instance:

- In the way he chose **single-mindedness**. Having prepared for his mission for around thirty years, he left his childhood home with its familiarity, comfort and the supporting love of his friends and family, for the unknown travelling life of the wandering preacher

(Mark 1:14, 15; Luke 4:14, 15). The stress of tearing himself away from the safety of what was known is not described in the Gospels, but it is simple to imagine. The unknown world outside daily life must have been reported in the form of stories and fantasy; there were no photographs or accurate statistics, and no information technology. As he considered the way ahead, Jesus could not rely on dependable communication. Maybe the security he had experienced during his adolescence and young adulthood had become constricting as he matured; nevertheless, breaking away is always at the risk of great upset and fraction. Moving house and changing jobs are counted among the most highly stressful events for us, even when we have a house and job to go to. Jesus had neither.

And yet Jesus was so tuned in to the opportunities inherent to this loss and focusing, that he urged the same course – if necessary – on those who were timid in making up their minds about where their priorities lay. He told the crowds that anyone who wanted to follow him must put that desire before the love of parents or siblings or even children.[1] Loyalty to him must be absolute. Working for the Kingdom of God had to come first at every moment, and anything that got in the way had to be abandoned. Activity or wealth or dependency or public ritual or even learning: all are secondary to the primary priority of furthering the purposes of God the Father. This is the underlying principle of nearly all the parables of Jesus, and is explicit in all his actions.

- Jesus' single-mindedness was tuned into **loving God first**. Then, as he told us, as you love yourself, love your neighbour.[2]

His behaviour constantly bore this out. For instance, when he said, 'If you save your greetings for your brothers, are you doing anything exceptional?'[3] he was voicing a principle he enacted frequently. Such as when he visited the hated Samaritans, or listened to the suspiciously foreign Syrophoenician, or accepted help from a stranger with a darker skin, or asked for forgiveness for the soldiers driving nails into his hands and feet. All these incidents occurred at times when Jesus was particularly exposed to stress, and one would expect his priorities to be concerned with guarding himself. Because he had no fear or prejudice or distrust inside himself to guard, he could face the stranger outside with love and compassion.

- Having put God first, Jesus declared that his priorities were **to care for the 'poor'** – the damaged in body, mind, emotions or spirit as well as those who were socially underprivileged.[4] He gave himself to each of these categories with the intensity of the present moment. The blueprint he gave us for the working out of our lives is to be seen in the Beatitudes (Matt. 5:3–10).

- Jesus demonstrated his priorities **in action**; he lived them as well as speaking about them. When he was faced with turmoil he acted out his convictions on top of explaining them vocally. He knew the most important thing was to keep in communication with his Father, so he regularly left the crowds to pray on his own (this is expanded in chapter 11). Whatever is genuine in our topmost priorities can be read in our behaviour even more clearly than in our proclaimed intentions. 'By their fruit you shall know them.'[5]

   'A man had two sons. He went and said to the first, "My boy, go and work in the vineyard today." He answered, "I will not go," but afterwards thought better of it and went. The man then went and said the same thing to the second who answered, "Certainly, sir," but did not go. "Which of the two did the father's will?" ' (Matt. 21:28–31)

- One of Jesus' priorities when the expectations upon him were peculiarly heavy, was that of **energy efficiency**.
   - When he was particularly pressed by the crowds and their demands for healing he would take one single needy person away from the public eye and heal them in private.[6]
   - Or he would answer a plea for healing from someone on behalf of another who was at a distance, without actually going there.[7]
   - Again, surprising though it may be to us today, when Jesus saw that his message was falling on deaf ears he didn't wait around to reinforce it, he didn't waste energy over-persuading those who were reluctant to believe in him. He simply left them.[8]
   - And when Jesus was foretelling the catastrophe of the future, he told his hearers to drop everything when they saw it, not even to spend energy in collecting possessions or checking their households.[9]

- On some occasions Jesus demonstrated how he could **re-direct the priorities of others** through his own behaviour. For instance, not only did he warn the ruling religious leaders of the effects of their misguidedness, he showed in practice how it could be redeemed.[10]

Having established the priorities to any problem facing Jesus, he then had to make his plans for action, decide how to use the time available, and organise his resources. Just like us.

Time Management: Planning, Deciding, Organising

The Son of God had to be a master of time management in order to achieve his aim in three short years. In this brief section we are looking only at the techniques in his behaviour when exposed to stress, techniques that we can do our best to copy.

- At the very first recorded sign of his outstanding powers, Jesus was in charge of his own timing. When his mother urged him to make public his distinctive ministry by offering him the opportunity to demonstrate it, he said, 'My hour has not come yet.' A little while later, on further consideration, he took the bull by the horns and performed his first public sign – when he wanted to do it, not just to please his mother.[11]

- After this Jesus travelled around within Galilee; he decided to avoid Judea, because the Jews were looking out for a chance to kill him. In spite of this danger, his brothers urged him to accompany them to the feast of the Tabernacles in Jerusalem (this was a bit of a challenge because actually they still didn't believe in him and wanted to call his bluff). However Jesus said, 'For me, the right time has not come yet but for you, any time is the right time . . . Go up to the festival yourselves: I am not going to this festival, because for me the time is not ripe yet.' In spite of that, after his brothers had left, Jesus decided for himself to go up to Jerusalem secretly (John 7:2–11).

- It is said that on visits to Jerusalem, 'They wanted to arrest him, but because his hour had not yet come no one laid a hand on him' (John 7:30) and again in the following chapter, 'No one arrested him because his hour had not yet come [his time had not yet run out]' (John 8:20). And meanwhile Jesus himself is saying, 'For a short time I am with you still; then I shall go back to the one who sent me. You will look for me and will not find me; where I am you cannot come' (John 7:33–4). Such short extracts illustrate a strong sense of time-worthiness that surrounds the whole of the three short years of Jesus' public life. He was apparently acutely aware of the need to use each moment in its appointed way, in order to strengthen God's ultimate purpose for his world. No moment was wasted, or misused. Can that be said about our use of the time given to us?

- The extended episode of the dying and death of Lazarus from Bethany is a prime example of the way Jesus took responsibility for the way he managed time. Lazarus and his two sisters are the only group of people – other than the disciples – that we know Jesus visited on a regular basis. They were special friends of his. And yet when the news of Lazarus' terminal illness arrived, Jesus quite deliberately postponed going to see him because the glory of God would be better served if he waited.[12] Jesus curbed his own natural desire to see his friend before he died; he was prepared instead to risk the pain of mourning, and misunderstanding. Because of this and his decision to put every ounce of his physical, psychological and spiritual energy into the effort of calling him back from the dead – not only was Lazarus raised, but the faith of both Martha and Mary was consolidated, that of the crowd was strengthened, and the disciples as a whole witnessed a foretaste of what was to happen a little later to Jesus himself. A whole constellation of outcomes to further the glory of God, which was always Jesus' first priority. What it cost him we can only begin to surmise; it is not often that any of us are called upon to take such a gamble with time as this.

- Jesus constantly warned those close to him about what was to happen in the future, both short-term and in the long-term. The words he spoke were unpalatable and unacceptable to them, so Jesus had to repeat them on several different occasions. He says, 'I have told you all this so you may not fall away' (John 16:1) and 'I did not tell you this from the beginning because I was with you; but now I am going . . .' (John 16:4–5). This will be examined further in chapter 12, but at this point notice the technique of including the 'so that . . .' or 'because . . .' phrase – always explaining the reasoning behind the decision to those who are going to be most affected by the change. Other people can take hold of our timing of our actions better if we take care to put into words how we have come to that decision.

The Organisation of the Environment

The popularity of Jesus grew, and the need for him to be circumspect and fully organised took on special importance. In order to avoid being overwhelmed physically and emotionally by the vast crowds that were drawn to him (sometimes they were so closed in on him he could scarcely breathe) he developed various ploys. If he put a bit of space between himself and the people he could remain authoritative while enabling them all to hear him better:

- So he would get into a boat and ask the disciples to push out from the shore a little way, or walk a few steps up a hillside, or get them to sit down while he remained standing.[13]
- When there were several thousands of people waiting to be fed, Jesus organised them into small groups so the distribution of bread became easier.[14]
- Various other occasions when Jesus used his remarkable capacity for forward planning and organisation have already been noted; those major events such as the sending out of the disciples on their first mission,[15] the procession into Jerusalem,[16] and the preparation of the Passover supper.[17]

Delegating Tasks

Jesus was surprisingly un-possessive of his role. Although they weren't very good at it, there are many accounts in the Gospels of the way he encouraged his disciples to heal the sick and cast out evil spirits.[18] He would set them very exact tasks, as we have seen in their instructions to collect the donkey for the ride into Jerusalem and for the preparation of the Passover supper.[19] More than that, when people specifically wanted to see him, Jesus would on occasion ask his disciples to go and mediate for him.[20]

Sometimes Jesus would share the glory of effecting a healing with the local priests of the synagogue, as he did with the ten lepers. He gave them a specific task, as relevant to their condition as the instruction he gave the blind man to wash his eyes.[21]

Setting Goals Realistically

Jesus set goals for himself that were realistic. Unlike us, Jesus resisted inappropriate demands, such as the requests for yet more signs.[22]

Most significant of all is the startling language used in the Gospels about the determination of Jesus Christ to go through the necessity of the final passion. Not only does he frequently attempt to prepare his disciples for the coming bewilderment and horror, but for himself 'as the time drew near for him to be taken up, he resolutely turned his face towards Jerusalem'; and 'through towns and villages he went, making his way towards Jerusalem'.[23] We get a glimpse of that non-deviating will, that un-deflectable purpose, that wholly committed energy of Jesus Christ which enabled him to interpret, throughout his experience of stress, the ultimate glory of God.

All these observations on how Jesus used organisational skills apply to us, in our own day. In addition, we can use our common sense in very simple but often neglected ways.

Making lists is an obvious but underrated start. The list can be in any order to begin with, and everything can be noted, including times for breaks, meals and daily chores. Then the number of minutes each item is expected to take is estimated in a column next to the list, and the total added. If there are more than 900 (60 × 15) – and this is rare! – then some things have to be curtailed or given a new time on another day. Throughout the day, I can have the satisfaction of crossing off each item as it is achieved.

Coping with interruptions: whatever I do, it is in God's time, for He created it; if this present interruption is in the cause of the Kingdom He will enable me to readjust and re-scramble the remainder of the day in order to accommodate it. If it isn't, I can reasonably suggest to the one who is interrupting that we make another date for addressing the issue at a mutually convenient later stage.

Shortening conversations: perhaps I can explore the use of putting my thoughts together more succinctly; avoid returning 'gossip' for 'gossip'; leave off spending time and energy in telling everyone how busy I am and what has yet to be done; letting people know at the start of a conversation or an interview how much time is available, and in this way enable them to pace themselves also.

Putting on record everything that doesn't have to be kept in my head. As it were, leaving space in my brain to move around and think, instead of lumbering it with the job of hanging on to facts and dates.

Unlike Jesus, we have for our use an enormous number of mechanical aids and high technology. Our capacity for storage of information and the speed of processing it has leapt ahead in our generation. He managed without computers and faxes, E-mail and dishwashers. Maybe we have to learn to be rather clever about which technology actually furthers our priorities, and which technology simply encourages us to take more on and clogs us up still further. We have to decide on our deepest priorities first.

The means we have of organising ourselves may be different to those available in first-century Galilee, but our aims and objectives can be very similar. It is not so much about what the means are, but about our determination to pursue our priorities. Like Jesus did.

•••••••••••• **11** ••••••••••••

Objectifying, Distancing, Withdrawing

> **TO COUNTERACT:**
>
> Submersion in over-
>   involvement
> Becoming drained, dried-out
> Scattered attention
> Scattered personhood

•••••••••••••••••••••••••••••

This is, perhaps, the most important chapter of this book. In our day we are faced with so much personal intrusion in the form of demands, challenges and expectations, that whatever persuades us to allow ourselves to get away from them has to be very valuable. Any suggestion that this is common sense is too mere; natural wisdom is not strong enough, it will be swept aside. It has to be an impelling argument if it is to make any dent in our obstinate conviction that we can manage and that we are indispensable.

Most of us are well and truly saddled with the popular notion that Jesus Christ, Son of God, was always available to those who came to him and unendingly accessible to all those who had any sort of difficulty. This is the overriding impression we get from those who wrote about him. The stories of Jesus' helping and healing activities are paramount in our perceptions of his life on earth. These accounts are written by his devoted followers long after their daily physical contact with him had ceased; their chief aim is to convince their readers of the Messiahship of their hero. The ordinary and consistent lifestyle that he designed for himself is not a matter of immediate interest, but the drama of his mind-switching miracles most definitely is. If we are to contact the response to stress modelled by Jesus (the human being) *in his behaviour*, we have to fine-tooth-comb the Gospel texts and find what is revealed between their lines.

76

We have been looking at the priorities which underpinned the organising skills of Jesus Christ. Now look at the **order** of the following piece.

– Having been on their first mission, the disciples returned
to Jesus .... *returning to base*
– They reported on all they had done .... *feed-back*
– Jesus took them away with him to a quiet place .... *withdrawal*
– The crowds found them out and followed, Jesus
welcome them .... *having been re-charged*
– He taught them .... *once again generously giving out of his resources*
– and cured those that were in need of healing ....
.... *having been re-saturated with the power of God*
(Luke 9:10–11)

This is a truly astonishing sequence. It is totally unlike anything we are familiar with today. What makes it difficult to assimilate is the utter matter-of-fact ordinariness of the telling, a sequence which to the disciples is such an everyday and accepted pattern that it needed no expansion, like dressing each morning or having breakfast. It is as though a newspaper article ran: 'and the sales team returned to the director and showed him their statistics. The director got places for them all on a chartered plane package to Cornwall where they sat around for a bit. The press found out and advertisers flooded the *Cornish Express* to join them. The director met the incomers at the station with open arms, revealed to them his sales secrets, and filled out the spaces in their selling methods. Everyone was happy.'

This is another piece from the Authorised Version:

> And the apostles gathered themselves together unto Jesus, and told him all things, both what they had done and what they had taught. And he said unto them, 'Come ye yourselves apart into a desert place and rest a while'; for there were many coming and going, and they had no leisure so much as to eat. And they departed into a desert place by ship privately. And the people saw them departing . . . and ran afoot thither out of all cities, and outwent them, and came together unto him. And Jesus, when he came out . . . was moved with compassion toward them . . . and he began to teach them many things.
>
> (Mark 6:30–4)

So Jesus was concerned not just for the needs of the crowds, but for the mental health of his disciples too. That in itself is rare today, that a manager should arrange to go on holiday with his support group to give them all a break. Add on to that that this same manager had no regret when the besieging, clamouring crowd chased them to their hide-out; and to top it all, he looked at them with love and pity and gave them more of what they wanted.

Now this piece:

> The news of Jesus kept spreading, and large crowds would gather to hear him and to have their illnesses cured: but he would go off to some deserted place and pray. (Luke 5:15–16)

It is a truly rare person,[1] who, met by someone in critical need, can turn around and walk in a different direction. Speaking for myself – and, I suspect, the large majority of 'caring' people – when I am met by someone appealing to me out of their acute need of the moment, I cannot resist offering them some sort of immediate solace. All need is acute to the one who is suffering it, and it boosts my own self-importance to feel that I have been appealed to; my inflated ego begins to tell me that I am the only one who can possibly help, and to imagine all the glory I will have in the gratitude and appreciation of the one I have 'helped'. I look forward to that lovely glow of proving once again how indispensable I am. Even though I acknowledge that I am nearly at the end of my tether, that I am worn out and only functioning at half-efficiency, still I'll take on one more person wanting my help. And as for a *crowd* of people in need . . . how did Jesus manage to resist the enormous pressures put upon him to attend to situations that would inevitably overload him? It is an astonishing fact that he did resist overload – there is no hint in the Gospels that he was anything but in full charge of all his responses, whatever the circumstances. From where did he gain the insight and strength to allow himself *not* to become sucked into other people's demands on him? How did he never get hooked into becoming over-involved?

Because he always respected the responsibility that each person holds for themselves; and he held this respect at the forefront of his consciousness. Jesus was deeply rooted in the will of God, and in order to keep in constant touch with every movement of His purposes, he had to spend large amounts of time listening to Him and basking in His love. Because he knew this type of enmeshment with God is available to each one of us, Jesus was prepared to step back and make space – he didn't have to act as mediator in all things. In addition, he needed to maintain the very gifts the Father had entrusted to him, so they would retain their complete usefulness.

At the time of the first century there was a well-established tradition of Jewish meditation. The techniques and opportunities for silent prayer and wordless contemplation were familiar to those well educated in the religious practices of the day. So familiar, perhaps, that there was no need for Jesus to expand upon them in his teaching, he just demonstrated their value in his daily life. We know he was well rehearsed in the stress management tools of detachment and withdrawal.

Look at the evidence of the way in which Jesus distanced himself, at times, from those who were demanding of him. There are four categories under which we can explore this ability to withdraw.[2]

1. The easiest to understand was his idea that when an intimate healing was to be successful, the person to be healed should be taken away from the watching crowds and be addressed in private. These occasions have already been noted.

   Mark 7:33 Jesus led him [the mute] away from the crowd, and
   Mark 8:23 Jesus took the blind man by the hand and led him out of the village.

2. The second is the common habit of Jesus to withdraw from the crowds in order to be with his disciples in privacy. It has been touched upon already, but here it is useful to note the number of incidents recorded. On such occasions the disciples would ask him to elaborate on some teaching they had not fully understood earlier in the day – as we might ask our parents when we were children to explain something we had heard them say at a party when at last we got home. Or they might all enjoy relaxing together, perhaps picnicking at the end of the day by the Sea of Galilee. More interesting is the reliance Jesus put on their readings of the temperature of the crowd, and the general sense of support he gained from the company of these twelve very ordinary men. For instance: from Mark –

   3:7 Jesus withdrew with his disciples to the lakeside.
   6:31 Then Jesus suggested, 'Let's get away from the crowds for a while and rest'.
   9:28 Later, when he was alone with his disciples in the house . . .
   10:10 When he was alone with his disciples . . .
   11:19 That evening as usual Jesus and the disciples left the city.

13:3   As he sat on the slopes of the Mount of Olives, four of the disciples questioned him alone . . .

from Luke –

9:10   Then he took them, and went aside privately.

and from John –

2:12   He left for a few days with his mother, brothers, and disciples [post-Cana].

11:54   He went to the edge of the desert with his disciples [before the passion].

3. More difficult to fathom, perhaps, is the manner in which Jesus could let go of the temptation to become heavily embroiled when he saw this as being unconstructive, even if it was with a fascinating situation. Jesus would take the deliberate decision to detach himself from the melee, to go off by himself. Sometimes he would distance himself from an argument which was about himself. Most of us would spend some time in defending our corner, in restoring our reputation, in refuting the charges made against us. But when he felt his opponents were so entrenched in their argument that nothing he said could shift them from their own ground, he would quite simply slip away.

For instance: from Matthew –

8:18   At the sight of the crowd surrounding him, Jesus crossed to the other side.

13:36   Leaving the crowds outside he went into the house.

12:15   Jesus knew this and withdrew from the district.

14:22   Jesus made the disciples embark, and cross to the other side, while he dismissed the crowd.

15:39   Jesus sent the people home and got into the boat and crossed over.

16:4   (While the religious leaders were trying to trap him) . . . and he left them, and went off (NJB); Jesus walked out on them (LB).

from Mark –

1:38   'Everyone is asking for you'; but Jesus said, 'We must go on to other towns'.

1:45   Jesus could not go into any town, but stayed outside in deserted places.

7:24   There he entered into a house and would have no man know it (AV).

8:13   So he got back into the boat and left them, and crossed to the other side.

from Luke –

4:43 . . . begged him to stay. He replied: 'No, I must go . . . '

5:16 There were vast crowds . . . but he often withdrew to the wilderness for prayer.

18:24 Jesus watched him go, and said, 'How hard it is . . . !' [the rich young ruler].

24:51 In the act of parting, Jesus blessed them . . .

from John –

4:1 When he knew greater crowds were coming to him . . . he left Judea and returned . . .

5:13 . . . for the place was crowded – but Jesus had slipped away. 'He kept himself hidden' (JB).

6:15 Jesus saw they were ready to make him their king, so he went higher into the mountains alone.

10:39 They started to arrest him. But he walked away and left them.

10:40 . . . and he went beyond the River Jordan to stay (post-confrontation chapter).

4. *Most enviable and hardest to digest of all, was Jesus' insistence that he needed to be on his own.*

For instance from Matthew –

14:23 . . . then he went up the hills by himself to pray.

from Mark –

1:35 Long before daybreak he went out into the wilderness to pray.

6:46 (Post feeding of 5,000) Afterwards he went up into the hills to pray.

from Luke –

4:42 Early next morning he went out into the desert.

6:12 He went into the mountains to pray, and prayed all night . . . [pre-choice of 12].

9:18 One day as he was alone, praying, he came over to his disciples and asked them . . .

9:28 He took . . . with him into the mountains to pray [pre-transfiguration].

11:1 When Jesus had been out praying, his disciples came and asked . . . [Paternoster].

21:37 . . . Each evening Jesus returned to spend the night on the Mount of Olives.

from John –

    7:53–8:1 They all went home, while Jesus went to the Mount of Olives. At daybreak he reappeared in the Temple.

    12:36 Jesus went away and was hidden from them.

Plus Gethsemane – when he withdrew from them a few paces (Luke 22:41).

Objectifying, detaching, distancing, withdrawing – each of these terms has its own nuance; each of them describes an attitude of mind that says, 'I don't have to be all things, all the time, to all people. It's OK to take time and find the place to be on my own; where I can be restored. I am responsible for my own predilection to burn-out. I *am not indispensable. God is.*'

The difference for the Christ-centred person, in contrast with those of other persuasions, is that we can see that Jesus Christ withdrew from the public gaze on various occasions with various goals; but his overall intention was to *disengage in order to re-engage.* It was not to get away or reject or express antipathy towards any of those who needed him. It was in order that he might attend to them and their needs with greater intensity and with the supreme concentration of the present-moment that was his singular style. Some world religions would have us become unimpassioned, and work towards attaining a state of total serenity leaving all desires and all pain behind. This is not the way Jesus modelled for us. Rather, he was so anchored to the bedrock of his Father's purpose for our world and the coming of the Kingdom of God, so secured to this foundation and sure-footed in his commitment to it, that nothing – but nothing – could shake this attachment. He was never detached in a superior way from the world, but so attached to God's love of humankind that he had to preserve his ability to serve it.

As Jesus said himself, 'He who does not gather, scattereth'. To remain strong, we have to make sure that we get the time and space we need to become gathered, collected, 'togethered'. Otherwise not only do we scatter our own energies, but also risk scattering the hope and energy of others.

The argument in the evidence is strong. It speaks for itself.

        Whatever my circumstances;
        However 'busy' I am;
   Whoever is demanding of me, needing me, appealing to me;
I can *always* make time to be present with God – and God alone –

to be with Him in stillness, single-pointedness, de-cluttered
enough to listen to Him
and be gathered into His purpose, His power, His peace.

- I know of someone who is so responsive to others' needs during his waking hours, that he sets his alarm for three o'clock every night, in order to get up and be on his own in the gaze of God. After his meditation he returns to bed and to sleep, knowing he is refurbished for the coming day.
- I know a mother of young children to whom this exercise was so important she emptied out the broom cupboard and put in there a patch of carpet and a prayer stool. The children knew that when the door of the broom cupboard was shut, she was not to be disturbed and she would come out a nicer mum with more energy for them. So they learnt it was in their own interest to let her have those few minutes on her own with God.
- I know a group of people who come from very different worlds; they are from business, and art, and home-making. They meet at 7 a.m. on Saturday mornings, while their families are still sleeping or watching children's TV, to be together in silence and stillness in the presence of God.

All these people insist that their groundedness in dealing with the stresses of their lives is centred on those times of (temporary) withdrawal when they become gathered, in the gazing love of God.

St Peter put it succinctly like this: 'Gird up the loins of your mind; be sober, and hope to the end' (1 Peter 1:13 AV).

Challenge and Change

To 'rehearse' or not?
Stability zones
Confronting limiting beliefs

TO COUNTERACT:

Making a mess of it!
Negative mental habits
Disbelief in oneself
Lack of confidence

• •

It was a crying shame. You didn't know whether to admire his persistence or bewail his obstinacy. Doug Try-hard somehow always managed to get it wrong. Doug was a nice enough man, and you had to be sorry for all the changes and difficulties that came at him out of thin air. He went at them like a bull, charging at them without fear or favour. But then after the worst had passed he went over and over what he had done, and how he had done it, and the mistakes he had made, all the while pulling himself down. However much you tried to sympathise, it affected all those around him – all those stories of misfitting circumstances and ill-judged decisions. It seemed as if he had never stopped to think things out.

The worst of it was that he started to misbelieve himself. He had lots going for him, but he could never see it. It wasn't self-pity exactly, but you knew that if you were in his company you couldn't be cheerful yourself, or be positive about your own affairs, for Doug had become such a moaner. In spite of his nice house and nice family, no one wanted to be with him for long. Shame really.

Jesus had quite a lot of ill-fitting circumstances to deal with too. He didn't have a house or a family in the ordinary understanding of those terms, or a regular job. No constant source of income, and he had to face changes in his company and his place every day. In spite of there being so much physical movement around him, when you got near him there was this uncanny feeling of being rooted, of being deeply secure. He certainly knew what he was about, however chancy his life seemed to be. This was remarkable, because among the thousands of people who watched him, there were some who were spying on him for mistakes and political incorrectness, and some who simply laid in wait for something exciting to happen (whether this was to be good or bad it didn't really matter to the sensation-seekers). Only very few really *believed* in him. His vigorous belief in himself and what he was doing was so unshakeable, it made it possible for those who were close to him to remain secure and optimistic.

How could this happen, stability at the centre of chance? Could we get somewhere near it too, this deep, tethered, outgoing sense of assuredness?

Jesus not only lived change, he welcomed it. He looked for change; that is why he came into the world, it is the substance of the re-incarnation. Jesus saw change as the vehicle for creativity and new life. *Conversion* itself means 'to change'; to change direction, to turn around and turn your face towards God. Jesus knew all about change and the conflict that seems to dog our attempts to change. Repentance involves change; putting into reverse my selfishness and turning to face God involves fundamental change. Jesus was always aware of the impact it made on others, and the effect it might have on those he loved. In terms of behavioural tactics, how did he manage change and conflict?

A. Preparation

(i) *Foreknowledge*

Jesus would give full warning to those closest to him about what was likely to happen in the days ahead. He did, occasionally, make use of the element of surprise, such as when he went up to Jerusalem having told his colleagues that he wouldn't; and he used surprise as a means of making people think, such as inviting himself to the houses of notorious people. The God of the New Testament is a God full of surprises. But in general Jesus would foretell major events; for instance he warned his hearers about the coming clash with the authorities, and predicted his torture and death.[1] He foretold other dramatic happenings – the destruction of the great golden Temple and the rout of Jerusalem,[2] and what was to the crowds the worst thing of all, the horror of the apocalypse.[3]

Jesus made use of these predictions to arm his hearers beforehand, in order to give them a chance to digest the news and face up to what was coming. Jesus obviously practised the theory that being forewarned is to be forearmed, and he expected others to benefit likewise as proper preparation for large events. From his studies of the prophecies in the Jewish holy writings and from his own reading of the times, Jesus intuited early on in his ministry that the changes he was introducing would inevitably lead to a clash with the religious and civil authorities. He knew they would attempt to wipe out his influence by crucifying him. This furious conflict between the cosmic powers of good and evil seems to have been very clear to Jesus himself, but at first he only alluded to it in veiled terms to others. He gave them stories about a king's son being murdered, about the necessity of enjoying the company of the bridegroom while he was present, and he urged people to make the most of the 'little while' they were together.[4] The full brunt of what was likely to happen he only allowed them to face as they actually approached the scene. In forearming himself, Jesus made sure that he was fit *physically* to stand the ordeal of the passion which lay ahead of him; that he was prepared *mentally* of the necessity for it; and that through his living prayer in the Garden of Gethsemane he was as accepting *emotionally* and in *spirit* as it was humanly possible to be.

(ii) Positives of the outcome

Underlying the predictions of Jesus is a second purpose. On nearly every occasion when such a warning is recorded, it ends on a note of hope. The destruction of the capital of Israel will be followed by a change to the new order; the apocalypse will be followed by the coming of God's Kingdom in all its fulness; the crucifixion will be followed by the resurrection. It's as though he wanted at all times to accentuate the purpose or *usefulness* that was inherent to the change.

All the while Jesus' message remains constant: *the responsibility for our actions is ours.* There are many translations of his original words and they include: 'Take care . . .', 'be on your guard . . .', 'take heed to yourselves . . .', 'keep watch . . .', 'keep awake . . .', 'stay awake . . .', 'hold yourselves ready . . .', 'be alert . . .', 'stand ready . . .', '*watch* . . .'.[5]

(iii) Counting the cost

Jesus told us firmly to count the cost before acting. All of Luke chapter 14 concerns various aspects of accounting for our decisions. It is summed up in verses 28–30. Jesus says, 'Which of you, intending to build a tower, would not first sit down and work out the cost to see if he had enough to complete it?' Otherwise people would say, 'Here is someone who started to build and was unable to finish' and they would make fun of it. Part of this procedure is to imagine myself in the coming situation, and visualise the details of how I would act. In the face of change, there are questions to be asked before exposing either myself or those around me to the risks that may have to be met along the way. I am to ask questions like:

- Is it going to be worth it? and to whom? Me? Others? God?
- What physical, mental, emotional or spiritual energy will it need?
- Have I got that amount?
- If I haven't, *where shall I go to get it*?
- What will it mean to others, immediately? soon? in the long term?
- What will others get out of it?
- What can I offer to God, for Him to use, and to transform for His own purposes?

No doubt Jesus asked these questions as he faced the changes in his life, and he expects us to be firm and responsible with them too. There are debits and credits to be weighed up,[6] risks to be assessed, and sometimes the actual stages to be rehearsed, either in fact – such as finding the location of the event and timing how long each step of the process will take – or in imagination. Trying to avoid unexpected intrusions, but allowing for some leeway. Careful planning can greatly reduce the hazards ahead. Not too much like Doug Try-hard.

B. Later

Reflecting later on the experience, as Mary did on the childhood of Jesus and the disciples did on the transfiguration,[7] has a different value. What is known as 'destructive rumination over past mistakes' has no part whatever in the Good News of Jesus – the suicide of Judas Iscariot was the direct result of such rumination. It has often been pointed out that much of Jesus' healing activity lay in undoing the effects of such drawn-out rehearsal over past unhappiness. Some experts say that the psychosomatic symptoms of those seeking Jesus' healing hand were the result of unfinished emotional trauma. The idea of 'if only . . . ' can be a hang-up. In the Gospels the emphasis is on 'what can I do about it *now*?' Suppressed conflict and unresolved emotional rumination can do immense damage in producing stress-signs. In a certain sense this is to do with conscious mind-control. If

I know that I have done my best, I acknowledge my mistakes and offer them to God to be resolved in His light,[8] then there is no more that I can do but leave the issue there with Him. Nowhere in the Gospels are we told that Jesus hankered over what had been. He garnered wisdom from the past, but always as a means of looking ahead to the ways of changing the now into the future.[9]

C. The Use of Stability Zones

Too often when we are in the throes of change and its potential for conflict we overlook the refreshment that lies in our 'stability zones'. When life is too full to stop and I am too harassed to let go, it can make the difference between the fractious, impetuous, draining behaviour that leads towards burn-out and the coping, creative, alert behaviour that brings new life. Stability zones are those areas when just for a few moments I can be aware that I am in a safe haven; it only takes a minute to switch off, a space so short that in general we override the opportunity and it passes off without acknowledgement or usefulness. The most obvious stability zone is the morning tea or coffee break; often this is ignored, or spent on the hoof complaining and agitating! It is something about being present to the moment, and it involves simple things like breathing out, pulling the shoulders down, thinking of one enjoyable thing and giving thanks for it. Stability zones are those moments when:

- I finally get into my car and 'clunck' the door, so I am on my own and can think my own thoughts for myself;
- there is friendly contact on the phone;
- an unexpected lull lets me sit in the garden for a short while;
- I get out to the loo and can practise the presence of God;
- I down tools for the day and take just a few moments savouring the relief before joining the queue to the exit;
- the baby is at last sleeping and I can stay still for a few seconds before turning my thoughts to the next job.

Jesus made use of stability zones in his quiet companionship of the twelve; in his times alone with his Father; when he walked ahead of his disciples striding down the road; when he 'prayed by himself' even though he was in their company. Every time he enjoyed a meal with others he was in a stability zone. What are yours? Register them mentally and even write them down to remind you when time gets impossible. Actively make use of them, as Jesus did.

Confronting Limiting Beliefs

When facing either change or conflict, or both, it is important to challenge some of the messages we give to ourselves that actually limit our freedom to choose wisely. Whether we are aware of it or not, in our minds we have a continual dialogue going on that has been called 'self-talk'. This dialogue is made up of inherited instructions that we seldom question, although they have been carried over from our distant past and may no longer be either appropriate or applicable to our present situation. The insistent internal commentary all too often consists of put-downs:

- you've bitten off more than you can chew this time all right;
- you're no good at this sort of thing, trying to do it just shows you up;
- you're hopeless, look at the mess you made of that!
- he's bigger than you; she's cleverer than you; they're all only out to get you!
- wait till they find out what a fraud you are!

Some of these messages we picked up as inexperienced children, and they have stayed in our subconscious long after they should have been replaced. It is a common analogy of stress that upfront I appear to others like a serene duck moving smoothly over the water – but underneath my feet are paddling like mad. Many of us put enormous energy into struggling to convince others we are not really struggling at all. Do we really need to use up our energy in that way? Is it a properly constructive way of facing change?

When we become aware that we are carrying these limiting beliefs around with us, we can consciously pick up the message and alter it. We may have learnt to react automatically with a phrase that had some substance to it years ago; since then we have undertaken that training, or fulfilled that experience adequately, or met that challenge successfully. We don't *have* to stay with negative self-talk after its sell-by date. Starting out on a new turn in my life while I still carry such denegrating ideas can do nothing but lower my chances: if I want to get to the most fruitful place, I will have to alter my internal dialogue.

Jesus had considerable experience of challenging the limiting beliefs that burdened people down. Most of his ministry was spent building people up away from their limiting beliefs, but here are just a few instances:

• The story of Nicodemus and his previous rigid boundaries to belief; as he came to Jesus he was trying to open them up but his belief was still tied and limited to 'miracles'. Jesus' answer to this position was that the 'wind blows where it pleases . . . you cannot tell where it comes from or where it is going. So it is with everyone who is born of the Spirit' (John 3:1–8). Opening boundaries.

- The idea of stretching the boundaries is made even more explicit in the case of the woman taken in adultery (John 8:3–11). As he took time to consider the prescribed and accepted horrific punishment for this act, Jesus says, 'Let the one among you who is guiltless be the first to throw a stone at her.'

- The great structure of fossilised rules which controlled all behaviour on the Jewish Sabbath was put under scrutiny when Jesus said, publicly, 'The Sabbath was made for man, not man for the Sabbath.'[10] There are too many instances of Jesus questioning these legalistic rites to include here so perhaps it is sufficient to quote three anecdotes of his behaviour.

  - On the Sabbath, he 'untied' the woman from the bonds that had been bending her over for eighteen years, at a time when 'religious' people confined themselves to untying only their beasts from their overnight stalls.

  - On the Sabbath, at a meal with suspicious Pharisees, Jesus restored a man who was drowning in his own tissue fluid, at a time when his hosts were limited to hauling out of water only a family member – or an ox.

  - On the Sabbath, in a synagogue, he told a man with a withered arm to stretch it out whole, at a time when his listeners could stretch out their arm to rescue only a sheep fallen into a hole.[11]

- Jesus made a point of challenging the limited belief of the disciples. On such occasions the language he is reported as using seems peculiarly strong to us; maybe it was said with a compassionate twinkle in his eye. 'O ye of little faith!' is the Authorised Version wording of Jesus to the two walking to Emmaus, 'Foolish men! So slow to believe!' (Luke 24:25); other translations describe Jesus as upbraiding them with their incredulity and obstinacy (NJB), their lack of faith and stubbornness (NRSV), their incredulity and dull-ness (REB; see also Mark 16:14). Limited and limiting beliefs – called 'hardness of heart' – were a source of anger and even despair to Jesus (Mark 3:5). It was something he found great difficulty in absorbing. After the euphoria of the experience of the transfigur-ation, Jesus said to the disciples who had been unable to heal in his temporary absence, 'Faithless generation, how much longer must I be among you?' (Mark 9:19) Even when his great friend Peter failed in his attempt to meet him walking over the water, Jesus exclaimed, 'You have so little faith, why did you doubt?' (Matt. 14:31) This continual fronting of the disciples with the limits of their belief has to be taken seriously. None the less the manner in which it was done and reported is expanded more fully in chapter 18.

• Jesus also challenged the ruling religious leaders on their limited beliefs and hard-heartedness. For instance, concerning the longevity of marriage (Matt. 19:8).

When I myself am looking at change, I can resonate with some of these men's inability to stretch attitudes, and their lack of flexibility in behaviour. Underlying all these are some of the deepest ideas I hold about myself. When I tell myself I am no good, that I am unlovable and unlovely, that I can't do it, then change will indeed be a mammoth task. In terms of stress and its management, there is another and equally disabling extreme. As a Christian I am sometimes tempted towards this extreme, when I tell myself that there should be no limit whatever to what I can demand of myself, and all my needs should be subjugated to everyone else's needs. My own selfhood gets in danger of disappearing in total collapse. Jesus said, 'With God, all things are possible', but that is very different to expecting of myself what I expect of God. It is a dangerous snare to think I can capture the limitlessness of God in my own preposterous and absurd goals. I *do* have a selfhood created for me by God; to be self-destructive in the expectation I have of that selfhood is hardly giving glory to Him for His gift. My Creator fully expects me to work within my limits; to know these, and do my utmost to use the tools He has given me for His Kingdom without too much damage is to respect His purposes.

E. What I Believe About Myself Must Be Realistic

Although with God all things are possible,[12] God wishes to companion me, not obliterate me. It is not so much what I want to do for Him, but more a case of what God wants of me.

Bearing Doug Try-hard in mind, there are two final points. He was not aware of the dangers of continuing to be curbed by the logic of the left brain; or of remaining within the boundaries of those things that are measurable; or of being compelled by the 'up' context of our current culture. He was unaware of the experience we shall explore in Parts 3 and 4.

Secondly, perhaps it is timely to reflect that we do not have to be over-influenced by the depression, violence and desperation of much of our present-day reporting. Inevitably we come across things that are tragic, distorted, misconceived. In order to avoid being sucked under the horror we have to learn not to dwell too long on the lurid bits. This is a pertinent and very topical mental skill, one that is frequently modelled by Jesus. Deliberately to set our minds on tracks leading to the glory of God, rather than allowing them to wallow in muck. As someone has observed – evil feeds on evil, good feeds on good. So:

> Whatsoever things are true,
> whatsoever things are honest and just,
> whatsoever things are pure, and lovely, and of good report,
> if there be any virtue or praise,
> think on these things.
>
> (Phil. 4:8 Abbreviated AV)

And the God of Peace shall be with you.

Picture-story of Blind Bartimaeus

Mark 10:46–52; Luke 18:35–43; Matt. 20:29–34

•••

Thaddaeus is speaking:

I am one of the lesser disciples, I stay on the edge of his closest circle. I love Jesus and believe in Jesus with the whole of my being, but my respect for him keeps me at a distance. That's all right by me, because from there I can watch him and see how he acts when other people are demanding of him. Sometimes it feels as though they want to consume him whole, they are so eager to take everything he has to offer them. It's as if they see a bright red apple and want to get great bites out of it so all their hurts will be instantly healed. It's astonishing how Jesus copes. Take the way he responded the other day to poor old Bartimaeus for example.

Bartimaeus is a really sad case. He's been around for a long time, sitting on the pavement just at the edge of Jericho, begging. He is the son of Timaeus — you know, that respected citizen who keeps coming up in the local news — and a subject of shame to him. No wonder; there his son sits on a tattered smelly blanket which is his only possession in the world. That blanket is his mattress, his coat and what he uses to collect the money and bits of food that people throw him. People are quite generous and Bartimaeus seems to prefer that sort of scrounging to being a 'poor relative' dependent on the heavy charity of his father. He's an awful whinger, always disgruntled, labelled a purposeless no-gooder. Mind you, he is blind, although he hasn't always been. As a young man he had lived a full life, but a foolish prank after a drinking bout landed him without the use of his eyes. The worst thing now is how he hates not being included in the debates that go on all around him, just because people think he can't 'see', as if he were a fool too.

This particular day had been a long one. We were totally exhausted and looking forward to making camp in the desert that night. I had watched over the last few weeks as Jesus' determination to get to Jerusalem became increasingly stern. He would not be deflected. He had told us that he was getting towards the end of his ministry, and I had sensed the increasing frustration

*and tension growing in him that his message was still so imperfectly under-
stood. There had been that keen and rich young lawyer – so well educated
he could have been of enormous promotional value if he had sided with Jesus.
There had been real rapport between the two of them, and the young man
had seemed to want to do anything for the coming Kingdom. Can you
imagine the pain and disappointment of Jesus when he finally decided to go
away? You could see in Jesus' face the acute hurt caused by this let-down,
but he didn't make a fuss or try to override the lawyer's own decision. Then
there was all that misunderstanding with the disciples – what were they going
to get out of giving everything up? Didn't Jesus realise what they had done
for him? As if Jesus hadn't 'done' anything for them! And to top it all, that
extraordinary scuffle when Zebedee's wife bustled up and asked for special
favours for her two sons in the next life; that was some cheek. Jesus was
gentle with her and didn't exactly put her down or refuse her request, but his
disappointment about the misunderstanding of his very basic teaching about
how to serve rather than be served was so sharp I nearly broke down myself.
But we turned and went on towards Jerusalem.*

*And then there he was, blind Bartimaeus, shouting and yelling and waving
that old battered cloak of his. The crowds were pushing Jesus along, each one
of them vying to get his attention. Those nearest to Bartimaeus told him to
belt up and stop making such a racket, but he wouldn't. The more people
tried to control his antics the wilder they became. Jesus stopped a moment,
and the whole crowd with him. Everybody watched, wondering if he was
going to let go some of the accumulating frustration and tension in a rebuke
to this rude display; Jesus was already drained and exceptionally tired, he
really had enough on his mind. How was he going to choose – how was
he going to play it? Would he go with the feelings of the crowd, and project
their impatience with the blind beggar? Would he brush him off as a persistent
but impertinent interloper? Or would he get rid of him simply by giving him
some sort of sop to keep him quiet? Which was Jesus' priority?*

*Jesus could hear the cries of Bartimaeus, and so the old beggar could easily
have heard him. But Jesus didn't call out to him direct, he asked one of the
disciples closest to him to go over and fetch him, as if Bartimaeus was really
someone special. I watched closely, and it was as if by asking someone to do
the bringing, Jesus had given himself a moment of space – inside not outside
– to draw on a hidden fund of energy and compassion. You could see his face
soften and 'listen'.*

*Jesus of course had pity, he could always feel sorry for others in need. But
this was something different. It was a sadness that someone also created by
God, his own Father, had had to live in this way, but it was also a sort of
recognition that there was something in Bartimaeus that recognised something*

in Jesus. Even without eyes to see. A resonance or sense of bonding between them. Maybe it was because Bartimaeus was the only person who had yet called out to him using his own name, Jesus, coupled to the fact that he came from the house of David, that great family from which everybody knew the Messiah would come. Maybe it was a moment of immense relief. This man, poor, begging, and thought to be 'not seeing', had glimpsed a corner of the truth.

The surprising thing was, that when they came together, face to face as it were, Jesus didn't just hand out what he had to give, like everyone else had done to the poor old man. Jesus took him seriously, as he had done the rich young lawyer, and respected his own autonomy. He actually asked the man what he wanted! not promising he could have it, like the fairy in the story who grants any old wish. But quite quietly and seriously he asked, 'What is it you are really after? What is it you want of me?' Bartimaeus was a little taken aback at that, and calmed down himself, letting all the excitement and indignation around just roll off him. Then, after a brief pause, he said so hardly anyone could hear, 'Teacher, let me see.'

He said nothing about the Kingdom, nothing about turning to God. Perhaps he felt that 'seeing' wholly meant looking at God, and allowing God to 'see' him in return. Anyway, Jesus seemed to think there was something like this in this request, and he made his eyes whole again, just like that.

In his keenness to come to Jesus, Bartimaeus had thrown off the dirty old blanket that had been with him so long as his only protection. Now he threw his arms in the air praising almighty God (please note – the unseen Yahweh had the praise, not directly the now-seen man Jesus) and all the crowd followed suit. The procession leaving Jericho that evening was lighter and brighter than the intrusive demanding one that had started out.

··

Summary

— halfway through the book

··

Note Jesus' ability to deal with his own stress by:

- Caring for the tools of his body.
- Disengaging in order to re-engage.
  This detachment from friends and family was to secure and deepen his *attachment* to the purposes of God. It was temporary in both place and time, and followed by giving his total presence to those he met on his return.
- Refusing to become sucked into other people's projections.
- Resisting the temptation to overload, whether this came in the form of demands from other people, or from a need to be needed, or an urge to 'prove' his teaching.
- His acceptance of people's expectations of his mission without rejecting them; he took them on board but in the process modified them.
- Insistence of respect for each person's autonomy of choice and decision-making, and their consequences.
- Sustained by delight and *hedonia* in God's creation.
- Always and always passing on the glory to his Father.

96

•••••••••• Part 3 ••••••••••

Skills of the Emotions

••••••••••••••••••••••••••••••

Taking Responsibility for Them

Recognising my internal dialogue
Owning my self-talk

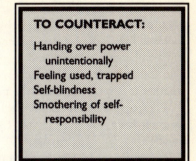

TO COUNTERACT:

Handing over power
   unintentionally
Feeling used, trapped
Self-blindness
Smothering of self-
   responsibility

•••••••••••••••••••••••••••••

We are dealing here with the stress management of common emotions, which is different to pastoral counselling or psychotherapeutic disclosure of emotions that have been traumatised. Stress management is about introducing the concept of *choice*, and it applies in the area of my emotions just as much as it applies to the tools of my body or mind. Before I can manage anything, I have to acknowledge that there is something that needs to be managed; and in the management of my emotions, I have first to recognise what is mine. Then can I take responsibility for it.[1]

Wayne was in prison; he was quiet, introverted, self-blaming. He had thought he never felt rage, that it was alien to him. At school he had been taught that Jesus was controlled and strong, never bothering other people with his feelings, so Wayne never expressed his either. As he grew up he played around with drugs a bit – but he could take them or leave them. One night he had been crossed while drinking with the boys, and he went home and took it out on his wife. She landed up in intensive care and he landed up in prison. He simply didn't know what had hit him, that explosion of fury didn't belong to the wife – that bloody eruption, where had it sprung from? He had never been 'violent' in his life!!

Are we being conned? If so, who by? The media? those around us?

99

ourselves? It's as if we are being coerced into buying a received attitude we didn't ask for. The context around us tells us to admire those things that are *up* and *visible*; we can cope with them. So the things that are *down* and *hidden* are ignored, they don't count; they have to be forgotten.

We all like to display the *up* emotions. They show we are confident and competent, cheerful and coping. Today we emphasise 'upness'. The following sort of sentence is common in daily management, whether it is speaking about the professions or about business.

Wake *Up*! We must Build *Up* *Up*-beat strategies for *Up*-grading: we must keep our end *Up*, stay *Up*, and *Up*-date for the *Up*-market situation.

It's revealing to look at the vocabulary we use daily. Consider this list.

High value terms:

START UP	WAKE UP	WORK UP	WIND UP
STAY UP	PUSH UP	FORCE UP	DRIVE UP
KEEP UP	STEP UP	PAY UP	GET UP
LOOK UP	SET UP	STAND UP	MAKE UP
KEEP MY END UP	PULL YOURSELF UP	BUILD UP	HEAD UP
SPEED UP	SHOW UP	CHEER UP	ADD UP
MOVE UP	BLOW UP	CLEAN UP	BOOT UP
stretch up	heave up	fire up	fill up
do up	climb up	hurry up	warm up
pick up	loosen up	tidy up	free up
roll up	eat up	drink up	stir up
hooked up	put up	gear up	stoke up
toughen up	sharpen up	winch up	run up

Add to those:

upbeat	up market	upgrade	upfront
upheld	upshot	upstart	up and coming
upwardly mobile	upstream	up with the Jones!	update
up-end	uptight	buoyed up	banged up
upheaval	upsurge	uproar	live up to . . .

The following are negative, but still imply high energy:

belt up	shut up	blow up	beat up
het up	wrought up	fed up	washed up
break up	burn up	tied up	'up yours!'

There are, of course, very many others, these are only a representative selection.

Now, compare these lists of **Up** words with the downbeat connotations we give to **Down** words: these mostly relate to things I must not allow myself to do:

Low value terms:
I must *not* get:

DOWNHEARTED	DOWNTRODDEN	PUT DOWN	TALKED DOWN
WORN DOWN	RUN DOWN	BLOWN DOWN	MOWN DOWN
SHUT DOWN	KNOCKED DOWN	DOWN AND OUT	

I must *not*:

BREAK DOWN	CLIMB DOWN	SLOW DOWN	STEP DOWN
BURN DOWN	FALL DOWN	STAY DOWN	GET DOWN

And yet, and yet
when I calm down, wind down, settle down, sit down, lie down, centre down . . .

that's when I can *strip down, reach down, bend down* and get *deep down* enough to – **touch base** – that place of deep stillness, where my deepest being can rest, and can take in, rather than give out.

And get *low down* enough to go through the doorway into the birthplace of Jesus.

The stress management principle of extending choice is perhaps at its most difficult when it is applied to the constant stream of dialogue that goes on inside me and is driven by old habits established in the distant past of my childhood. Many of these 'drivers' were appropriate when they were instilled by the well-meaning adults surrounding me and shaping my attitudes; but perhaps, over the years as I mature, they become outdated and inappropriate to my present situation. The voices that have been telling me how to behave and what to feel can become so much a matter of habit that I don't even bother to question them, I am hardly aware of their presence, let alone the power they have over my behaviour. Things like 'hit back', 'don't take the blame', 'keep your hands clean', 'don't let on that you're hurting', 'you made a mess of it last time, don't let it happen again' can rule our attitude towards others. All this effort to keep my end up and remain unblameable produces an enormous degree of unbidden stress. As I build up my armour against the world, the very place from which I should be getting my sustenance becomes unrecognisable, even by me.

Jesus knew all about the *up* emotions. He recognised joy and love and accomplishment in his own life. In spite of all the adulation of the crowds, he also was familiar with the uncomfortable emotions. We have seen how he used choice in his bodily behaviour as well as in his range of mental coping skills. We have seen that in order to choose we have to know what there is to choose from; and that part-knowledge necessarily means only part-choice. Jesus Christ never reacted out of habit, or out-of-date second-hand drivers. He responded to whatever came at him with total awareness of the choices that were available. More than that, he used the energy which sprang from his immediate emotions to fuel his cognitive response. His emotions, as recorded in the Gospels, were full and wide-ranging, neither dampened nor denied, but he recognised them and applied them with wholehearted respect for the specific matter in hand. Whether it was a positive or so-called negative emotion, he would neither ignore nor disown it, but accept it and apply it appropriately.

We do something different. I frequently don't like what I feel, so I lay it on the shoulders of the one facing me. '*You* make me so angry', I shout; 'He's afraid of me so *he* might attack me', I quail; '*You're* only jealous because I'm prettier', I argue. While the emotion is attached to someone or something else, I deprive myself of the power of doing anything about it, I am simply the victim. If I allow myself to feel the anger in me – it is basically mine after all – and the fear and the jealousy, then I can keep charge of it and retain the responsibility for working it out, even changing it. It won't build up, accumulate and eventually get out of hand, in the way that Wayne's did.

The so-called negative emotions are the unsocial ones. They are the ones that can be associated with uncomfortable or destructive behaviour, and a lot of the time we presume it is inevitable that they should be. Because of this presumption, and because such feelings as anger, resentment, jealousy, self-pity, and fear are unattractive in company, they get hidden away in an attempt to 'bury' them. We try hard to push them away – out of sight, out of mind. They may be out of our thinking for a while, but they have an energy and a power and vitality that will not be held down. Denying or rejecting the power of a feeling, whether it is a positive or a negative one, is like amputating something that is a bit of my body. It hampers my whole system, putting a limit on how I can make the most use of it.

Something else nasty might happen too. All too often when I have refused to admit this feeling to myself, I will unthinkingly project it out onto someone else where it doesn't belong. Instead of hating myself for it (that might be too dangerous) I hate the same thing in someone else. I fling out blame and accusation somewhere outside me, so I don't have to deal with it directly myself. Not only am I building up the probability of rows and injustice, but I am actually dumping the power that belongs to me somewhere else where I cannot make use of it at all.

There is another way, one that Jesus seems to have used. With my mind I can tell myself to take a good look at these less comfortable emotions, not simply for analysing them and then neatly folding them away with rationalisation (although this in itself is a useful tool at times), but to take one out and *feel* it. Stay with it, taste it, own it, it is mine, *of me*. I can learn to uncouple the feeling itself from the action or 'bad behaviour' it urges me to take up. I can just allow that the feeling is there, in me, before deciding what to do with it.

To recognise my own self-pity, for instance, doesn't mean I have to wallow in it. Not until I fully acknowledge it and understand that it comes from me, myself, and it was not put onto me by someone else, can I decide how to use the energy it generates. Without doing harm to others. The next chapter will explore this further.

Jesus was aware of his immediate emotions. When he was faced with acute suffering he felt anger mixed with sorrow, even grief. This component of anger in his heartfelt compassion was used as a fuel to reinforce and energise the activity of healing: his was no pallid, anaemic, wan, 'if only' type of helping. He needed to make use of the strength of both positive and negative to create the charge necessary. To both make the charge, and 'take charge' of it. So the wholeness he gave out for others was dynamic and powerful, and it was always dominated by his drive to charge the world with praise and glory.

References to the compassion and forgiving-ness of Jesus Christ are too numerous and well identified to list here. It is an interesting exercise to identify the number of other emotions which are registered in the Gospels as having been observed in the behaviour of Jesus. In one chapter in Mark alone (chapter 8) we read of his pity, disappointment, frustration, interiority, flash-irritability, puzzlement, compassion, self-enquiry, trust, self-disclosure, anger, conviction, warning, and finally his assurance of future glory. Examples of other emotions recorded elsewhere as being his are:

- *Grief, sadness, distress*:
  he was grieved to find them so obstinate – Mark 3:5
  at Gethsemane – Matt. 26:37–8; Mark 14:34
- *Weeping*:
  with Mary, at the death of Lazarus – John 11:35
  at the sight of Jerusalem – Luke 19:41
- *Alarm, and warning*:
  'there will be weeping and grinding of teeth' – Matt. 8:12;
      13:42,50; 22:13; 24:51; 25:30; Luke 13:28
  to Satan, after the temptations – 'Get behind me!' Matt. 4:10; Luke
      4:8
  with Simon, after his expostulation – 'Get behind me!' Matt. 16:23;
      Mark 8:33
- *Tenderness*:
  looking up to heaven he sighed, and said, '*Ephphatha*' – Mark 7:34
  with Mary: he gave a sigh that came straight from the heart – John
      11:33,38
- *Yearning*:
  'I have come to bring fire to the earth, and how I wish it were
      blazing already!' (JB) . . . 'How pent up I am until it is
      accomplished!' Luke 12:49–50 (LB)
  following the turning away of the rich aristocrat, Luke 18:24
  pre-passion – 'how I have longed to gather you under my wings',
      Matt. 23:37 (JB)
  at the last Passover – 'I have longed with great longing to eat this
      with you', Luke 22:15 (LB)
- *Pity*:
  he pitied them, and healed those who were sick – Matt. 14:14
  to the widow of Nain, on the loss of her only son: 'He felt sorry
      for her and said, "Don't cry." Then he went up and touched the
      bier [which was ritually unclean] and the bearers stood still, and
      he said . . . ' – Luke 7:13
  for the women watching and waiting as Jesus carried the cross, 'do
      not weep for me, weep for yourselves' – Luke 23:28,29
  for the crowds, in case they should faint from hunger on their way
      home – Matt. 15:32
- *Disappointment and frustration*:
  following the calming of the storm, 'Have you still no faith?' –
      Mark 4:40 (LB)
  'How many more miracles do you people want?' – Mark 8:12
      (LB)

'How long must I endure you?' – Mark 9:19 (REB)

- *Anger*:

  expressed in the startling 'Woes' directed at the Pharisees in Matt. 23:1–36; Mark 12:38–40; and Luke 11:39–52

  as in the fate of those who hurt children – Matt. 18:6; Mark 9:42; and Luke 17:2

  the upsetting of the trade in money in the Temple court: significant unanimity in the words 'you are turning my Father's house of prayer into a bandits' den!' – Matt. 21:12,13; Mark 11:15–17; Luke 19:45; and John 2:16

- *Empathy and insight*:

  in response to Thomas' doubt: 'Give me your hand; put it into my side' – John 20:27

  in response to the urgency of the longing of the two blind men: 'and Jesus stood still, and called them. "What do you want me to do for you?" ' – instant healing, Matt. 20:32 (REB)

  following a sick woman's touch of his cloak Jesus was 'at once aware of the power that had gone out of him, and he turned round . . . ' – Mark 5:30

- *Courage*:

  in the face of the full blandishments of the devil – Matt. 4:1–11; Mark 1:12–13; Luke 4:1–13

  at his capture, Jesus went forward to the arresting guard – Matt. 26:50; Mark 14:48–9; Luke 22:51–3; John 18:4,8

  silent before Pilate, even in the knowledge that Pilate's authority could be overwhelmed by that of God, should he ask for it – John 18:37

- *Joy*:

  Jesus is repeatedly reported as giving thanks, praise, glory to God his Father. 'Joy in heaven' is his way of describing the ultimate liberation when the lost is found, the sinner returns, the feast is full. See, for instance, Luke 15:5,6,7,9,20,24,32

  Specific instances where he revealed the importance to him of joy as a final goal are in John 16:20–2 where weeping is turned into rapture, anguish is turned into joy, labour results in new birth

  Jesus' own joy was in communion with his Father, as in his long prayer in John 17:1–26

  The ultimate act of joy was in the resurrection of Jesus after his crucifixion, and his return to the heavenly places at his ascension

Love permeates the entire life of Jesus. It is the drive and the fuel, just as his lifeblood is, and it runs through his veins. It colours every thought, every word, every task, every enjoyment, every prayer. It is expressed at its fullest in the last chapters of the Gospel that is most concerned with glory.

- 'Love one another as I have loved you' (John 13:34; 15:9 REB)
- Jesus had always loved those who were his; now he showed how perfect that love was (John 13:1 JB)
- 'I have loved them as much as you, Father, have loved me' (John 17:23 JB)
- 'Anyone who loves me will heed what I say; *then my Father will love him, and we will come to him and make our dwelling with him*' (John 14:23–4 REB)

Throughout his life Jesus knew of his own emotions, and how to deal with them. He also lived the principle that it is too simple to remain depressed and angry; he recognised the emotions he experienced but didn't remain with them. Instead he harnessed the energy that is part and parcel of all strong emotions and re-directed it with present-minded awareness and appropriate choice. We can see in the following chapter how this management works out. In our own case, of course, as we attempt to follow his modelling, we will need to pray for a considerable amount of divine grace to be poured down as well! In giving light to the blind, Jesus will respond to our pleas for light in our own self-blindness. Perhaps Wayne didn't know about prayer.

•••••••••• 14 ••••••••••

Managing Them – Without Harm to Others

Emotion IN or OUT

Anger, guilt, sorrow

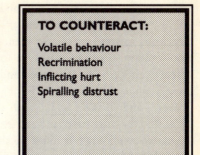

TO COUNTERACT:

Volatile behaviour
Recrimination
Inflicting hurt
Spiralling distrust

•••••••••••••••••••••••••••••

When we were designed and crafted by God, we were not only left with the tools that were necessary to forward God's Kingdom, we were left with the choice of managing them or mismanaging them.

'Keep watch on yourselves!' says Jesus over and over again. He puts the responsibility squarely on each of us to know ourselves and manage our own behaviour. Even in the light of his love and his forgiveness, Jesus the Christ does not hold back from giving terrible warnings about what follows from harmful behaviour. Take for instance the fate of anyone who 'causes the downfall' of a child: that person is to be drowned with a great millstone hanging around their neck.[1]

How we behave comes out of what we think, and how we think is often slanted by what we feel. If our feelings affect our thinking and the way we think affects our behaviour, we have first to recognise our deepest feelings, as we saw in the preceding chapter. That on its own is insufficient: we have also to manage them.

Our aims, in managing our emotions, must surely be those described by Jesus in Luke 17: to follow his instructions to forgive seventy times seven; to have even that grain of faith which moves mountains and transplants mulberry trees into the sea; and to live convinced that to do no more than our duty is not enough.[2]

The five basic emotions are love, joy, anger, guilt, and sorrow. Just as the five primary colours can be mixed and mingled to form every other colour, so every other emotion is a different mixture of these five basics. Sometimes they are turned outwards, and sometimes they are turned inwards. Grief is a combination of sorrow, anger and guilt; jealousy derives from a mixture of love and anger turned out; self-pity from sorrow and anger turned in. Some of the really down emotions are so complex we can lose sight of their source. And yet when I can find I am anchored and secured even in the low places, then I am truly blessed. It is on those days when I am floored (flawed?) and all is *not* well; when I am drained of the ups, and the highs, and the brightness, and achievement and optimism seem unreal; when my own known feelings are those of foulness and reproach and unusableness: that is when my attachment to God and His purposes is tried. That is when the management of the tools He has given me can help to ground me, if it has been well learned. Is there a pattern we can learn in the way that Jesus managed his own negative emotion?

Self-pity is a useful example to start with. Jesus himself had every reason to indulge in self-pity. He gave all of himself in response to the crowds, yet those with influence maligned and misjudged him. He left the glory of heaven, yet he had nowhere to call his own home. Having healed others at every turn, he was subjected to the knotted whips and jeers of the occupying soldiers. He lived his life as a member of the honourable house of David – registered in the first few hours of his life – yet his execution was pronounced by a petulant foreigner. There was in his life an enormous potential for smouldering self-pity, it could have become so overwhelming as to obliterate his entire mission. He took it in silence to God (was this in part why Jesus kept silence before Pilate? Was he offering to Him all the destructive urges that might have resulted in a last-minute reversal of his whole life?) and God re-converted the powerful energy into outward-looking forgiveness; forgiveness towards the very forces that were doing their utmost to destroy him. In offering the strength of the emotion for the purposes of God, he was aligning his human will alongside his Father's divine will. Without that act of attunement, God would not have co-operated.

Can this sort of pattern be applied to the way we try to handle our strongest emotions? We'll look at some of the most troublesome: anger, guilt, and sorrow. Love and joy will come into our discussion of relationships later.

Anger

There is a component of anger in many of the emotions assigned to Jesus in the previous chapter. In terms of stress management, there was some anger in the combination emotions of grief and frustration and disappointment that were quite frequently reported.[3] Jesus did not squash it totally. He did not always remain the meek and mild figure of Sunday School pictures; he did not put 'niceness' at the top of his priorities. According to the Gospel records he recognised anger in himself and expressed it in short, sharp expostulation.[4] 'How long must I put up with you!'; 'Haven't you understood *yet!*' Then the strength in the emotion was channelled into a positive action. For a specific instance see the picture-story that summarises Part 3 on p. 150. The one occasion on which it was acted out was in clearing the Temple courts of dishonest money dealing.[5] This is the supreme example of how Jesus managed anger, and he did it in a maturely calculated way.

As Jesus approached Jerusalem for what he knew was the last time, he must have been acutely aware of the awe and majesty of the house of God. His sense of justice and of occasion was harshly affronted by the display of corrupted trade; he knew it rode on the power of the religious authorities to exploit the pilgrims. Jesus' spontaneous rage at what he saw can only be imagined. One remarkable fact, only recorded by Mark, is that having noticed the state of the Temple courts, Jesus *left* them and spent time at Bethany considering what he should do about it. About two days later he returned; by then he had decided to challenge the Temple authorities in a dramatic way that couldn't fail to disturb them – he drove out those who were exchanging money, using a horse-whip and upturning loaded tables. Knowing that this would provoke a violent reaction on the part of the priests, he seemed unfearful of their reprisals. 'Why didn't you arrest me?' he challenged them.

Note that this incident is followed only a few verses later (Mark 11:25) with Jesus saying, 'when you stand in prayer, forgive whatever you have against anybody, so that your Father in heaven may forgive your failings too.'

What is more typical of us?

Most commonly, we hide anger, deny it, or put it squarely on the shoulders of someone else. It's not mine, it's yours, and it's your fault that I feel angry. Almost as if someone else had picked up a load of

dirt and thrown it at me, innocent bystander that I am. Or it is a
disturbance I don't relish the look of, so I close my inner eyes to it.
It's too hot for me to handle so I blow it on to you. Anger gets
bandied around, hurled from one person on to another, no one
wanting to own it and stop it going further.

To acknowledge that the anger belongs to me, and that it is being
fired in me because there is an accumulation of rotten tinder inside
me, is asking too much. My smothered feelings are sparked off by an
unrelated whiff of hot air and get blown out of all proportion. Flames
escape and catch on to hot kindling lying elsewhere and the whole
group gets set on fire. I myself pretend I hardly know where or what
started it; I only know I feel aggrieved and injured and the wounded
party, even though it was inside me that the conflagration started. All
because I had refused to admit a small spark of anger early on. I had
neither acknowledged its presence nor managed its force. I couldn't
let go of my precious image of 'nice' me.

Anger has been described as *what happens when I perceive that my
demands are not being met.* This definition covers even so-called 'righteous' anger, because what I want to happen isn't happening.

*I see an elderly woman limping across the road: a motorcycle zooms past her
only just avoiding running her down and I feel angry. My demand that
elderly people should be respected has been flouted. It may well be appropriate
anger, but it is none the less anger. If this happened outside my house on a
fairly regular basis I am likely to build up a considerable head of fury. If I
don't do something about it I will get stroppier with my children when they
are on their bikes, and with my workmates who think I'm a crank. If I feel
misunderstood and resentful a real fight is likely to break out. On the other
hand I might get sufficiently angry sufficiently often to decide actually to do
something about it. My anger might fuel a positive action; I might write a
letter to the local press, or visit the police station, or call on my local
councillor. It might even get a pedestrian crossing marked outside the sheltered
accommodation which is next to my home.*

Sometimes it is a practical idea to have a specified safety valve at hand
for those times I recognise I am storing up anger. Something that
will enable me to get rid of the head of steam I am trying to contain,
so that I can look at the ingredients of the anger in a calmer fashion,
and *then* decide what to do about it. Kicking the cat is hard on the
innocent cat, but kicking a cardboard box around the garden, or
stamping on the kitchen floor like a two-year-old in a tantrum,

or slamming saucepan lids together, or hurling pillows at the wall or screaming at the wind or yelling swear words in the shower – there are a myriad things I can think up to let off steam without harm to others. Sometimes these actions have to be kept for times when I am on my own. Some people may prefer to vocalise their feelings to someone else, someone who is a good listener and will absorb what they say without accepting the need to *do* something about it. Or many people find writing down their grievances helps to relieve the anger, or keeping a file in their personal computer – with a secret password – into which they can hammer out their worst expletives. When the hot air has been let out, then, and only then, when I have fully convinced myself that the anger is *mine*, can I consider how most productively to set about changing things for the better. While I am blaming other people, or the boss, or the government, or circumstances, or God, for the anger there is little I can do about it because I tell myself it is their problem and out of my hands. As soon as I understand that the emotion is *mine*, whatever triggered it, then I can take on the responsibility of using its energy to a useful purpose.

I may decide to go and say sorry; or to set about repairing the damage; or to start rebuilding the broken connections. Taking charge of my part in restoring the balance is now in my hands, not waiting outside me and something over which I have no control.

Guilt

This is a difficult fact to grasp: the word 'guilt' does not appear in the Authorised Version of the Gospels, nor the Jerusalem Bible nor the Good News Bible. There are two instances of the word 'guilty': one concerns the only unforgiveable sin – that of slandering and speaking evil of the Holy Spirit[6] – and the other concerns the yelling mob screaming out for the conviction of Jesus Christ.[7] 'What is your verdict?' asks the high priest of the crowd of onlookers; 'He is guilty; he should die', they respond.[8] The vast edifice of guilt feelings that some generations of Christian literature have devised, and which have been absorbed by devout followers of the Church, does not have its blueprint set in the Gospels. Guilt used as an immediate means of social control is familiar to every parent, and church dogma has not always been prepared to resist this temptation. There is considerable literature available which is concerned with uncovering past mistakes. Today we have no basis for continuing to tolerate the imposition of guilt where even Jesus did not do so.

The stress inherent in the vast expectations and demands being laid daily on Jesus, did *not* cause him to experience what we call 'guilt'. It is we in our self-pride who feel 'guilty' when we can't fulfil the things we think people are expecting of us, or those things we expect of ourselves.

We are taught that Jesus Christ experienced everything we experience, and certainly that he 'knew all things'. Perhaps the exception is what we know as 'guilt'. In John 8:7 we read of Jesus challenging the accusers of the woman caught in adultery that her punishment should be started by 'he that is without sin among you' ('he that is free from sin' REB). It's as if he knew there would be no one in that category, although he knew what it was like to be without sin. Jesus preached about contrition and repentance often; and on forgiveness often. 'If your brother does something wrong, go and have it out with him alone, between your two selves. If he listens to you, you have won back your brother. If he does not listen, take one or two others along with you' (Matt. 18:15). And for instance, 'My son, your sins are forgiven' (Luke 5:20). He tells people directly where they go wrong, but he never preaches on guilt.

What is more typical of us?

Here again is an anomaly. 'Guilt is strictly an English word; no other Germanic, or indeed Indo-European language has it, and it is not clear where it came from.'[9] It was not until the sixteenth century that the word came to mean the 'state of having wilfully offended'.[10] Since then our burden of personal guilt has grown so overdeveloped that the more important awareness of forgivenness and of forgivingness has become meagre and infrequent.

We have done some strange things with the idea of guilt.

– On the one hand, in an effort to limit the overwhelming sense of liability for all things wrong, guilt gets constructed into a series of duties against which I can measure my own worth: I tell myself that if I do fulfil the things I've *got* to do, ought to do, should do, then I will be free of guilt and see myself as a 'goodie'. Similarly, if I refrain from those things I mustn't do, shouldn't do, I've *got not* to do, I can once again see myself as a 'goodie'. The trouble with these *gottas* is that they are never-ending, and as soon as one set of oughts is fulfilled there is a whole set of others waiting for my attention; so the load of guilt, instead of becoming lighter, can get heavier.

– On the other hand, we have trivialised the word colloquially – 'Oh my dear, I feel so guilty, I forgot to sugar your tea'. Guilt can be so overburdening we have to attach it to minor offences in order to cope with it all.

Neither of these ploys are Christ-centred.

Some people's lives are riddled and ruined by feelings of guilt, however much the acts and attitudes which triggered the guilt are forgiven. Perhaps it is ourselves we can't forgive when we fall below the absurd constructs we set for ourselves; maybe it is related to an inverted sense of self-pride. Our living, loving, fiery God has risked creating beings who will often fall short of the mark, and in Jesus Christ we see total forgiveness offered to anyone who asks for it. At times this forgiveness is given even before it is asked for.[11] Who are we to hang obstinately on to our guilt, when the Lord of All, sinless himself, never put it onto us?

Guilt doesn't have a lot to do with actual sinning. The greatest of sinners may feel very little guilt. Sin is rectified by contrition, reparation and restoration, not by guilt.

So, when I am stressed by all the expectations I see coming at me which I know I cannot possibly fulfil, instead of allowing a crippling sense of guilt to descend on me I can:

– recognise it for what it is; *my* perception of how I have failed, probably based on inverted, imploded, false ideas of my own capability;
– make amends for the immediate triggers of guilt: say sorry, repair damage, build bridges, work for reconciliation;
– digest *seriously* that I am not required to be all things to all people;
– reform my aims in a way that is realistic and attainable, making smaller goals I can reasonably hope to gain;
– when I don't reach my goals, laugh at myself, say sorry to whomever I have harmed, talk to God about it, and start again. And again. And again.

Sorrow

Sorrow, and its more complex derivatives disappointment and grief, are clearly expressed by Jesus. His biographers record them with great poignancy. Perhaps the moment that is closest to our own experience is that in the incident of Luke 17:17; Jesus says to the one leper who returned to thank him after the confirmation of his healing, 'Didn't I heal ten men?' He expresses the spontaneous sorrow he felt when the remaining men were so preoccupied with their release from their dreaded disease, and telling their families and friends of their drama, that they had not returned to Jesus or to give glory to God. There was deep disappointment too, that those who failed were of his own people; the one who returned was a 'foreigner', a Samaritan. Jesus manages his emotion by expressing it but not acting it out inappropriately – he doesn't chase the others up and rub in their ingratitude as we might do, nor does he store up a grudge which might colour a later episode, as I might do.

All through the Gospels, it is very notable that Jesus' moments of deepest anguish are never 'swallowed' or disguised. They are acknowledged, and expressed, so those around him are aware of what he is going through. Yet he never transposes the weight of his own emotion onto the shoulders of others, and thereby multiply the torment. In each incident Jesus deals with the emotion himself in a way that is specific for that event. For instance:

- When he heard of the death of John, who was his cousin and his boyhood friend, and who had been the enthusiastic promoter of Jesus' own mission, it was news that appalled him. The wild but holy John had had his head – cut off on a royal whim – paraded round a drunken and jeering orgy in front of Herod. This was not only an obscenity, not only an immense personal grief, but it was a threat of powerful immediacy to Jesus. He responds by going off on his own to a remote area, to be alone (Matt. 14:13).

- As the final realisation came to Jesus that the only way to save his beloved, misguided, stiff-necked Jerusalem was by undergoing a similar public parade of humiliation himself, he wept. His disciples recorded his weeping, but what they remembered was something special. It was not only the depth of the weeping they experienced as it was wrenched out of his body, it was that Jesus wept not simply for himself, but for the future fate he knew of which Jerusalem would not take warning (Luke 19:41–4).

- Possibly it was the greatest let-down of all. Jesus, who was the teacher and soul-friend of the group of men he had chosen, had travelled with them, and companioned them, and loved them with every fibre of his being; then he discovered that one of them would lead his enemies to his most intimate resting place. Jesus was in deep distress. He declared it openly, 'One of you is going to betray me!' He resisted confronting Judas in front of the group – they might well have mobbed him – but used the ritual that was available in the moment to convey his knowledge under cover to Judas, with the instruction to get on with it if it had to be done. And then he carried on through the complex procedure of the evening with no further loading of blame. Instead he took steps to institute the greatest memorial of his love so it would be remembered through all ages. Anguish acknowledged, received, and transformed (Mark 14:17–25).

- A little while later, in the garden at the foot of the Mount of Olives, his anguish took the form of sweat and blood. He knew his disciples would not be able to cope with it, and he withdrew from them a little way. He asked them to stay with him, just to watch with him while he got on with the job of coming to terms with what was about to happen, as he had to accept in full what he had perceived only in glimpses before; in Gethsemane, Jesus takes his very urgent appeal to God in private, and goes apart on his own (Mark 14:33–5 etc.). He was disappointed, in all astonishing truth, that they couldn't manage even to stay awake, but there is no hint in the Gospels that he 'took it out on them' by projecting his dismay onto their frail and unready experience. He wouldn't put emotional responsibility onto people who were without the maturity to know what to do with it.

What is more typical of us?
We, as humans, deal with our sorrows in a vast array of different ways. There are some basic questions which apply to all of them.

- Is emotional responsibility something that is put onto me at the appropriate time, or is it something I have to learn to take on for myself? In the Gospels Jesus seems keen that we should take up as much as we can, but he doesn't heave it onto others just to ease himself of his own load.
- Do we accept our strong emotions-of-the-present even to ourselves? Or, to avoid pain and embarrassment and the risk of making fools of ourselves, do we prefer to cover them up, deny them, reject them? Put them down for fear of losing face if we act on them inappropriately?
- Do we acknowledge them straightly and plainly, as a way of owning them ourselves and to others, but equally without involving blame of others?

- Do we claim responsibility for them, or do we tend rather to project the uncomfortable ones onto other people and relieve ourselves of doing anything about transforming them?

What can we learn from the behavioural response of Jesus our Christ?

In Relationship

Personal connectedness

Listening, and being

listened to

Adjusting expectations

> **TO COUNTERACT:**
>
> Self-enclosure
> Isolation
> Icy-sufficiency
> Stunted growth

● ●

'We've been together for fifty-four years and now we're friends.
We have a bash at each other now and again, but sooner or later
we get around to being friends again.'

'To me, God is My-Lord-Who-Knows, yet is Friendly-With-
It. And Jesus as a man mirrors Him.'

'Mum, do you want to be called Gran, Chumma or Grandma?
You've got to have the same name for all the grandchildren.'

And to Simon, Jesus said, 'You shall be called Peter'.[1]

*A great many people learn very early on in life that 'Insecurity and Uncer-
tainty' is the name of the game. At some stage in our infancy our needs for
instant gratification are greater than what we receive, and we feel angry and
unsafe. The most loving parent has other needs also, and that proves to us
their fallibility in caring for us. We each of us have to learn how to be
separate.*

*Take Lindy for instance. As a young child she grew suspicious and wary.
In order to protect herself from as much let-down as possible, she pretended
she didn't need others, at all. She even pushed them away. When she got to
big school she experimented with trying to conform to the rules of the group*

so that she might get accepted, but she found them to be boring and restricting, so instead she went inside herself and amused herself with fictitious characters who always did what she wanted them to do. That was fun, and it was quite easy to let her imagination go, but it did make her uncommunicative. If she talked about her secret friends to others they laughed at them, and at that they went sort of fuzzy and unreliable, so she just kept them to herself. Eventually Lindy learnt to do most of the things her peer group did, just to avoid comment, but she didn't put too much passion into it. She got married in the usual sort of way, half-wondering what all the fuss was about, and although the house was kept tidy and the meals were on time she still kept her 'real' self to herself. When the first baby came there was a brief moment when she wanted to give of herself, to fulfil all her dependent baby's needs with her own breast milk, but she didn't bother to persevere with all those disturbed nights; it was easier when someone else could give the baby a bottle. So Lindy withdrew again into her secret world. The second baby was different; she was more confident as a mother, the baby was less demanding and she enjoyed looking after it more. She even started loosening up and laughing with the two children, and Lindy's husband noticed a new warmth in her sexual response to him. But by then he had developed another interest, someone he had met on his own at the pub who was unattached and positive and impassioned. So once a routine with the children was established he left quietly in the middle of the night with a note to Lindy speared onto her toothbrush (he knew she would never not clean her teeth in the morning), and with no forwarding address. Then the second child, her favourite, started having fits and ended up with brain damage, and quite suddenly Lindy didn't know where to turn. Her fantasy friends were no good to her now, they weren't real and they were totally empty.

She looked out at the neighbours passing her window. 'Those selfish self-satisfied prigs,' she wailed to herself, 'they don't know a fraction of what I am going through.' She had no inkling of how impenetrable she had become, nor of how Sally, next door, had felt cold-shouldered by her. Lindy didn't even know that Sally had a child with cerebral palsy, or that she was in contact with a friendly group of families who together supported each other. The waste of it all, the loneliness, the unnecessary isolation, the loss . . .

Of all the various relationships we can build, **friendship** is the one most celebrated by Jesus. It is also the one most devalued in our present culture. We have many contacts, acquaintances, and networking units, but long-term friends are rare. Friendship is a buffer to over-stress in three special ways:

(i) When I am in a state of high stress, whether it is positive and a means of launching me into a change I want, or whether it is negative and looks like destroying my self-confidence, what is needed is a friendly group of people who understand the situation and can be a platform of support. People who are good at both accepting me as I am and encouraging what I could be.

(ii) This sort of group can absorb the negative spin-offs of a difficult situation; it can continue to uphold and sustain me in spite of my irritability and self-dissatisfaction. Sometimes I will be the one to be there, returning the support.

(iii) There will be at least someone in such a circle who is prepared to listen, without any judgement and with minimal comments, while I get the worries out of my system.

(iv) Friends provide a wonderful platform for distraction and play and laughter.

If people are able to mismanage relationships, rather like Lindy, without even meaning to, how did Jesus the Christ manage them?

Personal connectedness

While he was learning to live with the unique range of expectations being flung at him,[2] Jesus devised a wholly new structure for dealing with personal connectedness. As Messiah, he could have chosen to live on an admired but isolated pinnacle. The expectations and projections coming at him were so massive that on their own they would have held him up there indefinitely. But Jesus chose something entirely different, and new.

– He was expected to be externally powerful, aggressive, and to take hold of the shape of outside events; instead he chose to reshape inside attitudes.

– He was expected to take dictatorial and military power; instead he turned power into a form of personal authority which stemmed from his inner communication with God his Father.

– He was expected to meet the popular desire for political power; instead this was sidestepped by taking on the full power of self-responsibility.

– He was expected to confront the established religious law, but instead he simplified and expanded it.

Most significant of all, the methods he used to transform the world on the widest scale, were the very ones that he applied to every personal relationship. He did away with double standards or disguises that exclude. He wanted to draw everyone *in*, keeping nobody *out*. As a starting point, these are some of the ways he behaved concerning *friends*:

1.

> **Jesus said, 'I do not call you slaves, but friends . . . I call you friends, because I have made known to you everything I have learnt . . . '** (John 15:13, 14, 15)

Between friends, Jesus modelled the opening-up of experience; the sharing of insight and understanding. This sharing has a qualification however: he told them everything he had learnt from the Father, everything that was good and constructive – this didn't necessarily include those things he had learnt from the 'other side', and his contact with demons and evil spirits. Friendship does *not* require the re-telling of destructive knowledge or the showing-off of familiarity with evil.

2.

> **'My friend, I am not being unjust to you; did we not agree . . . ?'** (Matt. 20:13)

Jesus demonstrated that friendship was to be in the context of mutual trust, whether this contract was spoken or unspoken. This is in strong contrast with the manipulative climate of friendships recorded in the Old Testament.

3.

> **'Friend, how did you get in here without a wedding robe?' And he was speechless. Then the king said, 'Bind him hand and foot and cast him into outer darkness'.** (Matt. 22:11-13 NRSV)

Friendship with Jesus implies a certain compliance with specific common values and allegiances. The term 'friend' is not applicable to any old body in any old guise. It carries responsibilities with it. Notice, however, that the 'imposter' is not turned out before he has been given the opportunity to stand up for his position, and refused it.

4.

> **'Friend, do what you are here for.' Then they came forward, seized Jesus, and arrested him.** (Matt. 26:50)

At the hour of perhaps his greatest tension and uncertainty, Jesus still hung on to his amazing tolerance for others, sustaining a capacity for ambiguity well beyond ours. He still gave room to 'the other' to behave as they deemed fit, still without judgement. Personal responsibility is rooted in the person who is acting, and even in this case it is not taken over by the one who is acted upon.

5.

> **'My friend, move up higher.'** (Luke 14:10)

An integral part in friendship as modelled by Jesus is the acceptance – even encouragement – of change. Just as Simon developed into Peter, and Thomas the Doubter changed into Thomas the Acclaimer, so also our friendships are not based on static circumstances but need to move as each new growth shows itself. This applies as much to each individual, so each can have a different rate of growing and a different name. There is no homogeneity to friendship.

Christian marriage, as contained within the concept of the twentieth-century nuclear family, expects us to put all our relationship needs into one basket – physically, emotionally, metaphorically and to confine all our deepest emotions within that small circle. This is to expect the almost impossible. Some argue that *in order to keep the family together* it is vital that some types of relationship are extended outside the tight family circle. Since the enlarged and inclusive 'Family' has virtually disappeared, the number of human repositories for our personal feelings, expectations and even projections are severely reduced. Where I could have complained to my great-aunt about the annoyance of my little sister, I now have only my father, mother, or brother to whom to unburden – and they live with my little sister also and are less inclined to forget than my great-aunt. In Jesus' time, several generations and varied members of those generations would have been geographically close, and between them could have shared the negative emotions of all, and harvested the collective wisdom of all. In our time, it is more common to retain strong feelings – positive or negative – and vent them strictly within the closed family. Close same-sex relationships outside the family, even though they are entirely non-sexual, are harder to maintain today. It makes for a very profound difficulty, and is complete antithesis to the practice of the early church.

All relationships are nurtured by tolerance, adjusting expectations, and listening. There are clues to our own behaviour in all of these from the ways Jesus responded.

Tolerance

How far does *our* tolerance go? Do we, for instance, allow for the inclusion of such a statement as that issued to the main Sunday papers: 'Many Christians are Lesbian, Gay or Bisexual and are happy with their sexuality, knowing that God returns their love and worship with affirmation and blessings'? Do we allow others to rejoice in their own insights, whether they are identical to ours or not? Jesus the Christ says, 'Why can you not judge for yourselves what is right?'[3]

Commitment to love and self-giving puts us in the way of being vulnerable, and all the attendant risks of being hurt. Jesus never flinched from that. He went out of his way to avoid the self-protecting measures we use – bombast, overreaction, all the range of 'how dare you!' and 'I told you!' and 'poor misunderstood me' behaviours. Even under the most severe stress, Jesus married tenderness with strength and gentleness with determination. His compassion for others always enabled him to see their point of view, his selfhood was never barricaded in such a way that others couldn't get in, no one ever felt excluded. Hand-in-hand with this openness goes the gift of self-responsibility: 'Hold yourselves in readiness' again and again.

This sort of tolerance is much more than the ordinary 'I'll just stand back awhile and let you do your own thing' sort of steadiness. The difference in the standing-alongside that Jesus expects of us is that when I am really upset by someone else, when my plans have been seriously put out of joint by another, when my friend turns into my enemy – in all these cases Jesus demands that I truly affirm that God loves that other (offending) person as much as He loves me. That whether I see myself as good wheat and the other as the weed or vice versa, and whether the sun is shining or the rain is raining, it is shining and raining equally on the wheat and the tares. He/she is no less loved by God than I am, and I am no more worthy of God's love than they are. This is a hard lesson to remember all the time!

Adjusting Expectations

In the very process of keeping relationships dynamic it is essential to readjust and update constantly the things I expect of the other person. This means a continual reappraisal and reinterpretation of how *they* are feeling about any situation, just as much as I might hope they are assessing how I am feeling. I have to be continually aware that my likes and dislikes are not necessarily the same as his/hers; and just as my likes and dislikes can change, so can hers/his, sometimes quite unpredictably. On occasion, taking the responses of the other for granted can be a sort of backhanded compliment, but at others it is an excuse for slothful empathy. The excitement and surprise of really long-term relationships – such as the marriage above lasting over fifty-four years – is the constant change and development in the growth of the spouse. This growth may happen in stages, and in different stages to each other. By each staying in parallel as it were with the other, without too many crossings-over and harping intrusions into the other's way of seeing things, we can give each other space to grow at our own rate. Jesus must have been driven to the edge of despair at times by the obstinacy and hanging-back of the disciples; at times they could make nothing of his words, and what he said was quite obscure to them. Somehow he put up with both the denseness and the lack of understanding of those around him.[4] He continually adjusted the expectations he had of them, and went on encouraging them and hoping in them however often they fell short, with patience and tolerance – and a lot of laughter. At times even the names he gave his friends changed, just as the affectionate and intimate names we give each other within families can vary from time to time.

As we go on alongside each other, Jesus advises us to humble ourselves and our large ideas as if we were little children; for, he says, of the delight and tolerance and excitement in them is born the greatest in the Kingdom of heaven.[5]

Listening

Above all, in order to get his expectations in some sort of realistic order, Jesus *listened*. We have seen how he constantly advocated others to listen (John 5:24 for example). Not with any idea already in his mind of what the speaker was wanting to say, as we most commonly do; nor with any sense of hurry or interruption. His attitude to whomever was speaking was that of a free-flowing two-way exchange, circulating, unpressurised, mutual. He delighted in being always approachable, in communicating, in being receptive. 'What do you want?' or 'what do you think?' was often on his lips.[6] His empathy, perspicacity, and insight was such that he could tolerate ambiguity to the furthest extent possible. '*Love your enemies,*' he insisted! (Matt. 5:43) 'You are *blessed* when people persecute you! Leap for joy!'[7]

When Jesus was under the most acute stress before his voluntary entry into his arrest: he made use of that moment to eat and drink with his closest followers. He chose this moment to tell them why they were his friends: because they co-operated with what he asked of them – a reference to their own response to him; and secondly, because they were a repository on earth for 'everything he knew'. In addition, at this high spot of his own need, as he was about to go into the torment of darkness himself, he took off his only 'guise' – his outer garment – and so stripped he stooped down to their feet and washed them, each in turn.[8]

What could Lindy have done that was different? Could she have trusted more, been prepared to be more open and vulnerable to others, even at the cost of sometimes bearing hurt? Could she have adjusted her expectations of her neighbours, of her husband, opening herself out a bit more in order to receive as well as give? Would such an opening actually have broadened her giving, as well as adding to the gifts offered to her? Would her own children have benefited by a wider horizon? If she had listened to them, would they have learnt to listen to her, in exchange sometimes?

Lindy had never paid attention to God. Was God ready to pay attention to her?

Letting Go
When and how

● ●

This will be a short chapter but it comes with a message that is pungent. The message is vehement and vigorous; it is astringent and penetrating and adds spice to every choice. It is about an attitude that ran as an undercurrent through all the decisions that Jesus made in the Gospels. *Jesus the Christ, Son of God, Redeemer of the world, didn't act as though he was indispensable.*

In chapter 11 we examined the mental priority given by Jesus to physical and geographical withdrawal. Making close relationships is about commitment, about binding our allegiances to another – or specified others. Surely emotional attachment is a Good Thing? How did Jesus approach this question?

Judging by the amount of space they are given in each of the Gospels, there are four outstanding personal relationships that were important to Jesus: Mary of Bethany,[1] John the disciple whom he loved and who leaned so close to him at the last supper,[2] Lazarus whom he brought back from being dead,[3] and his mother. In each case we are given clear indications of how Jesus, in spite of his special love for them, *gave them freedom from being enclosed by him* as a human being. He would not smother them, nor be smothered himself by them.

• When Mary, his mother – such an extraordinary and divinely chosen mother – started to urge him too far, he clearly made space between them so they could each take their own decisions (John 2:4). This space was reinforced when she, with his brothers, came looking for him because they were concerned for his mental health.[4] Jesus went so far as to proclaim the idea that a healthy distance must at some time be encouraged between parents and children if they are to grow and pursue their own allegiances as a necessary principle.[5]

- With John, the beloved disciple, Jesus knew he would be seeing him again after his resurrection in human form. And yet, as he was dying on the cross, he used his panting and pain-stricken breath to 'hand over' his prized and individual relationship with him. As his spirit was leaving his body, Jesus asked John to make a special bonding with his mother, and he asked his mother to accept John as the nearest replacement for her son (John 19:26,27). In the physical and emotional stress of parting, the behavioural response of Jesus is to detach – voluntarily and purposefully – from his own established and precious emotional relationships, but at the same time to make sure of the possibility that new ones can grow. From stress to glory.

- As for Lazarus, the letting-go is less specified. Lazarus and his sisters had hosted Jesus on many occasions, and the story of the emotional turmoil caused in Jesus by his death is movingly told (John 11:1–46). Yet once he is re-established in the household as alive and well, he is barely mentioned again. Jesus performed the miracle of raising Lazarus for the glory of God, not for the strengthening of their own relationship. It appears that neither were lumbered by indebtedness to the other. When Jesus returns for a final meal with them it is simply stated that Lazarus was there (John 12:2), no further interaction between them is recorded – Lazarus was 'free' to get on with his own life.

- The references to Mary are perhaps more numerous than any other person outside the circle of the twelve disciples. She is mentioned at various stages throughout the ministry of Jesus. She has the additional distinction of being the first person to whom he appeared after his resurrection. Yet at the exact point where her appalling sense of bewilderment and loss turns into ecstatic recognition, Jesus tells her she must separate herself. 'Don't cling,' he says; she may not cling *to him*, she must look to the Godhead for reassurance after he has ascended. From someone with whom she had a very close and ongoing relationship, this must have been a very unexpected and rather baffling response. But Jesus was releasing Mary from what could have been a tied-in, mutually-possessing type of intimacy to a wider and expanding ministry. '*Go*,' he said to her, spread your energy and talents, 'go and tell . . . '. An enlargement for Mary of her immediate concern for Jesus himself.

That is the crucial constituent of letting go; let go in order to widen, to expand, to grow. Let go in order to use the tools lent to me by God to even greater and larger effect. Let go my own desires and ambitions and immediate goals to include the expanded purposes of God. In the Garden of Gethsemane we have an example of the ultimate 'let go': letting go of what might seem good to me, what might let *me* out of a suffering predicament, into the overall, ultimate, overarching, long-visioned purposes of God.

Am I up to that – ??!!

It is the opposite of letting go in order to rid-myself-of . . .

Jesus Letting Go

Jesus said to the children, 'Come to me . . . '

To the exhausted he said, 'Come to me . . . '

To the blind beggar he said, 'Come to me . . . '

To the thirsty, he said, 'Come to me, drink of me, and you will never thirst again.'

But to Mary, one of the small band he loved the most, Jesus said, 'Do not cling to me; go, and tell . . . '

To the healed demoniac who wanted to follow him he said, 'Go . . . '

To the Samaritan woman he said, 'Go . . . '

As he left his disciples for the last time he said, 'Go . . . '

Perhaps the most challenging behaviour to modern pastoral thinking is the fact that, except for Lazarus and Mary, there is no evidence that Jesus followed up any incident of healing at all. Not even after the dramatic incidents of restoring life to the son of the widow of Nain, and to the daughter of Jairus. Both the demoniac named Legion and the rich young lawyer *asked* to follow Jesus; to both he said, No, not right now, continue on your own way. Come back later – perhaps.[6]

We ourselves of course do not carry the role of Jesus the Christ, and we can have no doubt that he made sure there were others around to support those who were newly healed and forgiven; none the less the way in which Jesus was prepared to hand back personal responsibility to those who had received help as soon as it was feasible, carries with it questions about our own dependence upon our need to be needed.

Twentieth-century Besetting Obsessions

Can we let these go? Would we be more effective in our work for the Kingdom of God if we did? Do the following cramp the glory of God?

- Our modern craving for comfort, a twentieth-century besetting obsession if ever there was one. Our drive after affluence, the desire continually to raise the living standards of our homes, to race after the latest fashion in clothes, furniture, aesthetics, food – are these things stress-relieving or stress-generating?
- The craving for control – this doesn't simply apply to the physical control of our environment or the mental control discussed in Part 2 of this book: what about the craving to dominate, manipulate, subdue, wrongfoot, downstage, the other? 'Putting them down' or conversely feeling 'put down' is a favourite daily game for most of us, if we look carefully enough. Are we prepared to give that up, let go that feeling of puppet power?
- The craving for certainty: it's as though we were paralysed by risk; that any intimation of chaos was a dead-end. In truth it is the lack of adventure, the absence of vulnerability, the deletion of trial that is the dead-end. Making everything accountable and open to compensation if anything goes wrong flattens all things to the lowest denominator and squashes their potential for growth. The search for certainty seems the answer when one is highly stressed, but it is illusory. Learning to live with uncertainty and to survive risk – perhaps even thrive on it – is a much surer base for making sense of stress.

Comfort, control, certainty[7] can temporarily boost my ego, but Jesus was prepared to let them all go. He didn't need the emotional twists and skirmishes we use in order to build up our own morale. His own personhood and wholeness were so self-authenticating he had no need to resort to such tricks. The more stress was thrown at him, the more transparent he became. It's what hits you when you look at him on the cross itself.

Finally, and more kindly! A common difficulty among those who

are naturally empathetic, and one which affects some of those who in
their professional capacity are exposed to the troubles of others, is
the problem of registering the pain of others, but not being dysfunc-
tioned by it. Jesus took on board an array of suffering and pain every
day that was more than most of us are asked to deal with in a lifetime.
He never seems to have been worn down or cowed by this quantity
of human damage. We have the new onslaught of mass despair
brought by word and image into the heart of our homes, but it is
removed and second-hand. Either way, how can one cope with the
sheer weight of dejection to which we are exposed?

It is difficult to theorise in words. It is difficult to describe with
logic. Perhaps the use of an image can help.

> In the place of deep stillness and deep relaxation hold in your
>   mind one image. One sole picture to the exclusion of everything
>   else.
> Right at the centre of your mind, one single image:
> It is of a domestic funnel.
> Nothing fancy or decorated, it is ordinary and mass-produced.
> A clear glass funnel.
> Looking straight at it, I see that it has no lid.
> The funnel accepts whatever is poured into it.
> It has no control over what comes, and it rejects nothing.
> Sometimes wine is poured into the funnel, sometimes vinegar;
>   sometimes milk, or it may be oil, or water.
> Just as the funnel has no lid, it also has no plug.
> So it doesn't cling to, or possess, anything.
> It doesn't hold anything back.
> It may be 'coloured' by what gets poured into it,
> but *everything flows through*.
> It may be that the direction of the fluid is changed,
> or its concentration is altered,
> but it all *flows through*, onto whatever is supporting it.
> The funnel is of no use unless it is supported, it will only fall over
>   sideways.
> My funnel is supported on a tripod, the tripod of the Trinity.
> Whatever flows into my funnel, flows out onto the seedbed of the
>   Holy Trinity.
> I may be shown how 'effluent' is converted into fertiliser,
> or I may never know.

I do know that nothing is wasted, and all I have to do is receive
   it, offer it, and let it go.
Stress into the Glory of God.

Thy will, Thy purpose, *Thy* power, *Thy* peace, not mine, O Lord
God.

17

Assertive Tactics

It's OK for me to be me,
and for you to be you

It was winter, and Jesus was in the Temple walking up and down. The Jews gathered round him and said, 'How much longer are you going to keep us in suspense? If you are the Christ, tell us openly.' Jesus replied, 'The Father and I are one.'

The Jews fetched stones to stone him, saying, 'Though you are only a man, you claim to be God.' So Jesus answered:

> Is it not written in your Law:
> 'I said, you are gods'? [Psalm 82:6]
> So it uses the word 'gods'
> Of those people to whom
> the word of God was addressed,
> – and scripture cannot be set aside
> . . . I said, 'I am Son of God.'
> If I am doing [my Father's work],
> then even if you refuse to believe in me,
> at least believe in the work I do;
> then you will know for certain
> that the Father is in me and I am in the Father.
> (John 10:23–38 abridged)

Whatever degree of stress assaulted Jesus, he never for an instant wavered in his all-encompassing love for his people. He was rooted and held steady by his devotion to his Father, his commitment to his ministry, and his service to the poor, the needy and the unknowing. But when we, as mortal Christians, attempt to follow this example, there are very specific dangers that can wreck not only all our efforts, but also the relationships we have with others around us, and even our very souls.

Deep, and sometimes deeply hidden, in our psyche are themes of motivation that can too easily be mismanaged. Their origins may be high-minded, but they can overbalance us, they can drive us too far. We seldom hear warnings about them from the pulpit, and our best friends resist speaking to us about them. We can only discover them for ourselves. If, by honest and unashamed listening, we can tune into the constant dialogue that goes on inside us, then we will begin to understand the barrage of secret directions with which we beat ourselves.

They are our *drivers*.

'Drivers' is an apt analogy. Most of the time we continue along a track of behaviour by habit, without being conscious of what is driving us, and we may go too far too fast. Once we become aware of the instructions that drive us, we can decide whether, for this particular moment in this particular set of circumstances, we are being driven appropriately. If we discover we are not, we can take the initiative and change the instructions. We can voluntarily disengage from the driver, until later when we want the same driver for a different set of circumstances. Understanding, and deciding whether to engage with or disengage from my internal drivers, gives me freedom from habitual behaviours and allows me to use my tools for the glory of God, especially when I am stressed.

The names of the commonest drivers are: Be Perfect! Please All Always! Be Strong! Hurry Up! Try Hard – Never Stop! The worst thing about these drivers is that they can lead me to create a false identity for myself, and my true God-given identity gets lost. For instance:

'Be Perfect!'

No one is perfect, or ever has been, except Jesus the Christ. If I set my goals upon being-the-one-who-is-perfect[1] I will be striving after something that is unattainable. It may make me blind to my own imperfections, or it may so exaggerate the guilt I feel for my failings that I become over-scrupulous. Those who live around a perfectionist often feel a sense of impatience, intolerance, irritability, and a lack of humour or light-heartedness around the person who is engaged full-time with their 'Be Perfect' driver. Sometimes there is a suppressed syndrome of hostility, a sense of me against the world, a need to prove that I can beat the world, which characterises the perfectionist. To put a lot of energy into accomplishing a task to the very best of one's ability is, of course, an excellent thing to do, but to carry this attitude over into *every* activity is very stress-making. Being unable to put it on one side while playing at home with the children, is not an excellent thing, and suggests a continuous employment of my 'Be Perfect!' driver. That not only increases my own personal stress, but the stress of those around me too.

'Please All Always!'

This speaks of another unrealistic goal and identity. If I set myself the task of *always* being pleasing, to everybody, the result will be that I so subdue my real wants and desires and genuine creativity for the sake of others, that I become veiled, and unreal. It is an interesting question – did Jesus 'Please Always'? If I *always* put the other first, listen to their opinions without expressing mine, denying every need of my own, suppressing any hint of conflict or genuine emotion, I may turn into a nothing, less than a shadow. This will be far from the vibrant reflection of that bit of the image of God He says He has put into me. Worse still, if two people driven totally by their 'Please All Always' driver are put into a room together, and perhaps asked to solve a problem between them, nothing will ever get done. Each will be concerned to 'please' the other without voicing their own ideas. Until people are willing to expose their own genuine convictions, there is no place for negotiation.

Choosing to please the other for a specific occasion – like going to a film that doesn't attract me on my son's birthday – is a very different matter to being so hooked into my 'Please All Always' driver that I never tell my husband how I would really like to spend my own birthday. He gets a kick out of pleasing me sometimes, and I deny him this if I never tell him how I am pleased. It is something of the same thing with God, our Father. He wants to know what we want, even if we are then prepared to give it up and let it go. Before we can do that, we have to know what it is we are prepared to let go.

'Be Strong!'

The person who engages their 'Be Strong' driver without let-up is the one who is always reliable, always available to hear another's woes, always ready with the right instruction. It's as if they have built a fortress around their vulnerabilities so they won't show. They are there for other people, but when it comes to exposing their own cracks in their defences they back off: being seen as 'weak' is not for them. It's difficult to get to know the real person inside the fortress, and many of them remain isolated. They have to do without knowing what true intimacy is. They are strong, and lonely. Unlike Jesus.

'Hurry Up!'

There is no vestige of an indication in the Gospels that Jesus ever 'hurried'. It is difficult to imagine him rushing, or eating speedily, or interrupting others by finishing their sentence for them. Whereas it has been said that we ourselves suffer from an epidemic of 'hurry-sickness'. The increasing speed of traffic, the demand that tasks should be completed yesterday, the use of the instant-return-answer fax machine, the ever-present computers and calculators and mobile phones, the availability of E-mail, food that is pre-processed and instant – all these things have contributed to the feeling that it is desirable to be fast and constantly on the go. Yet those who rush around their world miss the finer details in life, and the things that lie deeper, things that are below the surface and which 'ground' us. To be conscientious about deadlines, and to arrive punctually when we are expected, is of course common politeness; but to carry that sense of urgency into our off-duty is a travesty of the way God the Creator intended us to use our energy bank. At times we have to take responsibility for disengaging from that particular driver.

'Try Hard – Never Stop!'

If a group of people is asked 'What happens to someone who tries hard all the time?' the answer is immediate, 'They become awfully trying!' Not to mention tiring. Try-Hard doesn't necessarily achieve very much, but they must be seen to be trying. They are very judgemental on other people, because no one else is ever trying as hard as they are. The one who can never stop spreads stress around them. Did Jesus 'Try Hard'? It's a fascinating question.

There is a common factor to all these drivers. Those who find real difficulty with disengaging from their drivers are usually the ones who spend a lot of energy looking for approval. They find it feeds their security if others notice they do well with their driven behaviour. It can become a circular treadmill. I will be noticed if I try hard, so I try harder, and I get noticed so I try even harder; and so on, with each of the drivers. *I can change, and take charge of when I want to engage them, or to disengage from them.* It largely depends upon how I feel about my own personhood.

Personhood

Jesus had a strong sense of his own personhood. He described it in terms of metaphor, instead of in terms of responsibility as we tend to do. He didn't hold back in telling others who he was, and how he saw his relationship with the Father, from whom he drew his strength. If I start telling people about who I think I am it makes me feel as if I am conceited, or proud, or big-headed. In listening to others, and telling them how he thought of himself, Jesus actually *freed the other up* to talk about themselves. Prime examples of this are the accounts of the Samaritan woman at the well and the Syrophoenician woman.[2] If I acknowledge how I feel about things, it means the other has an equally valid chance of saying how they feel about the same things.

In the process of discovering my drivers, or perhaps as a result of that process, there will be a point at which I can claim 'I am!' I can say of a particular bundle of preferences and dislikes, of gifts and limitations, 'I recognise that, that's me!' The secret name of Yahweh in the Old Testament was 'I am', so holy it was unmentionable. If I have been sent out and commissioned by that 'I am', I can claim to nestle in its shadow as 'i am', even if it is only in a whisper. The sense of being unique (and of value on account of this uniqueness) can also be reinforced when I consciously let go of the roles and responsibilities I know I have taken on, and go into a place of being stripped of the very things I normally prize. More of this in Part 4.

In the Gospels, Jesus used the phrase 'I am . . . ' in a great variety of ways. He said:

I am the good shepherd –	John 10:11
I am the gate –	John 10:7,9
I am the vine –	John 15:1,5
I am thirsty –	John 19:28

I am living water –	(by inference, John 4:14; 7:37,38)
I am the bread of life –	John 6:35,48,51
I am the way, the truth, and the life –	John 14:6
I am the light of the world –	John 8:12
I am the resurrection and the life –	John 11:25
I am come that they might have life, and that they might have it more abundantly (AV) –	John 10:10
Before Abraham was, I am –	John 8:58
I am from above, I am not of this world –	John 8:22
Where I am, you cannot come –	John 7:34 (also see 8:22)
I am Son of God –	John 10:36
I am doing my Father's work. I am in the Father –	John 10:38
The Father and I are one –	John 10:30

Assertive Tactics

So we are led into the 'modern' techniques of assertiveness. The fundamental basics of Christian assertive tactics are threefold:

(i) I state to you how I feel, or think about, or see things, on the understanding that you will tell me how you feel or think about or see things. Telling you about myself is something I know about, because only I am an expert on my own experience. Similarly *you are the only expert on yours*.

(ii) So I avoid loading you with blame for the situation – or anyone else;

(iii) and I resist loading you with the responsibility of approving of my response to the situation.

I so easily and totally unreasonably fling: '*You* make me so angry!' 'It's *your* fault I feel like this!' 'If only *you* didn't – *I* wouldn't have to . . . !' 'You're a ★★★, it's you who does this to me!!' when the emotion is actually mine.

There is no single thing that makes everyone equally angry: starting out late for a party puts some people into a furore, while others take it without fuss. Being sworn at makes some people see red, while others remain unperturbed. Having my house broken into turns me into a trembling jelly of fear, my daughter into a weeping fit of grief, my spouse into a savage rage. *Our responses are different, and our responses are our own.* The fear, grief, and rage may have been triggered by the action of the thief, but they don't 'belong' to him. His fuel may be greed or hunger or retribution, but those are his emotions, not ours. We can't know what the other person's feelings are unless they tell us. We spend a great deal of energy and time on presuming what the other feels, and assuming they somehow know – or *ought* to know! – what I feel, without either of us voicing it.

Assertive tactics are about telling the other person what I feel, how I see a situation, and how I suggest changing it. This is not about selfishness, it is about honesty and clarity; when I let the other know about me, and how I see my role, the other is freed up to let me know about what belongs to him/her. As long as I spew out epithets that perhaps miss their mark totally, my anger will be met with defensive taunts or further aggression. Fury will pile upon fury, and a blazing row will result. Whereas, if I stick with what only I can truly authenticate, that is, the way that *I* am experiencing the situation, there can be no argument. They tell me how they are experiencing it, *which is an equally valid position*, and then we negotiate.

Conversely, not telling people about who I really am, results in stereotyping and misapprehension. An example of this is a catching piece published in the national press written by a public figure:

> 'The thing is, I don't particularly *want* to be a permanently pumped-up, ever-ready, multiple-partner, hard-core porno fantasy: the man you pick up at a disco, the one who, of course, naturally, stands to reason, can't get enough.' Resisting projections can be a tricky business![3]

Jesus dealt with projections and expectations in three stages: he acknowledged they existed, examined what could be done to improve the situation, and then he handed them on to his Father. 'A man ran up, knelt before him and put this question to him, 'Good master . . .' Jesus said to him, 'Why do you call me good? No one is good but God alone.'[4]

Two examples of incidents where Jesus used assertive tactics in the face of strong expectations that he would act differently, are:

- the story of the paralysed man let down through the roof to the feet of Jesus. The crowd around, and no doubt the man and his friends as well, were expecting that at the sight of the helpless patient Jesus would offer him healing. But Jesus was moved differently. The astounding and very public response from this little established and itinerant preacher, was to say, 'Take comfort, my friend, your sins are forgiven.'[5] Then, knowing the disturbance that this statement would create, he followed it with a demonstration of his personal authority – 'Get up, pick up your mat, and walk home.' And he did.

- when Jesus responded to the urgent appeal from the local ruler to come to the help of his twelve-year-old daughter, he was delayed on the way. Messengers ran up to tell the party that it was too late, the girl had died, but Jesus pressed on. It must have been some way, for by the time they arrived at the big house there was already a crowd of mourners and musicians bewailing the death of the little girl – perhaps they were people who wanted to curry favour with her powerful father, after all he was president of their synagogue. The way they sneered and scoffed at this 'ridiculous' healer who had failed to arrive in time, shows how they expected him to sneak away in shame and lie low. But undeterred, Jesus strode through the angry wailers, dismissed the intruders from the house, and went up to the bedroom. Lifting up her land in his, he simply said, 'Little girl, I tell you to get up.' And she did.[6]

Straightforward personal authority. No loading onto the other person, or other people. No scapegoating, nor even any need to edge others into making approving noises.[7] I am me, and responsible for the way I see the world, and you are you, responsible for the way you see the world. Of course things can change, and we can affect each other, but that happens best when the change is wanted and accepted, not imposed. The paralytic man went along with the action of his friends in dropping in front of Jesus, and the little girl must have said goodbye to her father as he left to see the 'healer' on her behalf – all the household knew where he was and where to find him. Assertiveness employed in a Christ-centred way is all about *it's OK for me to be me,* **and** *it's OK for you to be you.*

Warning: I'm Right!

Assertiveness is calm and unruffled; it is *not* to be confused with the 'I Know I'm Right' syndrome. The drive to know the right answer, to be seen to be in the right, is greatly encouraged in our culture. Ticking boxes on an instant reaction and getting it right is part of the measurement-mania that grips us. The physiological effects of 'I'm Right' go along with the hostility in the aggressive/defensive mode attached to all those others, who, unlike me, have got it wrong. This is one of the commonest predisposers to coronary heart disease. In this part of the world we are struggling with a scenario where our national experience of C.H.D. remains among the highest. Joan put it this way:

She told the story of finding her son's new trainers gone. The wet, muddy, loved trainers had been put on the back doorstep the previous evening when he had come into supper. In the morning they weren't there.

She exploded. 'Those were a Christmas present! It's jealousy – all the boys in the district envied them'; her voice rose with steaming ferocity – 'I'll get them; I'll make the **** pay! Those slimy, corrupt, low **** they'll soon squirm . . . ' Then she had to suppress her rage, her son's frustration had to be dealt with before school and her husband demanded his breakfast.

The blinding headache and rigid body – not to mention the fuzzy eyesight and screwed-up digestion – stayed with her the entire day.

Meanwhile the withered and homeless old man painfully picked his way across the icy roads in her son's shoes.

Jesus the Christ, Son of the High God, was inevitably always right. How did he avoid the attendant hostility? How did he re-tune the stress he received? How did he demonstrate the difference between '*I am Right!*' and 'Believe me'? We are told that the Roman centurion recognised in him an authority that resonated with his own ability to say, ' . . . come and they come; go and they go'.[8] This authority of inner personhood[9] is different to the acquired authority of *I am Right!* How?

Jesus knew he was right; but he knew it so securely (unlike any of us) that he didn't waste energy in pushing it down people's throats. His own sense of being right with God was all embracing, it didn't have to be thrust upon anyone. Do we *have* to be so keen to justify our rightness *all* the time? Can I just sometimes let it pass . . . ?

He said, 'Though I bear witness of myself, yet my record is true: *for I know whence I came, and whither I go*' (John 8:14 AV).

18

Counting My Blessings – and Laughing!

TO COUNTERACT:

GLOOM!
Self-importance
Pride

Counting my blessings is for Sunday School, and should be left there when I leave. Laughter is trivial, frivolous, superficial, worldly, nothing to do with maturity and gravitas. Maybe some people want to think this way: do I?

Among my blessings are the obvious ones, those things which are to do with my health, mobility, and my use of the senses; my mental activity; the power of my emotions; my family, and my range of relations; my house and material provision; my church and those who have held me up; my friends and social circle; the things I give thanks for in my environment and my job. And so on, ad infinitum. I may like to add in those people and those places that have lit up the way of the Spirit for me.

Then there is my *forgiven-ness*; the most staggering of all my blessings. Acknowledging stress is not the same as acknowledging sin, although there are some Christians who make the two sound very similar. Stress is not about fault, or blame, or debt, although at times I may feel it is close to it. Making sense of stress means looking at what is, at the demands that are real and the resources that do exist, and matching them up as far as possible for a positive outcome. For Jesus this outcome was the greater glory of God. Although a heightened sense of 'guilt' may be a stress-sign, it is not a necessary element of stress. None the less, awareness of my

140

own forgiven-ness rates a very high place on my list of blessings.

If ever I am in doubt of the need for forgiveness, I only have to glance over the tools mentioned in this book and the way I have neglected or misused them. Look at my hands – ordinary, everyday, commonplace, taken-for-granted fingers attached to the end of my arms. A complexity of engineering which I leave unexplored; a marvel of elasticity in the skin which holds it together, letting water out but not letting it in; the sense and sensuousness that lie in the fingertips; the fine-tuning of tendons and ligaments which allow minute adjustments of movement and of pressure; both symbol and action of strength and tenderness, power to express violence and harm, or sensitivity and healing.

With those hands held in front of you, upturned, try this small exercise:

> These are my hands. My hands, my own hands, attached to my body. Not yours.
> I put them in my pockets   [*do it*],   where they do nothing; no thing.
> I put them behind my back   [*do it*],   I am hiding them.
> I use them to cover my eyes   [*do it*],   so I can't see properly.
> I use them to cover my ears   [*do it*],   and I can't hear you.
> I put them over my mouth   [*do it*],   so I needn't talk to you.
> I push things away from me   [*do it*],   then I don't have to touch them.
> Do you still not feel the need for forgiveness?
> 'I'm sorry.'

Whenever I am aware of my forgiven-ness, my own forgiving-ness grows. And as I am forgiving, the awareness of my blessings grow.

This is a compelling fact: physiologically, whenever I count my blessings, or whenever I feel a bit more cheerful and whenever I smile, my body releases endorphins. These enzymes turn up naturally in my body; their jobs are to reduce the sensation of pain, to promote health, and to refuel hope and love and optimism and enthusiasm. So the actual secret workings inside the body God designed are on my side, helping me to be the person He wants me to be.

When Jesus sensed people were under stress, he used the gift of genuine reassurance. He must have experienced this deep need for reassurance himself, and found it with great fulsomeness as he spent time alone in communion with his Father. It must have been there that he learnt how to pass it on – 'Be of good cheer!' Jesus says again and again, and it comes from a deep well of creativity, from unboundaried hope. We have become spoilt and superficial. Our soap operas are larded with sentiments like 'I promise you everything is going to be all right: trust me', and they are voiced by characters who give us no foundation whatever for that trust! Jesus speaks with an authority – 'like an eruption of fresh air into a fetid room'.[1]

The Greek which is used to describe this reassurance is twofold; one verb emphasises 'cheer up, have courage', and the other 'fear not, be not dismayed'. For instance:

> 'do not be anxious . . . the Father knows your needs . . . ' (Matt. 6:25, 32)
>
> To the paralytic: 'Take heart, my son' (Matt. 9:2 REB; also Mark 2; Luke 5)
>
> To the woman touching his cloak: 'Take heart, my daughter' (Matt. 9:22 REB: 'be of good comfort' AV)
>
> Walking on the water, like a ghost: 'Take heart! It is I; do not be afraid' (Matt. 14:27 REB)
>
> To his three disciples, falling down after witnessing the trans-figuration: 'Stand up; do not be afraid' (Matt. 17:7; also Mark 9; Luke 9)
>
> Post-resurrection: 'Do not be afraid; go and take word to my brothers' (Matt. 28:10 REB)
>
> Awe at the vast haul of fish: 'Do not be afraid; from now on it is people you will be catching' (Luke 5:10; also Matt. 4:19, Mark 1:17)
>
> To the despised woman with the spikenard: 'Go in peace; your faith has saved you' (Luke 7:50; also Mark 14:3–9)
>
> 'Fear not, little flock' (Luke 12:32 AV)
>
> To the hated Zacchaeus: 'Today salvation has come to this house' Luke 19:9; 'In the world you will have suffering, but *take heart*! I have conquered the world' (John 16:33 REB)

We have, in addition, the full list of the Beatitudes – 'Happy are they . . . ' where Jesus turns topsy-turvey our ideas of what it is to be happy and blessed.[2] It has been estimated that the words of gladness and joy and delight are mentioned ninety-eight times in the Gospels alone. Jesus knew the power of the 'feel good factor'.

Jesus went further than just giving reassurance. He was so confident of the utter goodness of God he could laugh with us at our serious-ness, our cares-full-ness where we could be carefree with God. With many, it is a real problem to imagine Jesus laughing, and certainly there are very few pictures of him capturing a moment of laughter. When Nathanael came to him, having just met him, and rather pompously said, 'Rabbi, you are the Son of God, the king of Israel', Jesus replied, 'You believe this just because I saw you under a fig tree'(John 1:49–50). This light-hearted way of putting things into proportion, without putting the speaker down, is something that is often under-recognised in Jesus the Christ. But before exploring it further, it may be useful to distinguish between different types of laughter, both how we use it ourselves, and how we hear it from others.

There is *head* laughter, for instance. This is laughter that is based on the intellect, on wit, on knowing the 'in' jokes. Such laughter can be described as witty, ironic, clever, sophisticated, knowing; but it is often seen as cynical, sardonic, cutting, snide, sarcastic, contrived. It is divisive; you understand it or you don't, you are either part of it or you are not.

Heart laughter, on the other hand, comes from our emotional responses. It can be described as spontaneous, cheery and warm, sympathetic and understanding; or conversely it can be unkind, cruel, demoralising, malicious, putting down. Insecure laughter is irritating, anxious, nervous, agitated, defensive. It can also be blue and obscene. Once again, laughter from the heart can be heartening or dis-heartening, it is bipolar, divisive.

The laughter that comes from the *guts*, real belly-laughter, is *good*. It is wholesome and contagious. It is trusting, inclusive, companioning, there is nothing about it that is divisive. It is hospitable, welcoming, liberating, healing. It bonds people together. None the less today it is rare – when did you last have a good belly-laugh? Not a snigger, but a real let-go of a full-bodied laugh?

The sort of laughter which comes around the camp-fire meal at the close of a day out fishing, the sort of togetherness one feels at the end of a good meal in unpretentious company, the abandoned glee of children who feel totally loved, the spontaneous laughter that erupts when out walking on the hills – it has no reason, needs no trigger, it is simply about the joy of living. All the things that Jesus did and enjoyed.

The great masters of the spiritual life commend laughter. In *The Cloud of Unknowing* we are encouraged to be full of 'gamesomeness' with God; Dame Julian speaks often of the 'merriment of our courteous Lord'; Meister Eckhart said, 'God is at home; it is we who have gone for a walk'; and Thomas Traherne's themes of loving and laughing and jubilation saturate his work.[3] Laughter is akin to wholeness, to holiness, they said. But then laughter got a bad name among Christians in medieval times on account of the ribaldry which accompanied the Festival of Fools in church. For a few centuries writers were censorious about laughter, and held the theory it was a frivolous activity in the sight of Almighty God. Lately the delighted carefree laughter-in-prayer of the Celtic Christians is being re-discovered, and where stress has become such a heavy load in our own century a movement of the Spirit has thrown up such organisations as 'Clowns for Christ'[4] and 'Laughter Therapy'.[5]

Did Jesus Laugh?

Jesus Christ himself had an acute wit. It bubbled up out of a sense of the ridiculous and paradoxical – the sort of good humour that is embedded in the creation. Who else but a God of Laughter would create a flea with enough energy in its knees, which if it was transposed into a human's knees, could move a man to leap up to the top of the post office tower 20,000 times without flagging? Many of the remarks recorded in the Gospels, which have since been pored over with great solemnity, originated as humour – words which have a serious point wrapped up in light-hearted contradiction. In your imagination, if you were unschooled, having a day out near the lake with a group of friends, relaxed but enthralled by the charism of the speaker, how would you react to the following?

- The idea of a mulberry tree being whisked into the centre of the sea to grow? (Luke 17:6)
- Putting up with a great beam of oak in your own eye and, with it in place, trying to see the speck in your neighbour's? (Matt. 7:3–5)
- Imagining a loaded ship of the desert, a huge humped camel, attempting to squeeze through the hole in a needle? (Matt. 19:24; Mark 10:25; Luke 18:25)
- The stupendous idea of God sitting down to count hairs? or sparrows? or grains of sand? (Matt. 10:29,30; Luke 12:6,7)
- The ludicrous notion of taking your precious and sole source of light on a dark night, the lamp on which you depend to see, and deliberately putting it under a bucket? (Matt. 5:15; Mark 4:21)

- Being compared to a wandering fox, aimless and lost, that 'decides' not to make a lair? (Matt. 8:20; Luke 9:58)
- Trying, by swearing, to change a hair into either white or black? (Matt. 5:36)
- The picture of a blind man, hesitating to walk through a strange land prodding each footstep with a stick, and being prepared to show the way to another man – who was equally blind? (Matt. 15:14)
- Another picture, this time of a serious and respected religious leader, solemnly handling a strainer to exclude the pollutants in his meal. He strained out the gnat all right, but he failed to notice the camel entering his gullet! (Matt. 23:24)
- The comparison that a man might not be of more value than a sheep, or, for that matter, even than a sparrow! (Matt. 10:31)

Wouldn't such ridiculous images make you laugh?

Perhaps the most moving moments of all, which were relieved and lit-up by a chuckle of good humour, are the very ones that have been open to misrepresentation. The disciples were exhausted from a long day caring for thousands of people. They had been told by Jesus to row across the lake at night, and they were feeling fretful and anxious. There was no light from the moon or even the stars because a fog had settled on the lake, and a strong wind was battling against their progress. Jesus, having sent the crowds home, had gone off by himself, and the disciples were wondering where he was and how he was going to get home anyway. Although he too was exhausted, he had had the rewards of healing people, feeding them and all the appreciation and adulation that followed on from that. Perhaps they were unusually dispirited. Suddenly they sensed a ghost; it was coming towards them, sliding along on the top of the water. A terrifying sight at the best of times, but in the context of the dark weather it was magnified. They screamed. The 'ghost' called out to reassure them, 'It is I, Jesus' and Peter was so overwhelmed with relief and welcome he scrambled over the side of the boat to walk towards him. Would Jesus have chosen that moment to hammer him with reprimand? Jesus, the man filled with compassion and empathy and reassurance from his time on the mountain with God, would he have been derisive, while his friend sank?[6] He *might* have said, 'O you silly clown, it's me, you juggins, did you really think I came to alarm you?'

There is a somewhat similar occasion recorded after Jesus had died.

Two people who knew him well were walking disconsolately down the road away from Jerusalem. They were desperately disappointed, indeed hopeless and totally bewildered that their hero, the fruition of all their longings and ideals, had been killed like a criminal. Is that the occasion for Jesus – fresh with the exultation of having accomplished his task, having been resurrected as promised – to denigrate his grieving followers? (Luke 24:25) Or would he bring in a loving lightness of touch to lift them? Perhaps 'O you chumps, you sillies!' may be nearer the mark. Jesus' object was to restore trust and confidence, not to pull away the little they had left from under their feet.

The Effects of 'Healing' Laughter

Psychologically and physiologically laughter has profound effects which are usually under-appreciated. We'll take the bodily changes first.

- Every time I use the muscles of my face that spread my mouth into laughter, or the muscles of my abdomen that shake my sides with belly-laughter, I get into that part of the parasympathetic nervous system which releases endorphins and polypeptides responsible for feeling good, and feeling loving.
- The extra deep breaths induced by belly-laughter will increase the uptake of oxygen, so that fresh energy is spread throughout my body.
- The extra muscular activity speeds up the circulation of all the fluids in the body; blood goes round more efficiently, digestion is improved and the excretion of toxins is advanced.
- At the same time, there is an internal 'massage' of sluggish organs, which wakes them up to perform better.
- The effectiveness of the immune system is boosted and healing promoted. Some people have been so enthused by the healing effects of laughter that they have set up a charity whereby 'laughter wards' are established. These are places where patients can be prescribed a certain number of hours of watching comedy each day. The NHS has promoted 'laughter therapy' clinics in some areas in this country, with considerable acclaim.
- Laughter dissipates negative emotions and enlarges optimism, even where problems seem insoluble.
- The functions of the right brain are reinforced:

When I am laughing – I am not feeling victimised
When I am laughing – I am not fighting
When I am laughing – I am not being angry
When I am laughing – I am not blaming others

Some of these benefits overlap the psychological effects. Harry Williams expressed them with great succinctness and insight:

> When I laugh at myself I accept myself, and when I laugh at other people in genuine mirth I accept them. Self-acceptance in laughter is the very opposite of self-accusation or pride. For in the laughter I accept myself not because I'm some sort of super-person, but precisely because I'm not. There is nothing funny about a super-person. There is everything funny about a man who thinks he is.
>
> In laughing at my own claims to importance or regard I receive myself in a sort of loving forgiveness which is an echo of God's forgiveness of me. In much conventional contrition there is a selfishness and pride which are scarcely hidden. In our desperate self-concern we blame ourselves for not being the super-person we think we really are. But in laughter we sit light to ourselves. That is why laughter is the purest form of our response to God . . . For to sit light to yourself is true humility. Pride cannot rise to levity.[7]

A non-Christian writer expressed the effects of laughter on anger in a different but effective way:

> Anger – when your every cell is burning, and you become just a present flame; when every part of your body has become fiery and you have become anger – not just angry. In this moment of total present-mindedness one can become suddenly aware, and you can start laughing at the absurdity, the foolishness, the stupidity of the whole thing. But this is not suppression; this is laughter. You can laugh at yourself because you have transcended yourself. Never again will anger be capable of mastering you.[8]

Meister Eckhart put it like this:

> Do you want to know what goes on in the core of the Trinity?
> I will tell you:
> In the core of the Trinity the Father laughs –
> and gives birth to the Son;
> The Son laughs back at the Father –

and gives birth to the Spirit;
The whole Trinity laughs –
and gives birth to us.[9]

We shall be exploring the place of laughter in prayer further in chapter 23(5). I should like to end this chapter with a story.

A remote region of the Slovac countries was home to a number of Jews. They were seldom visited by a rabbi, and their questions and problems started to accumulate uncomfortably. The leaders decided the only thing to do was to invite a renowned rabbi to visit them, and somehow foot the expense. The day of his visitation was looked forward to with great expectation. Groups were formed to identify which particular problems they would put to him, and how to phrase the multitudinous questions that had been troubling them. How would he be able to address all their troubles in one short evening? Suspicion and jealousy and conflict grew between the groups, vying for a place on the programme.

The looked-for day arrived. The hall was filled to overflowing, agog with expectation. Then a little round man wearing a holy prayer cap arrived and settled himself on the platform with the leaders of the community. After being formally introduced, there was a pause. He obviously needed time to think over their position very seriously. Then he started smiling.

The visiting rabbi smiled to the person sitting on his left, and to the person sitting on his right. They smiled in return, and passed the smile on to those sitting next to them; they passed smiles on to the leading citizens in the front row. Soon the whole hall was smiling.

On the platform the Rabbi started a sort of a hum. He turned to his left and passed on the hum, then to his right to pass the hum on. The hum was caught by those in the front row, and soon the entire hall was humming.

Still nothing had been said. The Rabbi started chuckling to himself, and sort of rocking to and fro. He looked at his neighbour on the left, who started chuckling to himself and sort of rocking, and to his neighbour on the right, who started chuckling to himself and sort of rocking. Soon the entire hall was full of people chuckling to themselves and sort of rocking, in unison.

Then the Rabbi started to glow, to gurgle, to laugh. It was a full blown, let-go, no-reason laugh as perhaps only the Jewish people know. He turned to the important person on his left, and laughed with him. He turned to the important person on his right and laughed with him. Soon the entire hall was a mass of people rocking and rolling, holding their sides in waves of contagious laughter. No one knew what they were laughing at; there had been no joke to laugh at, they were just together, enjoying the laughter.

After about twenty minutes the Rabbi stopped laughing – his muscles were exhausted and could take no more. Quietly, the hall settled down, and the laughter slipped away. The Rabbi looked around — 'I hope all your problems have been solved?' he said, quite quietly.

God has given us a golden key to unlock some of the preposterous notions we carry around about ourselves. Are we too shy, or too pompous, to take it?

Picture–story of the Post–transfiguration

Matt. 17:1–18; Mark 9:2–28; Luke 9:28–43

•••

The happening of the transfiguration is told with equal verve in all three synoptic Gospels. It is one of those tremendous events from which each of those involved would have drawn something richly personal, too much to relay here. In the accounts we have there is a remarkable resonance with the themes we have looked at in Part 3. If we imagine what James may have told us about it, we may find out how Jesus was responsible for his own strong feelings, but refraining from loading them onto others; about his own relationships, and the way he managed to avoid being so caught up with them that he couldn't let them go; about Christian assertiveness; and even about a touch of humour. This could be James talking:

'There are just no words to describe it. For a long time we couldn't speak about it, even to each other. For Jesus, it must have been the climax of God's visible glory; the climax of his entire life. For Peter and John and me – why he had asked us to go with him we never knew – the vision of Jesus talking to those two, Elijah and Moses, as if they were his dearest friends, known since the beginning of time, knocked us back as if we were sleep-walking. He talked to them as if they were indescribably precious, his best friends he had known long ago. No wonder Peter thought of building a place for them to stay for a while. Jesus didn't think much of that idea, he said we couldn't hang on to the experience, we had to let it pass. Even though we were on our own, and could have spent as long as we liked up there, Jesus was never one to catch hold of anything – any one, any place, any time – as if his security lay there. He was anchored in God. After God Himself had spoken out of that dark, terrifying and overshadowing cloud, he seemed more determined to get on than ever. He said we had to go, back, to go back down the mountain again. We couldn't even try to re-capture that amazing experience. "On we go," he had said, "on we go, down to all those we left behind."*

150

'Jesus never actually explained why he had taken us with him. Usually he went off on his own to pray, not like that day. I was bothered about the ones who hadn't been asked — there must have been a lot of questioning and jealousy around. Perhaps there were shades of guilt, perhaps they felt they hadn't done enough of the right thing to get chosen — who knows? Then there they were, we could see them as we came down the mountain. The crowd around them seemed to be shaking their fists at them, what looked like anger and threat. From the exaltation of what we had just been through, to come plummeting down into all that suspicion and aggro and resentment, it took a lot of doing, I can tell you. Jesus had refused to hang on to the marvel on top of the mountain, and now he was resolute as he strode towards the middle of the row.

'As he approached, the whole crowd calmed down. What was it they were expecting? They seemed awed right enough, but there was an intense need too, they were hungry for drama, and I sensed it might turn nasty if they didn't get it. The remnant of the disciples hadn't been able to give them what they wanted, and there was some pretty hostile heckling from the know-alls among them. Maybe, in trying to regain Jesus' approval, some of the disciples had made out they were more used to healing people than they really were. Certainly the leaders of the crowd were very wound up about it. Jesus walked in and, by the way he moved, you knew he wasn't going to be waylaid by all that hassle. He went straight to the point; he was totally objective. He asked one direct question — "What's this argument about?", nothing to do with who's to blame or who did what.

'The father of a young boy waiting on the edge of the group spoke up. "I brought my son to be healed, but no one could do it." This just turned Jesus over. With one remark he showed how he felt and what he thought of the situation. He didn't single anyone out, but burst out with, "What an unbelieving and perverse lot you are!" Then with a hugh sigh of grief and yearning he said, "How long do I have to put up with this? How much longer must I go on?" We were left in no doubt of his feelings! But he didn't stay there for long; as if he wanted to draw us back into God's service he gave us a job to do — "go and bring the boy here," he said.

'So many of us scrambled to do what he wanted we must have scared the young fellow! The spirit of epilepsy inside him threw him around in a horrible way. Jesus stayed outwardly calm and objective, but I knew he was storming inside. He turned to the boy's father and asked him about the boy and his life, listening carefully for the answer. The father realised Jesus was full to the brim with different emotions and he wasn't at all sure which way he would react. "If it's at all possible . . . ," he started and Jesus replied (I think I caught a ghost of a smile), "If? Everything is possible! Believe!"

'The crowd was getting impatient, there was too much talk and not enough action for them. They started to draw in rather menacingly, one or two at the back seemed to be on the verge of hysteria. Jesus knew something had to be done, and quickly.

'And then there was the second momentous gathering of energy of the day. Not a gathering of glory like we had witnessed in the morning, but it was as if Jesus drew together all the energy from all the emotions of that day – the joy and then the parting; the grief, longing, and disappointment; the righteous anger, even despair – and all these he focused and hurled out at the tormenting spirit: "I command you, get out of him, and never go back!" It felt to me like a shaft of lightning, it had so much force and power.

'The effect was electric. The crowd stood motionless, and the father; the boy was motionless too. They said he was dead.

'Jesus stood drained for a moment, eyes closed, body limp.

'Then he saw the boy, resembling a corpse. Quietly and with infinite tenderness he bent down and touched his hand. Jesus bent right over and with his two hands under the child's arms, he drew him upright. He smiled, and the lad smiled back, standing firmly on his own two feet. Jesus let him go, back to his father.

'I don't know what happened later; they all went their own way. But before that, everyone – but everyone – was awestruck by the glory of God.'

•••••••••• Part 4 ••••••••••

Skills of the Spirit

••••••••••••••••••••••••••••

Finding the Significance of *This* Moment in *These* Circumstances

Present-mindedness

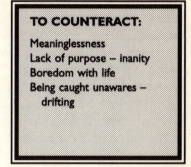

TO COUNTERACT:

Meaninglessness
Lack of purpose – inanity
Boredom with life
Being caught unawares –
    drifting

●●●●●●●●●●●●●●●●●●●●●●●●●●●●

Some readers may not like the idea of 'skills' to do with the level of the spirit – that area of our personality where we house our deepest values and purposes and direction. It is the place where I find out about the longings and questings and yearnings I seldom talk about, because they are so fundamental to me I prefer to just get on with it without looking too closely at how they work. Look at this incident:

The little girl was about two and a half, and she had to be kept socially 'quiet' by her parents as they waited. Then the nurse came in and 'Your turn', she said. The father picked up the fallen papers and put them neatly on the nearest chair, and in they went. About ten minutes later they reappeared calmly, talking about the groceries they'd get from the shop on their way home. It was as if they had left the room to go and pay for the papers.

Then it was our turn. My pregnant daughter climbed onto the couch and they smeared jelly on her abdomen. The scan pictures were a jigsaw puzzle of minute bones and organs, indecipherable. Then the sole of one tiny foot flashed onto the screen before it kicked out of sight. It was totally perfect; each toe was visible. So was the spine, exquisite in its symmetry. 'Two ventricles clear,' she said when the heart floated by, 'and a complete septrum', ticking off the observable organs. Length and breadth of the cranium; upper lip and palate with no cleft; measure the femur; two kidneys working; no gallstones; umbilical cord free, and it was done. 'You can go now,' she said kindly. Expertise expedited. Brilliant technology. Perfect pictures of a perfected marvel.

But oh! the significance! The awe of that constellation of miracles – seeing bones fit together, minute heart pumping freely, the face full and eyes 'winking', the limbs bending and stretching, the uncontainable wonder that had been contained. More, the fears of future conditions, the fears now ungrounded. The 'normality' that was beyond absorbing, beyond comprehending, beyond our designing. The significance of that small space is way outside verbal re-telling.

And yet, needs be, we got up, thanked the staff politely – no questions, thank you – and left through the waiting room.

'Your turn next,' she said to the waiting couple.

We live at such a speed of 'productivity' it is often impracticable for those being 'done to' to take in what is happening, so we get out of the habit of looking for significance. Besides, these are things we seldom bring up in a social context since they are considered private, and it is left to the individual to reach for them or not, as that individual decides. So they get left on one side and ignored. Assigning 'skills' to this area is like saying there are ways of using spades and keys and manuals which make significance more accessible, and its retrieval that bit easier. This is not a discussion of theology, but a concern for the stress due to *meaninglessness* which besets our society. Some experts say that this is the most fundamental of all our contexts of stressfulness. Organised religion is sometimes slow in taking on the colossal opportunity that lies in that last statement.

What do everyday people long for? Really yearn for? What '*gets to me*'? Is it a larger wage packet? A more exciting sex-life? To move away from this area? For my football team to win? Do I want more than anything else that my pain – or your pain – should go away? Or that I'm selected for this job/course/team/exhibition/contract/ . . . ? What do I sigh 'how long?' over?

In the passage recounted in the summary of Part 3, Jesus revealed his 'how long?' yearnings at least four times. At the top of the mountain he talked with Elijah and Moses about how long it would be before the culmination of his mission and his final passion; at the bottom of the mountain once again he yearned for the same culmination – 'How long must I stay with you? How long do I have to put up with you?'; and then he touched the longings of the father for his son (and no doubt the longings of the son himself) when he asked, 'How long has he been this way?' Jesus was always in contact with what he himself and other people *really* wanted.

For us, too, it is crucial to keep in touch with what we most deeply yearn for, what really motivates us as individual persons, because it is at this level that we can most profoundly change. In the last two decades we have been through a time of rampant demythologising; whatever good has emerged from that cleansing of idealism, we have been left with a rootlessness in daily life. In place of the codes we have discarded has grown something akin to a subversive trivialisation. This has great risks, because whatever it is that gives meaning to my life brings with it an identity. The 'who am I?' leads into 'who I am'. The stress of being without roots in the area of the spirit, of being without loyalties to a recognised set of values, easily turns into a sense of personal insignificance.

The first 'stress-skill' in the area of the spirit is to identify what my longings are and what set of meanings or significance is attached to them. Is my deepest longing never to grow old? or to repair injustice? or to understand the stars? or further the Kingdom of God on earth?

Throughout the Old Testament the longings of the people of God are being constantly verbalised, for instance in Job 6:8 (AV) – 'Oh that God would grant me the thing that I long for.' The quest of God's people for a full return into His favour and glory spread into Jesus' own longings that the purposes of God should be fulfilled. We can begin to taste this enveloping desire as we read Luke 12. First, some of the things Jesus says about us and our perceptions of significance:

– don't fool yourself (or others); he says, 'Everything now covered will be uncovered; everything now hidden will be made clear' (vv. 2–3);

– don't hoard trivia; he says, 'For wherever your treasure is, that is where your heart will be too' (v. 34).

– read the signs of the time; he says, 'How is it you do not know how to interpret these times? Why not judge for yourselves what is upright?' (vv. 56–7)

Then his own longings:

– 'I have come to bring fire to the earth, and how I wish it were blazing already! There is a baptism I must still receive, and what constraint I am under until it is completed!' (vv. 49–50) These words are strong; in other translations we have 'straightened', 'pained', 'pressed in the spirit till it is accomplished!' The NRSV uses the words, 'and what stress I am under until it is completed!'

And again Jesus' yearning:

– 'How often have I longed to gather your children together, as a hen gathers her brood under her wings; and you refused!'[1]

To return to the personal yearnings of each of us: can we identify them? Do we ever get anywhere near Jesus' deep desire for God's glory to be recognised? What about the longings of the three mothers in the earlier incident – the modern mum, the pregnant girl, and the prospective grandmother? Can we enhance the spiritual significance of our own lives?

Most of the time when Jesus is wanting to point up the importance of recognising significance, he uses metaphor in story or symbol. There are very many of them; almost everything around him becomes, in the hands of Jesus, a representation of the meaning of God's glory. Water, crumbs, sparrows, wind, wine, salt, stones, yeast, fruit, lamps, talents, sheep, coins – these are things we handle without much thought, common articles we pass over in the preoccupation of the moment. Jesus takes the everyday stuff of life to ask us to see in them the deeper significance of what we are doing. He wants us to be deeply rooted, rather than insecurely facile or superficial.

Take Ears!

Ears, that marvel of reception and balance we take so much for granted, forms an outstanding example of how Jesus taught us to understand significance. We seldom compliment each other on our ears, yet Jesus exclaims, 'Blessed are your ears!' and he continues, 'many prophets and upright people *longed* . . . to hear what you hear, and never heard it' (Matt. 13:16–17). He spoke in parables because the people 'listen without hearing or understanding' (v. 13). We, as the general people, are at risk of becoming so habituated to trivialising our deepest longings that we listen and listen, but never understand. Our ears are dulled to avoid using them to hear so that our hearts will understand and we will change our ways in order to be healed by God.[2] Jesus is exasperated still further: 'Do you *still* not understand, *still* not realise? Are your minds closed? Have you . . . ears and do not hear?'[3] [4] It is easy to imagine the gestures – the signs to convey a meaning – with which Jesus tried to get his point across about reading the significance in metaphor.

Today we are faced with the same difficulty. We avoid looking at what lies underneath the surface. Lately we have become reliant on being spoon-fed with quick-fix solutions, pre-packaged goodies and instant soundbites, so metaphor becomes even more distant. In a competitive and commercialised culture, immediate gratification is so much the norm that we have forgotten how it feels to thirst for significance, to hunger, to yearn at the deepest level in our search in the way with which the people of the New Testament were familiar.

Stress-skills

There are simple ways, simple 'skills' for bringing to mind at frequent intervals an awareness of what is happening *now, here,* between *us.*

- Present-mindedness, pausing for a split second to take in where I am at and where you are at, is becoming a sought-after skill. It is a distinct skill that can be taught and learned. Does its use bring me closer to God's purpose?
- Listening is another, listening to what the other person is really saying rather than what I think they mean to be saying; listening to what God is really saying, rather than what I would like Him to be saying; listening to what is happening inside me, instead of what I pretend on the outside because I want others to be impressed. This, also, is a skill to be taught and learned.
- Meditation, where I put aside all activity, whether the activity is physical or mental or emotional or spiritual, and stay there with what is at the very centre. Meditation helps me to decipher significance.

There is a more direct way than all these. If I decide that the most important thing in life for me is to get as closely as possible – however falteringly or spasmodically – alongside the model that Jesus left us of what it is to be human, I have a ready-made framework. However, we are not all Jesus, and we do not live in Israel in the first century. So he left us some further advice: *we are to turn to the Father.* Jesus uses this term of analogy to describe God; and even more intimately than that, He is a guide, a friend, a see-er-of-all, a tutor, a wise elder member of my family. He wants to delight in me as His child. This concept is full of amazement. None the less it carries with it some very practical ways of recognising stress, recognising significance, and offering clues about how to set about matching the two. There are several different ways to make this real:

1. Sometimes it's possible to go along with the Psalmist who says: 'I do not occupy myself with things that are too great and too marvellous for me. But I have calmed and quieted my soul, like a weaned child with its mother; my soul is like the weaned child that is within me.'[5] More of this in the following two chapters.

2. At other times I find I am the toddler who scrambles down from the security of his parent's lap and explores the world; I find that I have put a distance between that loving care and myself. I may become overly self-reliant, or lost and frightened.

3. When a lost child suddenly and unexpectedly sees the parent again coming round the corner, she/he runs excitedly and impetuously up to the parent; the child is welcomed with wide open arms and swung onto the shoulder of the parent.

4. Or sometimes, the wise parent keeps watch from a distance, allowing the child to make his own way and take his own decisions, taking the risk that some of those decisions may lead to further distractions, or even disaster.

5. Perhaps the child gets hurt, or bewildered, and loses track of her bearings. Then it isn't so much the child running after the parent, as the compassionate parent who runs after the child. God Himself searches after us, or nudges us, or even gives us a blinding flash of realisation. He is the pro-actor; it's not what I do or don't do, it's what He does.

6. Lastly, when he feels the child is strong enough, the parent might leave the child to work on a problem on his own. He won't be far away, but far enough for the child to feel he is in a dark night. When the light eventually returns, it will be brighter and lighter and more brilliant than ever before.

These are useful pictures to hold in mind when looking for the significance of *this* moment in *this* set of circumstances:

- Does the present behaviour match up with 1 . . . , 2 . . . , 3 . . . , 4 . . . , 5 . . . , or 6 . . . ?
- Is the present action or attitude working for God . . . , sent by God . . . , acting against God . . . , evidence of God Himself?
- What is the 'salt' that adds 'saltiness' to this present incident? Has the salt lost its flavour? Is it lacking 'salt'? What part have I had to play in giving 'flavour' to it?[6]

• Is there anything in this moment that adds to God's glory?

It's not surprising we get bewildered as we try to find a way through the labyrinth. Even Philip and Thomas, who had lived daily with Jesus in the flesh for three long and adventurous years, found it difficult. Jesus said to Philip, 'Have I been with you all this time, Philip, and you still do not know me?' (John 14:9); and to Thomas he said, 'Do not be unbelieving any more, but believe' (John 20:27).

He also said – to our enormous comfort when we are really stressed out and can find no meaning in anything anywhere, no significance relating to my life whatever – 'It is not the healthy who need a doctor, but those *who are in a wretched condition*',[7] he specifies it is those whom he has come to call. Do I yearn to believe?

Being as Well as Doing

Stripping, letting be, in contrast to 'proving'

> **TO COUNTERACT:**
>
> Dependence for 'worth' on my activity
> The need to 'prove' myself
> Comparing myself with others

••••••••••••••••••••••••

There were two people climbing a hill. At the topmost point they discovered a direction-finder. 'O look,' said one of them, 'Sydney is . . . miles away and New York only . . . miles. I didn't know that.'

The other just sat down and let the view do the speaking.

There were two people visiting an art exhibition. They stood together in front of the highly-acclaimed latest acquisition. One of them read avidly from the guidebook – dates, biography of the painter, context of the painting, style, colour and opinions of the artistry.

The other blocked all that out, and just stood still in the presence of the masterpiece.

There were two sisters concerned for their father as he lay dying. One of them straightened the sheets for him, tidied the bedroom, arranged the flowers, sprayed the air with a pleasant smell. She chatted quietly and reassuringly. The other stayed by the bed and held his hand, looking, without speech.

There were two monks praying. One read a chapter of Scripture, recited six psalms, made his heartfelt confession, and, in order to keep them 'fresh', prayed aloud three pages of intercessions.

The other emptied his mind and calmed his emotions and waited silently in the gaze of God.

These are not right or wrong ways to approach the tops of mountains, works of art, suffering people, or the Almighty Creator Creating. They are not to do with better or worse: they are about *choice*. Doing or being, active or still, both are valid and both rely for their effectiveness on the reality of the other. In ordinary life, most of us will tend to prefer one more than the other; when I am over-stressed, the being is paramount.

And that is a really strange thing. When I am over-pressed is just the time I *don't* want to risk dropping everything. I feel I am barely hanging on by my fingertips anyway, my only safety lies in the achievement of ticking off lists of 'things to do', because that gives me a sense of 'getting them *done*'. When the urge to stay with the safe active role is at its strongest, and even the thought of being unstructured is a threat, it is then that I need it most. Biologically, I will need to refurbish my energy from deep relaxation and sleep, as we have seen; we have looked at ways of budgeting mental and emotional energy by using cognitive and affective skills; if I want to receive at the level of the spirit, I have to empty my hands before they can be refilled. The layer of the spirit so easily becomes bogged down with duties and devotions and obligations, commandments and justifications, 'gottas' and guilts. When I am low and feel my resources have dried up, where is the renewal of energy at that level?

The Expenditure of Energy in the Layer of the Spirit

A great many of us are lavish in the use of our spiritual energy, we are spendthrift and squander it. It's not that we don't value it (unless we reject spirituality altogether), but we can use it up *inappropriately*. Most of us have a desperate conviction that we have to prove our worth. Somehow we have to deserve attention; to justify ourselves continually so that we can scramble up higher, do more and do more better. But for whom? This continual effort to measure up to some ethereal standard takes unlimited energy. But where is this measuring rod against which we gauge our progress? Who is it that we feel is waiting to pounce judgement on us? Sometimes it is the good opinion of others, sometimes it lays wait in my own self-esteem, but more deeply than either of these, we put this measuring rod into the hand of God.

Consider the following: Jesus told us: 'God so loved the world that he gave his only Son . . . ' (John 3:16), and when he arrived on earth to live our lives with us, he said:

- 'It was *not to judge* the world that God sent his Son, . . . but that through him the world might be saved. No one who puts his faith in him comes under judgement' (vv. 17–18). 'Those who live by the truth come to the light so that it may be clearly seen that God *is in all they do*' (v. 21).
- 'You judge by worldly standards; *I pass judgement on no one*' (John 8:15).[1]
- 'If anyone hears my words and disregards them, *I am not his judge*; I have not come to judge the world, but to save the world' (12:47,48).
- '*Do not judge*, and you will not be judged, because the judgements you give will be the judgements you will get, and the standard you use will be the standard used for you' (Matt. 7:1).[2]

It is a need from childhood, that I should set myself up against a gauge of good behaviour, so that I can gain approval and feel good. The most obvious spin-offs are ongoing competition and comparison with others. But this is a fantastical rod with which I beat myself. In Galatians we are told, 'Look to yourself, each one of you . . . Carry one another's burdens, and in this way you will fulfil the law of Christ. Each of you should examine his own conduct, and measure his achievement by comparing himself with himself and not with anyone else; for everyone has his own burden to bear.'[3]

Is there a way of being able to accept God's love and mercy and power, just because He made me me and no one else? Maybe then I wouldn't have to be so spendthrift with the energy He gives me, but could use it more constructively for His glory, not my own.

Obstacles to Being

Can we be prepared simply to try to be ourselves in the presence of God, uncluttered by comparison and competition? Firstly, we would really have to digest the fact that there is no way in the entire universe that God's attention – and even more important His love – can be either earned or deserved. It is simply there, and pure gift, waiting to be *received*. Then we have to face squarely the pile of obstacles which mounts almost unbearably high.

- What about the age-old question: which pleases God more, rational devotion that produces a pragmatic outcome, or the devotion that is beyond reason whose outcome is mystical? Does there have to be a 'preference' by God, or is there a place for both?
- There is the way we have been lumbered with left-brained insistence upon achievement, which forms the motorway of our culture today. Add to this our modern predilection for productivity scales and performance indicators – the service stations of achievement.
- The high programming of rationality is another motorway; to counterbalance these we have to be prepared to explore sideroads, and to be seen in lay-bys.
- We are also held back by an inbuilt aversion to the 'guilt' which we think will attack us if we stop *doing*.

Is it possible, in this day and age, to convince ourselves that we can get through this barrage of deterrents, and that in reaching the other side of it we will discover that limitless source of God's energy for His purpose in His way and His timing?

We know in fact that we were created to be human Beings, and we are turning ourselves into human Doings.[4] It doesn't all depend on me. God our Creator is on our side, proactively working for us.

The State of Being

It needs considerable conviction to grant ourselves the time and place to be stripped of those things we ordinarily prize. To let go our roles and responsibilities, our valued awards and qualifications, our cherished ambitions and long-held hopes, everything that normally I feel justifies my existence to others, and simply to Be. But Jesus himself was unimpressed by the habit of the 'hypocrites and the heathen' to pray in public,[5] or their leaders' reliance on physical display,[6] and neither was he pleased by the religious rulers who were unwilling to align themselves with him 'because they loved the praise of men more than the praise of God'.[7] He spoke more about what prayer shouldn't be than about what it should. That he showed by example, rather than by words.

Jesus' Example

In the recorded teaching of Jesus the Christ there is minimal discussion on *how* we approach God. The emphasis is on following

Christ and *doing* it. But how do we *do* something that requires no *doing*? We learn a lot from watching how he went about it.

– When the disciples asked, 'What must we *do* if we are to carry out God's work?' Jesus said, 'This is carrying out God's work' – and we are all set up for a nice containable list of Dos – 'you must *believe* in the one he has sent'. Nothing about what to Do, the primary necessity is simply to believe.[8]

– The immediate reaction to his baptism and the heavenly voice from God acclaiming Jesus was – to absent himself from everyone and *go away* into the desert. Astonishing.

– Jesus preached regularly in the syngogue[9] and attended the regular festivals, but he also made a point of getting away into the wide open spaces on his own. He deliberately made *choices*.

– Looking again at the long list of indications concerning when and how Jesus withdrew (see chapter 11) it is remarkable how many of them immediately *preceded* some important event. It is almost as if it became a deliberate habit, that Jesus would prepare for major change or decision in stillness, to practise Being with God and hearing Him *before* Doing the action.[10]

– Most of us spend a lot of energy trying to outdo the people around us; we take the way of one-upmanship into our work, our social life, and all our relationships. The Son of Man told us *simply to do for others what we would want them to do for us*.[11] No more and no less; the rest is about Being with them, alongside them. I don't want others persistently to down-stage me, how is it I have grown so good at putting them down? Being isn't about competing, it's more about being together. Allowing each one of us to be each one of us, individually and uniquely designed and created by God, without any need to be who we are not. As is so often quoted from St Augustine, but seldom lived out: 'God loves each one of us as if we were the only one to love'.

– Jesus' response to the sisters Martha and Mary was appropriate to each different occasion. In one incident he advised Martha that Mary was making the most of his presence simply by *being with him* as he talked, and that too much elaborate preparation on Martha's part was not necessary. Unfortunately sometimes this incident has been taken as a stereotype of varying forms of house-wifery: it is a single account applicable to a specific occasion. However it does typify Jesus' preference for Being (where it is practical) over a rather self-important Doing.

- In the first century in Palestine there was a considerable body of learning about wordless prayer. It was focused in the practice of the teachings of the Kabbalah. Claims have been made that before their destruction under the influence of the age of the Enlightenment, 'Jewish systems of meditation may have been among the most advanced in the world.'[12] Jesus himself would have been familiar with the techniques of this type of *still prayer*, which included the use of the mantra and a single-pointed wordless communion and adoration. How else would he have used those long hours spent in remote areas?

What Has All This Got to Do with the Management of Stress?

I am put in mind of a true happening. Arriving at an unfamiliar cathedral city, I was made welcome in one of the beautiful ancient houses in the Close. At around 11 p.m. I went to my bedroom on the top floor, while my hosts were bedded down two floors below. In the very early hours of the morning the house was shaken by powerful gusts of a sudden storm. This was no ordinary storm. I was up amongst the tops of the trees that swayed and cracked and brushed up against my window. The lightening flashed dramatically, and the thunder raged as if it had been pent up for centuries for this one storm. As I watched fascinated and dumbstruck through my casement, I was mindful of the storms which preceded the manifestation of God to Elijah (1 Kings 19:12). He wasn't in the rain, nor in the wind, nor in the thunder: His presence is made known in the soft murmuring sound that succeeds the fury and the noise.

Eventually 'my' storm petered out. It just seemed quite suddenly to run out of energy. I looked for the wonderful fresh calmness that always follows, for the still small voice, for the contrasting peace that signals the sigh of the world around – relief that the violence is over.

What I actually heard was something quite different. The created order had been taken over by high technology. The looked-for stillness, the gain and glory of the natural process, had been invaded. The place of still Being had been taken over by the screaming of a hundred electronic burglar alarms.

What an analogy of our present world!

Still, With God

Can I allow God to love me in my nothingness?

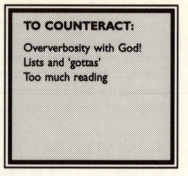

TO COUNTERACT:

Ooververbosity with God!
Lists and 'gottas'
Too much reading

•••••••••••••••••••••••••••••

So I have decided with my will that there may be something in this Being-ness, the state of Letting Go to Let God. Maybe I start reading some of the spiritual masters – it may well be that the power of these writings will be sufficient to get me started.[1] But if the practice of Beingness is to continue, it must derive from a deeply-rooted sense that it is something I yearn for more than anything else, not merely because someone else has recommended it. This is not a mild sort of pastime – I have to be aware of the pressures stacked against it; it will require commitment and determination, and a sort of obstinacy that won't be deflected. Most of all, it has to be driven by the conviction that I *want* to undertake this journey into God. Without this as a goal, this high priority, this personalised desire, it won't happen and Being will be stale.

Starting from Where We Are

Something very strange has been happening in our society. At the beginning of chapter 13 we looked at the way it shows itself in the everyday words we use, without any special consciousness of it. Our common verbs and adjectives reflect the emphasis of our culture, whether we want it to be so or not. That collection of the terms we commonly use to describe high energy output are mostly verbs –

doing words! It may be useful to glance through them again, at this stage.

The counterbalance to *up* activity is to calm down, wind down, settle down, sit down, lie down, centre down – that is where I can *strip down*, *reach down*, *bend down*, and get *deep down*; deep down enough to touch the deep stillness where my deepest being can take in rather than give out.

This exercise gives us a graphic example of the insidious pressures we are up against. In some cultures, time taken out to ponder and pray and mull is revered. In ours, we imagine we have found a superior way – we fax an instant reply. Conclusions must be offered 'on the hoof'; mealtimes are working times, time for digestion seems unnecessary; mobile phones mean I can be 'on the go' at every intimate and private moment. The most important thing is to be 'up and running' and to be seen to be up and running.

But slowly we are learning: unless we give ourselves experience in the deep-down level of living, our body/mind/emotion/spirit will grab it by foreclosing with a breakdown. We lose balance, physically or mentally or emotionally or spiritually.

Allowing the Deeps

It is not a matter of looking for 'benefits' – these will vary and sometimes be so indistinct as to be unidentifiable. It is a priority, a need, a yearning simply to be me with God, still with God, stripped with God. We are dealing with a place of no words, and words will not do to contain what results. This is not about spiritual excitability – the appropriate place for that is on different occasions such as communal prayer and praise for instance. There may be times when God grants consolations of feelings of peacefulness or blessedness or purposefulness or even 'visions' but these are not an 'aim'. We don't go into Stillness with this as an aim. There is the story of a young monk who came to his spiritual director with a sense of triumph; 'Father,' he crowed, 'I have been sent a manifestation!!' 'Don't let it bother you,' came the reply, 'ignore it and it will soon go away.' Benefits and results are not there to be looked for,[2] but through the mercy and grace of God He will provide whatever the soul most needs in the time and manner that He sees fit.

Jesus valued public worship and large religious festivals and verbal use of the Scriptures. There are also significant points to be made from the example of Jesus' use of Stillness.

Jesus' Example

Transfer to others: There is nowhere in the Gospels where Jesus imposed his preferred style of approaching God onto others.

- He went away on his own, but didn't insist that those around him did the same;
- he witnessed in their company how he prayed, but didn't demand they did likewise;
- he waited until they asked him how to pray and then gave them his own prayer;[3]
- virtually the only specific instruction he left them was to forgive others, to persist,[4] and to pray in secret.[5]

The glory is God's: In spite of all his time of being still with God, Jesus never kept the 'glory' which came out of this communion, or which came out of his 'works', for himself; he always deflected it immediately onto God.

Jesus' practice: In the first chapter of what is considered to be the earliest Gospel, St Mark, it is recorded that 'In the morning, long before dawn, Jesus got up and left the house and went off to a lonely place and prayed there' (Mark 1:35). This was the day immediately after the whole town had come crowding round the door at sunset, and he had cured many who had diseases and 'driven out many devils'. In order to deal with his exhaustion, after a modicum of sleep, he had taken himself out into the wilderness to experience a degree of closeness with God and an intensity of communion that we tend to shy away from. A few chapters later, Jesus goes across the lake with his disciples for some privacy as he looks for a way to deal with the shock of John's death. A huge crowd finds out where they are and follows. In such circumstances, you or I would be likely to turn on the crowd with some bitterness (or worse!), but Jesus welcomes them, and they spend the whole day listening to him preach. Then from somewhere he finds the energy to take pity on them and feed them – five thousand men and also the women and children with them. Finally, when in spite of the mood of elation, he must have been drained and exhausted and over-stressed by the vast demands made upon him, he asks his friends to take the boat back home while he disperses the crowd. *And then* he walks off up the hill to regain his balance and energy by praying in stillness alone (Mark 6:46[6]).

Physical satisfaction is inadequate: Another time Jesus demonstrates that he is not dependent on 'bread' for nourishment. Although he enjoys food and feasting, and a great many of his deepest analogies are based on eating and drinking, he makes it clear that he has other ways of being refilled, other sources of nourishment that are non-material (John 4:32). More than physical bread, his greatest source of infilling is the deep assurance that the work he was sent by the Father to do already is reaping a harvest.

The place of not-knowing: Even the Son of Man didn't know everything, didn't feel he had to have all the answers all the time. 'As for that day or hour' – the second coming for which we have to be on the alert – 'nobody knows it, neither the angels in heaven nor the Son; no one but the Father' (Mark 13:32).

Can I, too, voluntarily lay aside those things I might ordinarily use to bolster my own ego? Particularly when I am highly stressed, this is a crunch question: do I allow God to love me only on account of my 'becauses'?

Because I have appealed to Him . . . , because I've been to church . . ., because I visited . . . , because I have tried to be faithful to his commands. . . , because I have given to charity . . . , because I controlled my temper . . . , because I didn't follow up that tasty bit of temptation . . . , and so on?

If I drop *all* my 'becauses', can I allow God to love me in my nothingness? Can I give up the effort of holding on, get off the treadmill of getting others to recognise me, stop pretending to God I am better – or worse – than I really am and just rest with Him simply being me? I don't have to like myself, or approve of myself, or stop wanting to change parts of myself, but I do have to realise how ridiculous are the poses I adopt, most particularly in the presence of the One who designed and created me in the first place.

Can I allow God to love me in my nothingness? To lay aside, even for the shortest while, all the things I use as scaffolding, the things I have worked for and even for which I may be grateful, as if they were simply clutter in the channel between God and my soul, may seem to be a scary idea. Dame Julian writes that God wants a silly soul to come to Him plainly, nakedly, and homely; the author of *The Cloud of Unknowing* speaks of 'that bare blind feeling of your own being'. Jesus tells us we are to be as little children – no skills to rely on, no achievements to boast of, no knowledge with which to confound others. To be in a place where I am unskilled, inexperienced, unknowing; where I am open to marvel and wonder and mystery; where I am non-doing, non-possessing, non-cluttered; that is to be in the place where I am totally non-deserving; only totally loved.

> The child who isn't in the know, who doesn't understand . . .
> The child who gets it wrong, isn't 'right', is vulnerable . . .
> The child who gets lost . . .
> The child who is bruised and torn . . .
> The child who has had a bash at it and made a mess of it and
>   messed things up . . .
> This is the child who runs to the parent's lap
> With eagerness and need and *relief*.

A Practical Example

It's time to look at a very practical example. Perhaps you, the reader, want to try it out. Make a date for it; that is, resist the thought that a quick run through the next page or so will get you a rough idea of what it's about and you'll try it later, some other time. Make a date *now*, while you have your diary with you, just as if someone had rung you up for an appointment. Write it in, so it is unalterable, so that neither you nor your secretary nor your family can say you are free to do something else at that time. Write in 'Being Still with God' for a half-hour block. It doesn't matter what time of day or night you choose. Ideally it should be when you know your energy and concentration will be at their highest: if you are an early morning person, write it in then. If you are normally sluggish first thing, it is *not* the time to experiment with dropping everything, as if it was a case of using up non-productive time anyway. Stillness needs a strong ability to focus. Similarly if you are ordinarily very tired before you go to bed, that is not the appropriate time for this date. Some people make time mid-morning, after they have sorted the post and before they start the day's project; others like to put aside time when they return home in the evening, before their evening meal. Studies have shown that a person is unlikely to be able to draw on a strong degree of focusing power immediately after a good meal. It is a better idea to have some leisure immediately after eating and to keep the time of being still with God later, perhaps halfway through the evening.

Preparation

So, you've made your mind up and you've made a date. Now you have to make sure of

- the place. Somewhere where you can't hear the phone – or you've taken it off the hook – nor the front door. A place that is quiet and comfortable; the next thing is to
- experiment with your best bodily position. If you are going to do something that is unusual for you, you can give yourself a shorthand message by taking up a non-usual position. Whether you decide to sit on an upright chair, or on a meditation stool, or to kneel with a hassock or a pile of books between your knees (between them, not under them), or to lie flat on the floor, or with your legs at a right angle up the wall or supported at a right angle on a chair, the position should be comfortable but concentrated for you.
- Decide beforehand how much time is going to be given to this practice.
- Then it's important to let others know that you want time on your own and you do not want to be disturbed. Some people find it helpful to have a notice on the door to remind others not to disturb you for a little while, and to state the time when you will be available again.

Experience suggests that at least five minutes should be allowed for the settling down and preparation, and at least five minutes for a stable return. In between people vary from five to twenty-five minutes of complete stillness. For most people, psychologists tell us that expecting acute concentration to last longer than that is unreasonable and the stillness dissipates and peters out ineffectively. Until the mind becomes used to its own best-practice and the gauging of time becomes no problem, it is a good idea to enclose the decided number of minutes onto a tape by winding forward on an empty cassette; then record some very quiet and gentle music to alert you when the chosen number of minutes is up.

In place of these preparations, you could form or join a group. Apart from the thousands of church prayer groups and home prayer groups – and many of these will be for vocal prayer rather than stillness – there are around a thousand small groups meeting for sharing silence together. These may be affiliated to the Julian Meetings or the Christian Meditation organisation, the Fellowship of Contemplative Prayer[7] or they may be Buddhist or secular open centres.

The date has arrived

It's very simple. First of all, having made sure that you are unlikely to be interrupted, you might like to draw the curtains to minimise distractions. If gentle music helps you to wind down, that's fine, but some people find music itself can be a diversion. Take up the position you prefer, and make sure there is nothing tight around your body to restrict your circulation.

- Take a long breath *out* – let go of the exhaustion and negativities and doubts and questions – let them all out with your out-breath. If you have got into the way of belly-breathing as described in chapter 4, this is the time to use it.
- Then just let everything go into the hands of God who made you.
- Let the physical energy drain out of your muscles, let it melt and flow into whatever it is that is supporting you. Allow the energy supplied to you by God to return into His hands just for the next little while – He will see to it that you receive it back when it is needed again, and by then it will be cleansed and refreshed for the next job you do for Him.
- Let the mental energy supplied to you by God your Creator drain away. The very gifts God has given you – or rather lent you – let Him have them back into His keeping for a little while. He will take care of your powers of reasoning and planning and controlling until you next want them; they are not necessary for this moment, hand them back to God.
- The tools and skills you have in the area of your emotions – even the strong affective prayers of 'My God, I love you' or 'Jesus, I'm sorry' – even these are better kept for a different time. For now, let all your emotions, whether they are positive or negative, sink into where they came from, the heart of God. Let your emotional self rest in the care of Him who made you; rest, relax, give over to Him, be still.
- Even the deepest level of all: those yearnings and longings and journeyings of the spirit, let them go too for this moment. God will carry them for you for a while, they will be safe in His keeping.

When you feel that you are still, and uncluttered, and waiting, you may like to become single-pointed by the use of one word. Very gently repeat this word to yourself, not thinking *about* it but letting it speak for itself as it sinks slowly and simply deeper and deeper into your deepest soul. Like the mustard seed, but inverted! Its growth will be going down into secret depths of your consciousness and becoming rooted there; later it may erupt up and out into your behaviour but not now. For this moment the one word will match each out-breath – taking in the presence of God with the in-breath, and re-stating the one word in the out-breath. Stay with the one idea, but it may help at first to reinforce it with a changing sound. For instance:

Jesus said: 'I will give you rest. *Rest*[8] in me, and I in you . . . '

. . . *rest* . . .

Jesus said: 'Abide in me, as I in you . . . '

. . . *abide* . . .

Jesus said: 'Dwell in me, as I in you . . . '

. . . *dwell* . . .

Jesus said: 'Stay in me, as I in you . . . '

. . . *stay* . . .

Jesus said: 'Remain with me, as I with you . . . '

. . . *remain* . . .

Jesus said: 'Make your home in me, as I make my home in you . . . '

. . . *make my home* . . .

Jesus said: 'Continue with me, and I with you . . . '

. . . *continue* . . . [9]

It may be that a person will want to take one of these words to repeat for a week, or a month, or a year; or they might like to change the sound each few minutes. Neither is right or wrong, each soul will find its own way to be still with God.

Coming out

It is important that sufficient time is given to the return to the active world; this must not be hurried. On the physiological level, the body has been submerged in the slowed-down responses of the parasympathetic nervous system.[10] To return too suddenly to the active sympathetic nervous system can be a shock. Spiritually, time must be allowed for absorption of the experience and for the recollection of energy. A useful way of returning to the normal level of activity is this:

- Very quietly and gently take back the tools in the level of the spirit that you previously put into the hands of God; perhaps you will find they have been fine-tuned by Him as He held them, and their usefulness is now increased. Just be aware of it; if this has happened, accept it.
- Very quietly and gently take back the tools in the level of the emotions from the hands of God. Maybe now there will be a better sense of proportion about them. It's no use making an effort over this, but absorb it if it is there.
- Very quietly and gently take back the tools in the level of the mind from the hands of God. Sometimes He will have added to them a clearer perspective about what He wants of you. Don't use this moment to strive for it, but receive it if it is there.
- Finally, still keeping the sense of stillness within you, very gently and quietly take back the tools in the level of the body from the hands of God. He will have added new life to them. Allow energy to return from the ground of your being into your feet, draw it up into your legs; let it return to your trunk and be aware once again of how your body feels now, here, at this moment – feel the chair, floor, clothes, cushions, that are touching it; let energy return up your trunk into your shoulders and arms, neck and head, and bring into the front of your consciousness whatever it is that you are hearing now, this moment – maybe it is voices outside, or music on the tape, or traffic or bird song. Come right back into where you are, what you are, when you are. Always with thanksgiving for the 'Shalom' God has granted you.[11]

Postscript: Stilling with God is for anyone; but it is not an 'ought' for *every*one, and there are some, a very few, who for some reason or another do not take to it. If it doesn't feel right for you, leave it alone. Maybe at another time it will be worth trying again. Stilling with God should not be effortful, although at first it may take a little persistence. It should not be a duty. But those who make a weekly, daily, or twice-daily practice of it find it becomes essential to productive living – productive, that is, for the purposes of God both for themselves and for what He wants them to do for others.

None the less there are some warnings that need to be mentioned.

- If the practice of Being Still with God leads to any sort of 'spiritual snobbery' it is being done for Me, not for God.
- If the practice of Being Still with God results in a spiritual grabbing

for more! more! it can develop into a sort of 'spiritual lust', a greed to experience everything any soul has ever described. It is then being done for Me, not for God. He will send me whatever He sees right to send me in His time and where I am at; there is no indication in the teaching or practice of Jesus in the Gospels that he expects us to stretch and strive beyond what is in our capacity. God will always be the one looking for us, all we have to do is put ourselves in His way and receive. Like yeast, salt, lamps, it is we who do the receiving before we can be of any use to God.

– If the practice of Being Still with God encourages me to feel I have found the way, and all other ways are not the right way, then it is being done for Me, not for God. This is of particular importance for those who are asked to companion others on this way. Until fairly recently, much of the writing and leading in spirituality has been done by men. There is an evolving consciousness that the way some women receive God in Stillness is not the same as the way many men approach God in Stillness. More accurately, this is not gender-specific but more to do with the prominence of the anima or the animus in any individual. This is not the place to expand on this growing awareness, but to point up the great delicacy that is appropriate whenever there is sharing at this deep level of prayer, particularly between people of different genders.

Lastly, some people have noticed that as they strip off their spiritual 'camouflage' in the practice of Being Still with God they uncover things which they didn't recognise previously and which are distinctly uncomfortable. They may be alerted to some sort of spiritual ambition, or an earlier spiritual cowardice or rigidity, or even something like personal obstinacy, that is regretted. If these things, and others you may recognise within your own soul, seem to block the way it is good to take them to a wise soul-friend. Or it may be that in His mercy God allows you to recognise them and put them down at the foot of the cross in contrition, so that Jesus the Christ can take them up and deal with them directly. The only response to such grace is continual thanksgiving.

22

Together, the Hurt Body of Christ

Vulnerability – is there any 'use' to it

> **TO COUNTERACT:**
>
> Complacency
> Lack of urgency!
> Isolationism
> Individualism

This may be rather a strange chapter; it will not be saying some of the more expected things about *Integrating **Wholeness***. It is difficult to write; I hope it won't end up difficult to read.

Mrs Queenie Trim was very keen on her Rights. She had a right to a good life, so there wasn't anything to be thankful for, it was simply her right. She had a right to good health; she paid her taxes regularly as well as her private insurance premiums, so quite rightly she expected each illness to be taken care of and taken away; if she needed a triple transplant of heart, lungs and liver of course she would expect it to be done, it was her right.

She had a right to a decent house and good job; nothing special about that. The campaign for less pollution around her home, and less traffic in her road, interested her, though she enjoyed her own car and expected to go door-to-door wherever she wanted to go, of course. It wasn't her car that was the problem, it was all the others.

Queenie knew she had a right to good service – people in shops and garages and travel agents had to do things the way she wanted them done, naturally. And she had a right to be considered and respected and taken note of. It wasn't asking anything out of the ordinary, it was her right. She didn't like being put out, it went against the grain, she shouldn't have to be put in a position where she would feel upset. She had a right not to be harassed or distressed or put out.

Mrs Queenie Trim was very keen on her rights. After all, when she had got them, then she'd be free to think of the rights of others. Stress was certainly something to be got rid of – she could only start caring for others once her own life was stress-free.

Jesus Christ did *not* say, 'I have come to bring an easy life'. (He never mentioned 'rights'.) Jesus Christ said, 'Do you think that I have come to bring peace to the earth? No, I tell you, but rather division. From now on five in one household will be divided, three against two, two against three; father against son and son against father; mother against daughter and daughter against mother.'[1] He also said, 'In the world you shall have suffering';[2] 'I have come not to send peace but to bring a sword'[3] and 'the kingdom of Heaven has been subjected to violence and the violent are taking it by storm'.[4] He also said, 'Look, I am sending you out as sheep among wolves; so be cunning as snakes and yet as innocent as doves.'[5] Can you picture what happens to sheep when they are sent among wolves? In each of their various contexts, these strange sayings have something to tell us of the way Jesus spoke about stress. Then Jesus said, 'I have come to the sick – *those in a wretched condition*'.[6]

What Can Possibly Be the Meaning of All This?

This is a brief look at what Jesus did and said when he himself was under the greatest imaginable stress.

1. In the Garden of Gethsemane, while he faced the appalling apprehension of what was to happen to him if he went through with his arrest and trial and crucifixion, he was also wrestling with the temptation (for us, unimaginable) of knowing he could get out of it all by calling down whole armies of angels to dispel the evil. It was at this point that he told his closest friends, '*Now* is my soul troubled, tormented, in turmoil'.[7] What happened in the Garden of Gethsemane is beyond our full comprehension. An incident that occurred a little earlier is perhaps more accessible to us, and a bit closer to what we could possibly feel in ourselves.

2. Jesus knew he was approaching the climax of his mission, the end of his work on earth as a man, and the closure of his life. He had been emotionally affirmed by the poured perfume at supper in Bethany, and by the elation of the crowds as he processed into Jerusalem riding on a young donkey. These events resonated with

the revered ancient prophecies, but none the less they were encircled with ambiguous messages both for the disciples and for the masses of enthralled people. So Jesus' position was still unclear. Jerusalem was swarming with visitors from foreign countries in the capital for the religious festival of the Passover; from among them some Greeks approached the disciples. They were rather diffident about the wisdom and timing of their enquiry and the propriety of their intrusion, but nevertheless, coming from their highly-educated and philosophical background they were impelled to search for Jesus. They talked to Philip first; he wasn't sure that Jesus should be interrupted, so he asked Andrew. These Greeks must have been pretty persuasive, because in spite of his friends' sensitivity to the mental, emotional and spiritual load being carried by Jesus at that moment, they decided after all to bring the strangers to him. Was it an intellectual empathy that ran between them? Jesus didn't respond to them by asking social questions; he immediately and spontaneously told them what he was feeling. He told these foreigners he was about to lose his life, just like a grain of wheat which has to fall into the dark ground and be hidden before it can produce a great harvest; and that this eventual fruitfulness would prove to be his 'glorification'; nevertheless at this particular time his soul was in turmoil. 'What shall I say?' he questions; the Son is asking whether he should ask the Father, 'Abba, save me from this hour'? And then comes this astonishing statement: '*But it is for this very reason I came to this hour.*'

For the stress and the turmoil. *For* the struggles you and I have to deal with. *For* the very upside-down, inside-out, unclear uncertainties of life. It is not what comes at us that counts but *how we deal with it.*

This incident ends with glory. Not resolution, nor extraction from the trouble, nor armies of angels to do the work for him, but with confirmation of glory. Jesus cries out – in juxtaposition with his acute stress – 'Father, glorify your name!' A yearning appeal, a full-bodied cry from his heart and mind and soul, imploring God to make good come out of this appalling struggle. The response from heaven is an audible reaching-down, being-with, fully-supportive voice, 'I have glorified it, and will again glorify it.'[8]

3. A little later in time, at the very point of entry into that astonishing sequence of misunderstanding, misrepresentation, twisted truth, political manipulation, personal vendetta, mythic drama, brutal

torture, Jesus once again says, 'I came into the world for this one purpose – to speak about the truth' (GNB) – 'to bear witness to the truth' (REB).[9] Does Jesus put *purposefulness* into pain?

What Does All This Mean For Us?

A great friend of mine called Penny, whose spine is irrevocably crumbling and thereby the pain is constant, said to me, 'Obviously some of us have got to be in the soup – that's where Jesus is, isn't he?' Is there a way of making sense out of hurting, out of stress? If stress is the modern counterpart to suffering, is it something that can be used as a doorway into the heart of God? Is this the framework of the spirituality that is missing from much of our thinking on stress? Nowhere in the Gospels are we called upon to 'fit' into the world and into its claims for Rights. Maybe we are so keen on keeping ourselves protected and unflawed that we are actually denying ourselves the crucial significance of stress. Our carefully maintained veneer of being unstained by 'the soup' in which we are floundering actually prevents us from tasting the soup! It's only when we taste it that we can change it. The four Gospel writers imply we should be aware of our hurting and the hurting of others; that vulnerability is of supreme importance. 'And', says Penny from the depth of her vulnerability, 'if we listen for our Belovedness, it will come, every day.'

Vulnerability: its place and value

This is another surprise. Another point that is pregnant with consequence but in today's climate is counter-cultural. Jesus said, 'The poor you have always with you' (John 12:8 JB). He is saying that we are to be continually responsible to, and accountable for, the 'poor'; he counts those who are 'poor' as being especially 'blessed'. That's a difficult one to swallow from our so-called vantage point of comfortable affluence. It's not a case of one last swinge at poverty and it will be gone forever, and our consciences will be freed. The state of being in need – of someone, somewhere, being in a wretched condition – *is always to be with us*. The problems will not go away, but we are given a concern, a commitment, and an obligation to them that is lifelong. This should be enough to occupy us, but there is something else. In their presence we are provided with continual lessons to learn:

• about our own pride and complacency and *in*vulnerability;

- about Jesus' view of *the inconsequence of Muchness*. Jesus insisted again and again that sparrows are valuable, that children show the way, that the widow's mite is as joyfully accepted as the rich man's fortune, that the hurt and damaged and flailing are even more triumphantly received than the do-gooders, and that even two swords are 'enough'! (Luke 22:3) Over and over again this theme punctures our over-blown ideas on the desirability of having much. In the Gospels, having much of anything other than loving belief, doesn't count for much.

- about the fact that once we become invulnerable, we become unapproachable. Others can't get to us, I can't hear myself, and I make it difficult for God to reach me. Jesus the Christ himself demonstrates the extraordinary and essential value of vulnerability. When he is at his most vulnerable, surrounded by resentment and suspicion and intentions to kill, helpless and to all intents hopeless, it is at that point Jesus says, 'I am [the Messiah], and you will see the Son of man seated at the right hand of the Power and coming with the clouds of heaven.'[10]

The temptation to get away from stress

Being vulnerable means I remain open to hurt. The risks of stress and distress remain real. The temptation to eliminate stress is strong; as is the temptation to appear I am coping and in control. That stance is peculiarly prominent today. Jesus said, 'Pray that you do not fall when you are tempted.'[11] In the Gospels we are left with no doubt about the struggle Jesus had to go through. Eventually he reached a stage where he could offer to God the choice of whether he went through with his passion or not. Some look at this fateful struggle and read it as a direct object lesson concerning one human being and how he handled a situation where other human beings threw every sort of mistrust and disbelief at him. Others approach these events as having the significance of a cosmic sequence, one with such mystical potency and portent that the future of the whole of creation was poised on Jesus' response. Either way it is not difficult to see how Jesus the man was tempted to evade the horror of the unrolling drama. For instance, in Mark 8:31–4 we read:

> Then Jesus began to teach them that the Son of man was destined to suffer grievously, and to be rejected, . . . and to be put to death, . . . and he said all this quite openly. Then, taking him aside, Peter tried to rebuke him. But turning and seeing his

disciples, Jesus rebuked Peter and said to him, 'Get behind me, Satan! You are thinking not as God thinks, but as human beings do.'

This is almost identical wording to that used to describe the similar incident after the transfiguration.[12] Peter had touched on a raw nerve, a rawly sensitive temptation buried deeply inside Jesus to think the unthinkable, to question God's plan for the means of salvation. The forcefulness of Jesus' response to Peter gives us a clue to the force of the struggle going on within.

You and I would fall short in these circumstances. As with Peter, if someone I loved very dearly was about to face suffering, I would do everything in my power to deflect either the suffering itself or dissuade the one I loved from going into it. Presumably in our daily lives and loves this is the proper way to go about it. But Jesus implies that there are times when a person with sufficient insight into God's will can actually choose to go through the pain because in some way it can be used. Such a decision calls for immeasurable honour.

In a similar way, I would be inflamed with rage just as Peter was against the party sent to arrest Jesus, but he was told to put away his sword.[13] In this case Jesus resisted protection by his friends, and in addition he resisted the temptation of calling down legions of angels from heaven to come to his defence. He knew that the whole world's salvation would have been stifled had he been whisked into safety by a horde of flying champions.

If difficulties are useful, are we to look for them?

We have all come across, at one time or another, the old tribal assumption that the harder the life, the finer the type of character that emerges; that suffering brings with it a universal nobility. In this century these high-sounding assertions have been seriously challenged. None of us would wish trouble, stress, turmoil on any other. The more we can relieve each other of pain and hurt the better for them and the better for us. We no longer regard poverty as 'noble' – thank goodness – and even the doctrine of redemptive suffering has been subjected to hard and rueful scrutiny. Of course we must never seek or contrive difficulty, or feel merited by it. None the less, the God we look to for strength and nurture and grace is a God who allows the full gamut of human emotions to touch even those who are closest to Him. None, not even those who are the most devoted to Him, are spared gloom, despair, depression, hurt, failing, stress. We are encouraged by Jesus to pray for 'protection' and 'deliverance' from evil; and yet hurt, if it is offered, may have the role of opening us up and stretching us. It is not *always* the first and most important concern that I should hide away from the hurt, or shut it down, or deny it.

Where does this lead?

In the last chapter we looked at Being as well as Doing, and Being Me with God. But God wants me to Be with others too. If I can learn that it's OK to disclose myself to God, take off all my coverings in His presence, maybe I can learn to be less guarded and more transparent with others too. Perhaps if I allow to myself my own vulnerability to stress, and to God, I can learn to allow others to see it too. My turmoils, stresses, temptations, questions, doubts and fears. I don't want to be a wailer, but I don't want to be a pretender either. If I give up my false front I can choose, and allow others into my choosing.

> The man who could calm the wind and the waves;
> the man who could feed 12,000 people and leave seven baskets over;
> the man who could call upon legions of angels to defend him –
> at one particular moment in time
> **chose** to take the path of profoundly economic use of energy in that he
> **chose** to be done to rather than to do to; and he
> **chose** to absorb totally the worst evil without reflecting it
> *because he knew, and in his body witnessed, that suffering is usable by God.*
> If this is to happen, it first has to be given and accepted,
> so that in turn it can be given back to God.

Where God is, and faith in Him is real, there is *always* love and hope. And when suffering is acknowledged and handed to him with willingness, He can *always* use it.

Together – the Hurt Body of Christ

We are all, each and individually, to be witnesses to vulnerability; and our weaknesses and inadequacies and doubtings and hurtings can be offered to God to be used by God. Together we can share our pain and support each other in our pain. Together we can learn to be

the hurt body of Christ;
  the leaking vessels of Christ;
    the flawed messengers of Christ;
      the wounded healers for Christ.

We are equipped by God to comprehend, forgive, and fill in each other's leaks, and flaws, and wounds, forbearing one another as He forbears us. The glory is not in our perfectionism, but in what Christ makes of our offering. The way Christ fills up our offered inadequacies often demonstrates His power seeping through our 'cracks'; the very things we are least proud of may be the material He needs to demonstrate His power. The way Christ handles them proves that Light and Power are stronger than *any* dark.[14]

Togetherness

We have to be the body of Christ together. The foot has to do foot-like things because it cannot take the place of the eye. The eye has to content itself to work from one place because it cannot move around in space like the hand. The hand has to work in the public gaze and not in secret like the liver. Each and every organ is dependent on the others to work together for the good of the others. No part needs to compete with the other or try to be the other. Even secular studies have shown how group support promotes good cheer, confidence, competence, creativity, hardiness, and the ability to re-tune stress for the common gain. This is so much more so when we know we are held together by the One who fills the space between us.

So where have we travelled in this 'difficult' chapter? From the strange and hard sayings of Jesus our Christ we have seen how he admitted to turmoil and (i) told others about it and (ii) offered it to God for His use. We have looked at the temptation that always attaches itself to any sort of stress or suffering, that of getting rid of it as soon as possible. But coming face to face with the struggle enables me to acknowledge my vulnerability, and so touch the hurting places of others. And when we companion each other in coping with our various failings, in learning to use the different tools and skills with which we have been equipped, together we can be the body of Christ.

Throughout this chapter there has run another theme. Could 'stress' be seen as today's counterpart to 'suffering'? As the major infections, social malformations and political devastations that have dogged the human race in previous centuries come more under our control, and as in some parts of the world they are being replaced by commonly accepted human rights, is 'stress' the equivalent challenge to the things of the spirit? Does stress, and the way we handle the tools we have in our keeping to cope with it, become the means whereby we recognise the significance of body, mind, feeling and spirit to each of us and to each other?

Does all this make Mrs Trim's life – full as it is with self-protection – feel rather dry?

'Go Into Peace'

Jesus distinctly states that it is *his* peace he gives us, not the peace known by the world. Peace known by the world means an absence of conflict; the peace of Jesus Christ is that deep, deep assurance that we are each one of us totally loved right at the centre of the conflict. God doesn't remove those he loves *out* of the conflict, He is there beside us and loving us right *in* the conflict. The peace of God is about wholeness in spite of hurt and scars, beingness in the face of activity, centredness on Him even when we are surrounded by distractions and fightings.

The former Archbishop of Canterbury, Donald Coggan, has pointed to two incidents in the Gospels where Jesus uses the idea of this special peace, the peace that is beyond ordinary understanding, in a special and different way. In these two stories Jesus suggests a particular movement towards this peace. It is not something given to us in a lump, suddenly. It is a dynamic moving 'into' . . .

The first incident is where the woman who had the wretched condition of a flow of blood continuously for twelve years, had dared to touch the hem of Jesus' coat:

> . . . and she *felt in herself* that she had been cured of her complaint . . . Then, seeing herself discovered, the woman came forward, frightened and trembling because she knew what had happened to her; falling at his feet she explained in front of all the people why she had touched him and how she had been cured at that very moment. She told Jesus the whole truth. He said, 'My daughter, your faith has restored you to health; be free of your complaint and *go into peace*.'[15]

The second incident also concerns a woman, the one with a bad reputation in the town. This one dared to enter a private house where Jesus was dining with an eminent citizen. She waited behind him, weeping, and as her tears fell on his feet, she wiped them away with her hair; then she covered his feet with kisses and anointed them with scented ointment. Following the knowing complaint of his host, Jesus said, ' . . . I tell you that her sins, many as they are, have been forgiven her because she has shown such great love. . . .' Then Jesus said to the woman, 'Your faith has saved you. *Go into peace.*'[16]

'*Shalom*' to you, the reader.

•••••••••••••• **SUMMARY OF PART 3** ••••••••••••••

Picture-story of Legion

Luke 8:22–39; Matt 8:28–34; Mark 5:1–20

•••

My name's Hagar, and I don't like hogs. I hate cooking and sweeping and gossiping and all that girls-stuff even more. I like strong walking and feeling the storms and talking to the wind. Because I'm not like the other girls they pushed me out to join the swineherds, those who watch over the wild pigs away from our home in Gadara. I don't talk to them much; I think my own thoughts and keep out of their way. I use my eyes and ears more than they know I do; it's easier if I let them think I'm stupid.

Like that time when the Jewish preacher came over to our coast. That was a day full of shocks! The hogs graze the tops of the cliff, and in the rocks and caves below are people turned out of the town (a bit like me really) who are crazy. Whether they were crazy after they were pushed away or before is a different story, but among them there's a man who was right round the bend and worse – he slashed himself with sharp edges and screamed and ranted. We were all terrified by him. They tied him up with chains. The others taunted him and threw stones at him but I was too scared; besides, I'd had a hint of what it was like to not belong, to be thought out of my wits, to be jeered at because I wasn't like the others. He was a bit of an enigma too: I guessed he had 'touched the other world' like me, but while I kept mine to myself his had been beaten out of him. He had turned to hatred and disillusion and self-destruction. He felt totally let down; with me it was just in part. He could never find sense in all the different voices which were pulling at him; there were times when I could get my different selves to lay down together.

When the storm came that day, the others took shelter. I stayed out to be in it. The usual sight of Galilee on the other side of the sea had been swamped by darkness. The sudden fierce wind lashed the water into crossfire waves — anyone in a boat was put under ferocious threat. It was unforgettable, the noise and the turmoil. A gap in the darkness showed up a fishing boat with about twelve or so men in it, fighting for their lives, terrified and bewildered, a bit like the lunatic when he felt really bad. Then, glued as I was to the sight, I saw one of the men stand up and he seemed to talk to the waves and wind! Just as if they were naughty children. Then they went still . . . It flashed into my mind — that man was godlike: not because of the storm, because of the stillness.

It was the same man who stepped out onto the rocks here. The lunatic had seen it all, and before anyone had time to draw breath he had flung himself, still naked and bleeding, down in front of the visitor and called out to him by the most sacred name 'Son of the Most High God'. That's a name we would only think in a whisper, and here the lunatic was shrieking it out loud. It made even me tremble.

'Jesus' was the name they gave the stranger. Straightaway he asked the madman what name he gave himself. I liked the one he chose: 'My name is Legion', he yelled — I could follow that.

He was manic, a maniac; over-filled with delusions, premonitions, fantasies which tugged at him from every direction. The demons within had 'seen' the aweful power of Jesus who could calm storms and disperse furies. They didn't take to the idea of instant annihilation. They spoke out loud to this imperious person as if they were on equal terms, almost bargaining with him. It was as if they recognised the intensity of pure spiritual power. Perhaps for Jesus, it was the first time this out-loud acknowledgement had happened. 'Put us into the hogs', they said. Legion was powerless, rigid, gripped between the powers of evil and good.

Then, quite suddenly, he was emptied. Nothing-ed. Shed: of distractions and hurts and evil spirits, the lot. A moment of complete nothingness.

At that the loving poured in. I have never seen nor met such loving; from the top of the cliff where I stood watching, I not only saw but I, too, caught the loving. Enough loving to last for the rest of his life. A love which gave him the power to go off and cry out all over the city what Jesus had done.

It also gave me, Hagar, the one who was put-out and put-down, the courage to tell you this story.

Part 5

At the Centre

Affirming That Bit of the Image of God That Is In Me

And in you, too

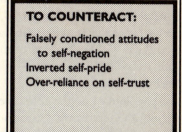

TO COUNTERACT:

Falsely conditioned attitudes
   to self-negation
Inverted self-pride
Over-reliance on self-trust

•••••••••••••••••••••••••••••

I am a bag of tools for God. Not for me, but for God. Maybe some of those tools have become rusty, or ignored, or forgotten. Maybe some are still in the box they came in, unopened, or maybe I have rushed into trying them out without first reading the maker's instructions. Sometimes I use these tools for my own glory and I feel great, and big-headed, and proud; my ego gets a great boost and I feel I am admired. At others – and for the one who is following the way of Christ this is preferable – I use these tools for others, and to the glory of the One who lent them to me. These tools are not mine to do what I want with, although I often forget and treat them as such. They are on loan, and they all have to be given back. The tools, on their own, don't even reflect the 'worth' of what is essentially me, they just happen to be what I have been lent. Helen Ward puts it very succinctly:

> We know that we owe our life and gifts wholly to the gratuitous love of God . . . My personal gifts are not 'me' but gifts, *they are purely for my use, needing neither justification nor concealment.* They are not statements about my human worth.[1]

Once I accept that all my 'gifts' are simply tools that have been lent to me by God for His use, I can go a bit further. There is an 'I' that holds these tools, and the nature of that 'I' makes a difference to how they are used. Maybe that 'I' happens to be hot-tempered, or unusually tall, or short-sighted, or born with a special need; whether that 'I' is advantaged or disadvantaged, the characteristics of this custodial 'I' need to be recognised. And then, we are told that somewhere hidden inside the 'I', even when it is in a mess, there lives a bit of the Image of God and something of the Kingdom of God (Luke 17:21). In terms of managing the stress I am confronted with today, and in terms of being Christ-centred, *all* these things need to be addressed.

We've looked at the four sides of the personality, body, mind, emotions and spirit, and the various skills that can be located in them. They could be arranged like this chart: but notice, there is a gap in the middle.

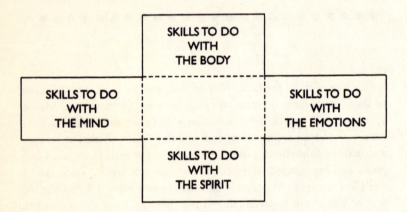

We have all come across people who are expert at the things to do with the body: those who cultivate physical fitness to the extreme. Maybe some of them get out of touch with the things to do with the spirit. We know of others who have brilliant minds, and cultivate their mental tools as far as they can go: maybe they live in an academic sphere where the needs of the body can get neglected. There are others we know who are very good at identifying feelings, their own and others': perhaps some of them forget to give reason sufficient weight, when it is appropriate. There are also those who get so wrapped up in the things of the spirit they live in ivory towers and lose touch with their feelings. So what is it that binds the four areas together, that makes connections between them, and makes for proper balance? I would like to suggest there are five important issues that together glue the whole personality into the purposes of God.

(1) Getting to Know Myself

Many Christians have a particular dilemma to meet. We know from our own experience that we work most creatively and with the greatest love and dedication when we ourselves, as individuals, feel loved and have a certain degree of self-worth. But in the Gospels Jesus says unequivocably, '*Deny thyself* . . . Take up thy cross and follow me'. It has been suggested that the emphasis is on 'denying your selfish desires' or 'putting aside your own pleasures, your selfish ambition'[2] – those things we do simply to indulge and gratify our self-centredness. The original words used do not imply that it is right to rubbish or destroy or annihilate the selfhood God has given us.[3] Significantly, this command is immediately followed by Jesus posing a new question: of what value is it to gain the whole world and lose or 'forfeit' one's true self?[4] If I use the tools I have been lent to boost my own Ego, to gain glory for myself, I might find that in the meantime I have lost sight of the 'me' He created – and of what use is that? Conversely, if I continually put myself down, there is a danger I might eradicate the bit of the Image of God that He has put in me – and where is the usefulness in that?

In the preliminary discussion of this book we saw that Jesus Christ as human being put a strong emphasis on self-assessment. When I am in a stressful condition I am in dire need of some yardstick about caring for myself, and caring for others; loving the self given me by my Creator, and loving Him. Loving myself *as* I love my neighbour. Not necessarily liking my self (or my neighbour), but learning about it, loving it, and rooting out the self-bloating bits. I need to recognise:

- my own capacities, tools, limitations, addictions, drivers;
- my essential need for a modicum of self-esteem;
- my own uniqueness, and the uniqueness of you too;
- that I make mistakes, frequently, and that it is often my fault; but that with the astonishing mercy of God I can recover from them;
- that it is never too late, and that an old dog *can* learn new tricks.

As I find out about the self which God has given me, I may discover layers of defensiveness; very gradually these can be melted so my behaviour towards others becomes less defended. I can reclaim the pieces that have been covered over for years, take responsibility for them, offer them back to God, and then my behaviour towards others will become less self-righteous. I will learn that these things can happen both in me and in you, we are both imperfect, so my behaviour towards you becomes less intolerant. As I grow in realisation of the forgiven-ness that the One who created both of us showers on us, it becomes more real that we are *all* and *each* of unique value to God. The way through life becomes exciting and crammed with marvel.

Jesus knew who he was very securely: he said, 'For I know where I have come from and where I am going' (John 8:14), and he expects us to be able to stand just as firmly in our own space.[5] *How* can I learn what is my innermost strength, my genuine authenticity, as against all those things I do because I 'ought to'? And at the same time avoid augmenting my own ego?

A filled-out version of the Chart 'Stress-Skills for Wholeness' is included as Appendix 8.

(2) 'I Wants', 'Wannas', and 'Gottas'

Each self is a totally special and unrepeatable bundle of attributes with a separate goal, not to be compared with any other. Jesus said to Peter, who was comparing his fate to John's, 'If I want him to stay until I return, what is that to you?' (John 21:22) We are each a unique selection of 'I wants', of 'wannas', and of 'gottas'. We tend to load them up with right and wrong, with niceness and guilt. Perhaps for a moment it would be useful to look at them quite objectively.

The '*I wants*' are the easiest to identify. They consist of 'I want the largest slice of cake', 'I want . . . to get your job', 'I want . . . to sit around eating chocolates while you do all the chores', 'I want . . . to be listened to endlessly by everyone else but never listen to them'. They are easily identifiable as downright selfishness.

The '*wannas*', in contrast, are not about selfishness. They are about living out of the part of me that is genuinely me, the Me God created me to be. When I don't know who that me is, it can be unwrapped, bit by bit, by using the tools discussed in Part 4: the me I unwrap when I experience significance and being and being still and allowing God to love me in my nothingness. When I can do the things that come out of my 'wannas', they are coloured with more energy, more commitment, more verve, more creativity, and they prove to be more productive, than those things I do out of what I have been told to do.

The '*gottas*', on the other hand, are the things I do that spring out of duty. The 'ought tos', the 'have tos', the 'musts' that have been handed down to us. Most of our lives, most of the time, most of us live out of our gottas. Undoubtedly we have obligations and contracts and vows. We do *have* to do our jobs, make a livelihood, get dressed, care for sick dependants. From the stress management point of view, it makes all the difference if I do these things only because I've got to, or because I genuinely want to. If they are wanna-gottas. Do I, today, keep myself clean because as a child I was told to do so by my 'betters', or because as an adult I prefer to be clean rather than dirty? The first is a 'gotta', second-hand, inherited conditioning, and the second is a 'wanna', something coming out of my present choice. I 'gotta' attend an overfamiliar lecture by my boss, while I 'wanna' be with my ailing child.

Some parents, before they make any suggestion or request to their children, make it clear to them that 'this is a "would-you-like?", not a "please-will-you?" ' (or, when appropriate, the reverse!). There is a distinct difference. It can become a useful rule of thumb to ask myself, before undertaking anything or when deciding between choices, 'Is this a "wanna" (a would-you-like?) or a "gotta" (a please-will-you?)?' If it relates truly to the me God wants me to be, it will feel like a gut-level 'wanna' – it will be in tune with my deepest hunches and intuitions about what is 'good', even if it is sacrificial. Alternatively it may feel like a head-imposed 'gotta'; sometimes these have to be undertaken even though they may be stressful, but it is good to have more of the former and fewer of the latter. Sometimes the glory of God shines through the genuine, deepest wannas, more than the conditioned, martyrish, gottas.[6]

The strange thing is that the more I can live out of my 'wannas', the closer I will be growing towards what God intended me to be. The more I live out of my 'gottas', the more risk I run of being solely duty-bound. If I pray because I ought to, I've been told to, it's my duty, it's likely to be more about justifying myself than overflowing with glory to God. The other way of praying used to be described by Michael Ramsay – his great bushy eyebrows working up and down with enthusiasm – is to pray 'because I want, to want, to want to love God'. I pray because I choose to, long to, yearn to, I can't manage without it, however inadequately I do it.

The supreme example in the Gospels of acting out of the 'wanna' level comes in the episode where a leper says to Jesus, 'If you want to/choose to, you can make me well again'; and Jesus replies with eagerness, 'I do want to! I do choose to! Be healed!'[7]

(3) Topsy-turvy: Giving It Away!

Having discovered something of myself, I then have a choice about what to do with it. As someone once exclaimed to me:

> All this talk about finding myself, what do I do with me then?
> Hug me to myself?
> Give me to someone else? someone personal and intimate?
> Give me away to good causes and wide charitable works?
> Does God want my me?

This is a particular and peculiar genius of Christianity. The better I am at owning who I am, the more authenticity it will have when I offer my 'I am' back to God.

Jesus expresses this choice of keeping my life to myself or giving it to him on many occasions; but it all seems so topsy-turvy. He who clings to life loses it; he who loses his life saves it. As Helen Ward continues:

> We know also that we come from humus, the earth, and share its frailty. Humility establishes us in the truth about ourselves, the truth about our utter reliance on God . . . This humility grounds me in confidence in God: I know my life is in His hands, not mine . . . neither my failure and inadequacy nor any measure of success can fundamentally alter that truth. The only fear left to me is of *trying to take myself out of His hands.*[8]

So I want to put my 'me' back into His hands. Give my me to Him. The teaching of Jesus is suffused through and through with this topsy-turvy situation:

- The first shall be last and the last first (Matt. 20:16,26).
- The one who wants to be greatest of all must be the slave of all (Mark 10:31,44).
- He who takes the best seat is asked to go lower; he who lowers himself is asked to go higher (Luke 14:7–14).
- He who is honoured now is despised later (Luke 13:30).
- The student is no better than his teacher, and can reach no higher than the level of the teacher (Luke 6:40).

- The servant is no better than his master, and the master no better than his servant.
- The messenger is no more important than the one who sends him (John 13:16).

Among other stories which invert our 'normal' set of social values, there is the wonderful account of the master returning to find his servants waiting and ready for him: the master himself takes off his coat, seats them down at table, and waits on them.[9] This story prepares us for the ultimate topsy-turvy act of Jesus our Christ taking on the form of a servant and washing the hot dirty feet of his friends at the final supper.

(4) But God Does Not Want Us to Be Servile

Jesus is vehement and unrelenting that we keep our own self-responsibility for our choices and decisions.

I have to claim something as me, and include it in my own authenticity, before I am free to give it away. Constantly, constantly, Jesus is doing just this. Every time he resists being sucked into other people's expectations of him, every time he considers a suggestion before choosing whether to act upon it or not, every time he takes the initiative, he is accepting the authorship of that choice. There is nothing easy or loose about this. There is no 'passing the buck' on to God, no servility to God; it is a fully virile authorship of his decisions. He chooses the appropriate tool (lent by God), uses it to match the circumstances with appropriate skill (taught by God), and hands the glory back to God where it belongs. He knows his own tools, applies them, and returns the interest. Just like the 'successful' servant in the parable of the travelling king who hands out talents, he makes the most of what he is lent and hands back the interest. Eventually the master compliments his servant by increasing the area of responsibility given to him.[10]

There is a suggestion of mutuality here; of give and take; the opposite of insisting on servility. In another sense we can refuse to accept this generous gift of responsibility by insisting on remaining obstinately servile; or by refusing to receive from others, imposing our service on them without accepting their gift in return. Jesus expressed his joy in receiving, as well as giving.

(5) Our Crazy Gratitude

Too often we forget to thank our Father for the profligate gifts He showers upon us. The natural and immediate response of true thankfulness and forgiven-ness is – laughter. The Celtic way of praying was so infused with the goodness and immediacy of God it erupted in laughter. This was a laughter that threw up every problem and all difficulties into God's keeping. Letting go of them into His care, His oversight; giving over the stupid idea that we need to cling on to their control, throwing over the ludicrous notion that we have all the answers, laughing at the preposterous expectations we have of ourselves and of each other. Care-full-ness being transformed into care-less-ness. Abandoning myself to the merriment of knowing: *God is always there*!

The following is a typical Celtic way of praying, on a dull day with a heavy load:

> I *am* walking with the Father –
> I am *walking* with the Son –
> I am walking *with* the Spirit –
> The three-fold all-kindly,
> Ho! Ho! Ho! *Three-in-One*!

These are the five issues that lock us into the explosion of the glory of God. *So Of What Is Glory?*

Jesus Christ's response to stress was to face it and re-tune it to Glory, the Glory of his Father. The *English Etymological Dictionary* gives these synonyms: splendour, resplendent beauty, exalted honour, halo, nimbus, exultation. All given to God as a result of *how* His Son dealt with stress.

Our Lord Jesus Christ appears to equate 'glory' with:
- giving the credit he is offered for himself back to God who owns it;
- involving the transformation of what could be seen as 'wounds' directly into 'worship' of God; and
- resisting being hooked into overload: ultimately the glory is God's, so to allow himself to become overcharged with stress, or over-whelmed with other's expectations, is hardly going to add to it. We wrestle with a besetting temptation to over-extend ourselves, usually in an effort to grab glory (ultimately for ourselves?). Jesus astonishingly resists overload.[11]

What Did 'Glory' Mean to Jesus?

'Let your light so shine before men, that they may see your good works and glorify your Father which is in heaven.' (Matt. 5:16 AV)

As he approached the final consummation of his mission, as he was about to take his leave from his closest earthly friends, Jesus said:

This sickness will not end in death, but it is for God's glory so that through it the Son of God may be glorified. (John 11:4)

Now has the Son of man been glorified, and in him *God has* been glorified. If God has been glorified in him, God will in turn glorify him in himself, and will glorify him very soon. (John 13:31–2)

It is to the glory of my Father that you should bear much fruit and be my disciples. (John 15:8)

In his high priestly prayer directed to God, Jesus says:

I have glorified you on earth by finishing the work that you gave me to do. Now, Father, glorify me with that glory I had with you before the world ever existed. (John 17:4–5)

And then, eventually, the final expression of mutuality:

All I have is yours and all you have is mine, and in them I am glorified. (John 17:10)

I have given them the glory you gave to me, that they may be one as we are one. (John 17:22)

Obviously, we are not equal with God as Jesus the Christ is – but if all things are possible with God we can at least reciprocate:

This is life eternal: to know you, the only true God, and Jesus Christ, whom you have sent. (John 17:3)

'Would you like to be an angel?' asked my all-powerful and adored Dad. I looked at the open window: there it gleamed, the invitation to join the high tropical clouds and dance in the vibrant sky. I was six, and Dad and I were enjoying an early morning cup of tea on my father's bed.

'O-oh yes! please!' I said. No hesitation.

'Just get up and close the door would you?'

That just about sums it up. The life-lasting bewilderment that of necessity my deepest and highest yearnings have to be translated into ordinary humdrum behaviour; and there isn't even any acknowledgement for the pain that that involves. We're all in it, but sometimes the continual closing of doors means that the longing itself gets shut out, and the chores become labour without joy. This book has been about different ways of taking on those tasks – as we all have to do and about which hundreds of books are written – but with an added dimension; the one that is too often left out by manuals on stress management. Tools in the body, mind, and emotions are well identified and described, but there is still the too-easily-quashed level where we strain at the leash to reach something we are not-quite-yet. This deepest part must be recognised also, and supplied with tools that work. Then we can begin to make sense of the stress supplied with our creation as a blueprint for survival. God's purpose; His presence; His power; His plenty; His peace.

So we have come full circle. At the beginning we started out to describe the tools with which we have been equipped to meet the stresses which are a part of God's strategy for our survival. We have tried to simplify things by looking at different layers of the personality, although in practice they overlap and merge. Our journey is about finding our way through the maze to the Godhead at the centre, but we are not on our own, we have a Guide who is also our Precursor and our Goal in the personhood of Jesus our Christ. The Celtic understanding of Christ-centredness has a lot to offer us. I would like (I wanna!) to end with a prayer derived from their prayer. For us who have worked together on this book – both me and my long-suffering family, and all those who have produced it, handled it, and read it, I pray:

> Loving Father, hold us;
> Living Son, enfold us;
> Fiery Spirit, mould us;
> Triune God, uphold us –
> To the furtherment of your Kingdom.
> Amen.

•••••••• Appendices ••••••••

Appendices

Appendices

The following pages have been included for the use of those who would find them useful as handouts in training courses. Permission to reproduce them by photocopying is given by the author and the publisher with the purchase of this book.

1. The Celtic Knot representing the Four Areas of the Personality.
2. Outline of medieval wall painting: Christ, Master of Tools.
3. The Chart of Differences between being In Control and In Charge (Chapter 9).
4. Record of Jesus' ability to withdraw (Chapter 11).
5. Our Culture of **UP**-ness (Chapter 13).
6. Handout concerning Laughter (Chapter 18).
7. Differences between Sleep and Chosen Stillness (Chapters 20 and 21).
8. Chart of the Stress-skills for Wholeness (Chapter 23).
9a. Suggested Headings for Work Groups looking at Stress-skills as used by Jesus in the Gospels.
9b. The names of these skills.
10. How Jesus 'coped'.
11. Addresses of Organisations concerned with Stillness.

Celtic Knot: the Four Areas of the Personality

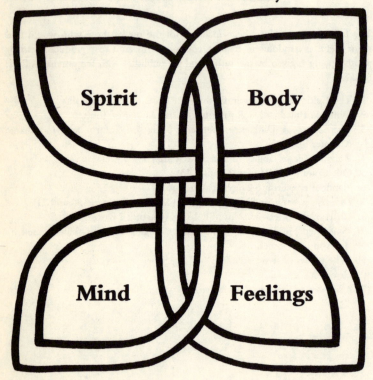

Christ, Master of Tools

Outline of a medieval wall-painting in St Just-in-Penwith, Cornwall (overleaf)

NOTE

- In this mural the figure of Jesus is stripped for work.
- The figure is surrounded by images of the tools ordinary people used to make their living; these are being offered to Jesus Christ for his use and his blessing.
- The whole of the body language expresses the way in which Christ individually accepts and cherishes each tool.
- It is my supposition (not authenticated) that in view of the erratic lay-out of the tools, each image was put there by the tradesperson of the village. There is no coercion or order about the placing of the tools, certainly no hierarchy, and each is offered voluntarily and by choice.
- The size, worth, proportions of the tools are unimportant. Jesus Christ is not much impressed by muchness. That they are there, and valued, is important. The corn-rick (just above the ladder bottom right corner) is smaller than the fisherman's reel! (by the left shoulder of the outlined figure)
- The tools are his, really; it is he who has *lent* them to the individual artisans for their use. They are placed near him by their stewards for his care and oversight.

If it was possible to construct a chart of the difference between being In Control and being In Charge it might go something like this:

IN CONTROL	IN CHARGE
'That which serves to check, restrain, or hinder; power of authority to check'	'Care, cargo, custody; the person or thing entrusted to the keeping of another'
'to exercise restraint or sway over'	'the exercise of care; trust'[1]
When 'I am in control', I limit the other's opportunity to be in control or to be right	When I am 'in charge' of the tools I carry, I can choose which to use, when to use them, and when to hand them over to others
I am attempting to eliminate risk	Some risk adds to life's variety and interest
I can't risk relaxing, being wrong, letting go, being 'shown up' – I have to demonstrate I'm 'best'	I don't mind being wrong and making mistakes; I am not threatened by being unskilled – others can often do it better
Extract from the promotion of a business stress management course: 'Take Control: Once and For All'	When I don't know, it gives others space to tell me what they know
In Control of myself, often means I am controlling of others	Being In Charge of my own responses, ideally means freeing others up to express theirs

There is a very fundamental difference between being in control of oneself and the ability to be in charge of one's responses. The one in control is powerfully

1. From Collins' *Dictionary of Derivations*. These definitions are substantially supported by the Oxford *Dictionary of Etymology* and the *Dictionary of Word Origins* (Columbia, 1990).

protected and defended, even armed. This can easily turn into one of 'me' against 'others'. Do I have a need to be protected, defended, or armed about my 'rightness'? Can I sometimes let go of it?

Do I want always to be absolutist?

In the Gospels, is Jesus the Christ *in control*?

It is remarkable in the New Testament, and something that radiates from the man whose life is recorded there – the *new thing* that he came to give his life for is that:

Jesus Christ welcomes each one of us as a *guest*, not simply as a pupil; God wants each of us to be his *ally*, not merely his slave.

Record of Jesus Christ's Ability to Withdraw:

whether for prayer, on his own;
or rest in the company of the disciples (support group);
or extract one person from the crowd to heal in privacy;
or decision to detach, and resist being hooked into 'overload'.

Matthew

8:18 At the sight of the crowd surrounding him, Jesus crossed to the other side.
13:36 Leaving the crowds outside he went into the house.
12:15 Jesus knew this and withdrew from the district.
14:23 . . . then he went up the hill by himself to pray.
15:39 Jesus sent the people home and got into the boat and crossed over.
16:4 (Religious leaders trying to trap him) . . . and he left them, and went off (NJB).

Mark

1:35 Long before daybreak he went out into the wilderness to pray.
1:38 'Everyone is asking for you' – 'We must go on to other towns'.
1:45 Jesus could not go into any town, but stayed outside in deserted places.
3:7 Jesus withdrew with his disciples to the lakeside.
6:46 [post-feeding of 5,000] Afterwards he went up into the hills to pray.
6:31 Then Jesus suggested, 'Let's get away from the crowds for a while and rest'; for so many people were coming and going they scarcely had time to eat.
7:24 There he entered into a house and would have no man know it (AV).
7:33 Jesus led him [the mute] away from the crowd.
8:13 So he got back into the boat and left them, and crossed to the other side.
8:23 Jesus took the blind man by the hand and led him out of the village [spittle].
9:28 Later, when he was alone with his disciples in the house . . .
10:10 When he was alone with his disciples . . .
11:19 That evening as usual Jesus and the disciples left the city.
13:3 As he sat on the slopes of the Mount of Olives four of the disciples got alone with him . . .

Luke

4:42 Early next morning he went out into the desert.

4:43 . . . begged him to stay. He replied: 'No, I must go . . .'

5:16 vast crowds . . . but he often withdrew to the wilderness for prayer.

6:12 He went into the mountains to pray, and prayed all night . . . [pre-choice of 12].

9:10 Then he took them, and went aside privately into a desert place.

9:18 One day as he was alone, praying, he came over to his disciples and asked them . . .

9:28 He took Peter (and James and John) with him into the mountains to pray [pre-transfiguration].

11:1 When Jesus had been out praying, his disciples came and asked . . . [Paternoster].

18:24 Jesus watched him go, and said, 'How hard it is . . . !' [rich young ruler]

21:37 Each evening Jesus returned to spend the night on the Mount of Olives.

24:51 In the act of parting, Jesus blessed them . . .

John

2:12 He left for a few days with his mother, brothers, and disciples [post-Cana].

4:1 When he knew greater crowds were coming to him . . . he left Judea and returned . . .

5:13 . . . for the place was crowded – Jesus had slipped away. 'He kept himself hidden' (JB).

6:15 Jesus saw they were ready to make him their king, so he went higher into the mountains alone.

7:53/8:1 They all went home, while Jesus went to the Mount of Olives.

10:39 They started to arrest him. But he walked away and left them.

10:40 . . . and went beyond the River Jordan to stay [post confrontation chapter].

11:54 He went to the edge of the desert with his disciples [pre-passion].

12:36 Jesus went away and was hidden from them.

Plus Gethsemane – and he withdrew from them a few paces (Luke 22:41).

Our Culture of 'Up-ness'

*We must Wake **Up**! We must Build **Up** **Up**-beat strategies for **Up**-grading: we must keep our end **Up**, stay **Up**, and **Up**-date for the **Up**-market situation.*

It's revealing to look at the vocabulary we use daily. Consider this list.

High value terms:

START UP	WAKE UP	WORK UP	WIND UP
STAY UP	PUSH UP	FORCE UP	DRIVE UP
KEEP UP	STEP UP	PAY UP	GET UP
LOOK UP	SET UP	STAND UP	MAKE UP
KEEP MY END UP	PULL YOURSELF UP	BUILD UP	HEAD UP
SPEED UP	SHOW UP	CHEER UP	ADD UP
MOVE UP	BLOW UP	CLEAN UP	BOOT UP
stretch up	heave up	fire up	fill up
do up	climb up	hurry up	warm up
pick up	loosen up	tidy up	free up
roll up	eat up	drink up	stir up
hooked up	put up	gear up	stoke up
toughen up	sharpen up	winch up	run up

Add to those:

upbeat	up market	upgrade	upfront
upheld	upshot	upstart	up and coming
upwardly mobile	upstream	up with the Jones!	update
up-end	uptight	buoyed up	banged up
upheaval	upsurge	uproar	live up to ...

These are negative, but still involve high energy:

belt up	shut up	blow up	tied up
het up	wrought up	fed up	washed up
break up	burn up	beat up	'up yours!'

There are, of course, very many others, these are only a representative selection.

Now, compare these lists of **Up** words with the downbeat connotations we give to **Down** words: these mostly relate to things I must not allow myself to do:

Low value terms

I must *not* get:

DOWNHEARTED	DOWNTRODDEN	PUT DOWN	TALKED DOWN
WORN DOWN	RUN DOWN	BLOWN DOWN	MOWN DOWN
SHUT DOWN	KNOCKED DOWN	DOWN AND OUT	

I must *not*:

BREAK DOWN	CLIMB DOWN	SLOW DOWN	STEP DOWN
BURN DOWN	FALL DOWN	STAY DOWN	GET DOWN

And yet, and yet
When I calm down, wind down, settle down, sit down, lie down, centre down . . .

that's when I can *strip down, reach down, bend down* and get *deep down* enough to

touch base – that place of deep stillness, where my deepest being can rest and can take in, rather than give out.

And get *low down* enough to go through the doorway into the birthplace of Jesus.

The Gift of Laughter

When I am laughing – I am not feeling victimised
When I am laughing – I am not fighting
When I am laughing – I am not being angry
When I am laughing – I am not blaming others

The physical effects of laughter:
Increase of O2 uptake
circulation of all fluids in the body is speeded up
internal 'massage' of sluggish organs
release of endorphins
immune efficiency boosted and healing promoted
negative emotions dissipated and optimism enlarged
right brain functions reinforced

Explore the positive and negative words attached to

• head laughter
• heart laughter
• belly laughter

• Jesus Christ and Laughter

When I laugh at myself I accept myself, and when I laugh at other people
in genuine mirth I accept them. Self-acceptance in laughter is the very
opposite of self-accusation or pride. For in the laughter I accept myself not
because I'm some sort of super-person, but precisely because I'm not. There
is nothing funny about a super-person. There is everything funny about a
man who thinks he is.

In laughing at my own claims to importance or regard I receive myself
in a sort of loving forgiveness which is an echo of God's forgiveness of me.
In much conventional contrition there is a selfishness and pride which are
scarcely hidden. In our desperate self-concern we blame ourselves for not
being the super-person we think we really are. But in laughter we sit light
to ourselves. That is why laughter is the purest form of our response to

God. . . . For to sit light to yourself is true humility. Pride cannot rise to levity. (Harry Williams, *Tensions*, 1976, p. 111)

Anger – when your every cell is burning, and you become just a present flame; when every part of your body has become fiery and you have become anger – not just angry. In this moment of total present-mindedness one can become suddenly aware, and you can start laughing at the absurdity, the foolishness, the stupidity of the whole thing. But this is not suppression; this is laughter. You can laugh at yourself because you have transcended yourself. Never again will anger be capable of mastering you. (Osho)

Do you want to know what goes on in the core of the Trinity?
I will tell you:
In the core of the Trinity the Father laughs –
and gives birth to the Son;
The Son laughs back at the Father –
and gives birth to the Spirit;
The whole Trinity laughs –
and gives birth to us.

Meister Eckhart

Differences between Sleep and Chosen Stillness:

SLEEP	STILLNESS
Mental state: Unconscious – unaware	Conscious – alert
Breathing: Erratic	Regular, low, abdominal
Exchange of gases: as normal	Minimal, as essential
Immune System: as normal, or lessened if agitated	Raised efficiency
Healing Process: " " " " " "	Speeded up
Blood Pressure: " " or increased if agitated	Lowered
Pulse Rate: " " " " " "	Lowered
Basal Metabolic Rate: Lowered 8% after 5/6 hours	Lowered 20% in 3 mins
Blood Sugar Level: unchanged	Lowered – no energy needed
Emotional Energy: Rapid Eye Movement *Mental Energy:* excited	Minimal – focused attention
Physical Energy: muscles in tension, perhaps	Minimal: muscle fibres long – deeply relaxed

Stress-skills for wholeness

SKILLS OF THE BODY

Responsibility for my body is MINE
exercise, diet, fluids, relaxation

The Use of the Senses
observation; celebration; enjoyment

Use of the Physical Response Package
sympathetic/parasympathetic
nervous systems

Appropriate Breathing
head, heart, belly

Finding Like-minded Support
choosing a support group

Diminished by Pain?
the stress of continuing pain

SKILLS OF THE MIND

The Use of Reason, Logic and Control
Jesus as 'Manager'

The Use of Choice

The Other Person's Point of View

Organisational Skills
selecting priorities
time management
task delegation
setting goals realistically

Objectifying, Distancing, Withdrawing

Challenge and Change

AT THE CENTRE

Recognising Me
accepting my own uniqueness, and yours
making room for self-esteem

AFFIRMING THAT BIT OF THE IMAGE OF
GOD THAT HE HAS PUT IN ME – *AND IN
YOU TOO*
With God, all things are possible

SKILLS OF THE EMOTIONS

Taking Responsibility for Them
recognising my own self-talk

Managing Them – Without Harm to Others
joy, anger, love, grief, guilt

In Relationship
listening, and being listened to;
adjusting my expectations

Letting Go
when and how

Assertive Tactics: It's Ok for Me to be Me
– and for You to be You

Counting My Blessings – and Laughing!
avoiding approval seeking and scapegoating

SKILLS OF THE SPIRIT

Finding the Significance of *This* Moment in
These Circumstances

Being as Well as Doing
the non-rational mysteries
stripping, meditation, wordless prayer;
receptivity

Still, with God
Me, in My Nothingness

Together – the Hurt Body of Christ
vulnerability/hardness;
hope, good-cheer, confidence, creativity

Jesus Christ was the recipient of more demands and expectations than anyone else who has ever lived. Yet he retained an astonishing resistance to *overload*. He made deliberate use of all the stress-tools which God the Creator had provided, and in doing so he demonstrated a totally stunning ability to choose which tool was appropriate for which circumstances.

Look at a few of these *tools*; how did Jesus apply his *choice* in using them?

In our records of the earthly life of Jesus, where do we find him choosing:

A between *now or later?*

B between *being assertive, or staying passive?*

C between *involving this person, or encouraging separation?*

D between *engaging in this action, or withdrawing from it?*

E between *expressing this feeling (e.g. anger, sorrow), or shutting it down?*

F between *doing it myself* (because I do it better), *or letting another do it?*

G between *seeing the other's point of view, and yet not doing things for the good opinion of others?*

H between *stoic asceticism, or finding renewal in enjoyment?*

I between *knowing I am unique, and allowing others their uniqueness too?*

J between *Doing-for-others, or Being-with-God?*

A Time management/present-mindedness

B Assertive tactics

C Objectifying

D Detachment

E Emotion management

F Task delegation

G Listening; responding not reacting

H Allowing *hedonia*!

I Respect for the other's difference

J Communing with the Father

NB Jesus reduced the expectations coming at him, by simply telling others not to tell!!

How Jesus 'Coped'

1. *First and foremost*, every thought

every emotion   was underpinned by Jesus' communion

every word   with his Father.

every action

2. *Jesus consciously used his ability to resist overload*:
   He took on board the expectations that came at him, considered them, and then re-tuned them to the glory of God. He never rejected or denied them (as we do so often), but they were deflected to God (as we don't). Others' expectations were never allowed to be corrosive, nor to corrode, his own sense of purpose or 'Being'ness.

3. *Jesus therefore maintained his own Personhood*:
   Giving, he wasn't depleted;
   Knowing, he wasn't depressed;
   Acting, he wasn't de-powered –
   because he refused to be hooked by the projections of others onto him, or be sucked into their expectations of him.

4. *In his daily living Jesus used, maintained*, and *enjoyed* his own human tools:
   His human equipment, supplied by God, was the same as ours – eating, drinking, exercising, sleeping, sensing, assessing.
   He used these tools without either misusing or abusing them.

5. *Jesus took on the responsibility of creating for himself his own support group*:
   He was proactive in finding those to accompany him on his journey, however inept they were or inadequate, and he accepted them as his close companions.

6. *Jesus **knew**, he was totally loved, totally **delighted in, by God:***
   And he shared this delight with liberality and generosity with those he found 'in a wretched condition', knowing it was inexhaustible, but respecting his own exhaustibility.

THANKS BE TO GOD

Addresses of Organisations concerned with Stillness

For the practice of relaxation and meditation in groups in England, both local and national, apply to the following addresses:

Julian Meetings, 32 Grosvenor Rd, Norwich, NR2 2PZ

Christian Meditation Centre, 29 Campden Hill Rd, Kensington, London W8 7DX

The Fellowship of Contemplative Prayer, The Vicarage, Tanworth-in-Arden, Solihull, West Midlands B94 5EB

Servants of Christ the King, Austin Thorburn, 28 Blacklands Rd, Benson, Oxon OX10 6NW

Quiet Gardens, The Administrator, Stoke Park Farm, Park Rd, Stoke Poges Bucks SL2 4PG

National Retreat Association, The Central Hall, 256 Bermondsey St., London SE1 3UJ

Cultural Country Retreats, Orchard Cottage, Broadstreet Common, Guildford, Surrey GU3 3BN

and for not specifically Christian quietness:

Relaxation for Living, 168/170 Oaklands Drive, Weybridge, Surrey KT13 9ET

Open Centres: Avlis Farm, Lower Stanton-St-Quintin, Nr Chippenham, Wilts. SN14 6DA

Notes

Introduction

1. (i) Jesus spoke directly to the specific beliefs of his questioner, who was a Sadducee, and one of a sect of priests who argued for the existence of life after death. Jesus quotes: 'God said: "I am the God of Abraham, the God of Isaac and the God of Jacob." Therefore He is God, not of the dead, but of the living. You are very much mistaken.'

   (ii) 'Pay Caesar what belongs to Caesar – and God what belongs to God.' The questioning Pharisees and Herodians who were each hooked into their own power – 'were amazed at him.'

2. It is interesting to note that while Deut. 10:12, 11:13, and 30:6 all speak of a commandment to love the Lord God with heart and soul, Deut. 6:5 and 2 Kings 23:25 list heart, soul, and might. It is only in the New Testament that 'mind' is introduced to the commandment. In Matt. 22:34ff., we are told that in reply to the Sadducees and Pharisees, Jesus talks of the heart, soul, and mind, and in Luke 10:27 it is the lawyer who says in reply to Jesus, 'You must love the Lord with all your heart, soul, strength and mind'. This extract comes from Mark 12:30 (LB).

3. The roots of the word as described in the *Oxford Etymological Dictionary*.

4. By Father Raimon Pannikar, the holder of doctorates in science, philosophy and theology, who speaks eleven languages, is the author of forty books and a visiting professor of a hundred universities.

5. Luke 12:48 REB.

6. Mark 10:29–30 and Luke 18:29.

7. For ease of reading and clarity of meaning, wherever the Trinitarian Godhead is indicated I have employed a capital 'H' for He/His/Him; wherever the meaning applies to Jesus living on this earth as a human man, I have used the lower case 'h'. And simply from traditional usage and the lessening of awkwardness, our full-gendered God has been lumbered throughout with the masculine personal pronoun!

8. Those readers interested in enquiring further about the training course entitled 'Christ, Stress and Glory' (which is accredited), please write to the author at: The Corner Stone, 50B Hyde St., Winchester, Hants, SO23 7DY.

9. *Revelations of Divine Love* (1373), transcribed by Dom Hudleston (Burns Oates, 1927).

Preliminary Discussion

1. The way in which the extension of this attitude can become self-delusory is discussed in chapter 3.
2. Quotations are taken from *The Living New Testament*, paraphrased by Kenneth Taylor (Hodder & Stoughton, London, 1967).
3. See Matt. 10:17; 13:23; Mark 13:21, 33–6; 14:38; Luke 12:40; 21:34.
4. The most obvious incidents of this rare reproof are when people demand a 'sign' – that is, when they demand greedily and unreasonably, yet *another* sign. See Matt. 12:38–9; 16:4; Mark 8:12; Luke 11:29–30; John 4:48.
5. For instance, see Matt. 8:4,30; 9:26; 9:30; 12:16; 16:20; 17:9. Mark 1:34,44; 3:12; 7:24; 7:36; 8:26; 8:30; 9:9. Luke 4:35; 4:41; 5:14; 8:56; 9:21.
6. There are a few further references that resonate with the point made here: when Jesus sent out the twelve apostles he said, 'As you go, proclaim that the kingdom of Heaven is close at hand', and before they left, he said, 'What I say to you in the dark, tell in the daylight; what you hear in whispers, proclaim from the housetops', Matt.10:7,27. Neither of these sentences appear in the other Gospels.
7. The accounts of this strong authority include the reaction of the people of his home town – Matt.7:29; Mark 1:22; the reaction of the religious 'authorities' – Matt. 21:23; Luke 4:36; and the reaction of the people of the town in Samaria who said to the woman: 'Now we believe no longer because of what you [the woman] told us; we have heard him ourselves and we know that he is indeed the Saviour of the world' (John 4:42).
8. See further discussion in chapter 17.

Chapter 1

1. John 2:1–11.
2. Luke 7:44; John 4:7,14; 7:37–8; 13:5; 19:28.
3. Luke 11:37–8; 19:5\Matt. 22:1–10; Luke 14:16–24\Matt.12:1; Mark 2:23; Luke 6:1\Matt. 14:16–21; Mark 6:35–44; Mark 8:1–9; Luke 9:12–17; John 6:5–13\Mark 5:43; Luke 8:55\ Luke 24:30,41; John 21:5,12\ Matt. 26:26; Mark 14:22; Luke 22:19.
4. Matt. 6:25; Luke 12:22.
5. E.g. Matt. 9:35; 15:21; 19:1; Mark 10:32.
6. Matt. 8:24; Mark 4:38; Luke 8:23.
7. Mark 7:33; 8:23; John 9:6\ Luke 10:34\ John 8:6\ Luke 24:39; John 20:20,27.
8. There are too many references to touch in the Gospels to record here! You may like to make a note of your own as this book proceeds.
9. Matt.13:36; Mark 6:31; 9:28; 10:10; 11:19; John 2:12; 3:22.

10. Matt.11:28–9; some translations use the phrase 'restoration for your souls'.

Chapter 2

1. Luke 2:14 in REB, GNB and JB respectively.
2. Matt. 3:17 REB; also Mark 1:11; Luke 3:22.
3. Matt. 17:5 NJB; also Mark 9:7; Luke 9:35.
4. John 12:28.
5. Isa. 6:9–10 (my italic), quoted by Jesus in Matt. 13:14–15. See also Isa. 43:8–9; Deut. 29:3; Jer. 5:21–4; Ezek. 12:2: 'Son of man, you are living among a tribe of rebels who have eyes and never see, they have ears and never hear, because they are a tribe of rebels.'
6. (My italic.) Matt. 11:15; 13:9, 15, 16; 13:43. Mark 4:9, 23; 7:16; 8:18. Luke 8:8; 9:44; 14:35.
7. Crowds touching his clothes: Matt. 14:36. Mark 3:10; 6:56; 8:22. Luke 6:19; 18:15. The woman with the haemorrhage: Matt. 9:20; Mark 5:27; Luke 8:44. Jesus with the children: Matt. 19:13; Mark 10:13; Luke 18:15.
8. For instance, see Matt. 9:18; Mark 5:23; 6:5; 7:32; 8:23, 25; 16:18; Luke 4:40; 13:13.
9. Mark 10:16 JB.
10. Lepers touched: Matt. 8:3; Mark 1:41; Luke 5:13. Fevered woman touched: Matt. 8:15. Eyes touched: Matt. 20:34; Mark 8:23, 25. Tongue touched: Mark 7:33. Bleeding ear touched: Luke 22:51. Bier touched: Luke 7:14.
11. Woman from Samaria: John 4:7–30; woman from Syrophoenicia: Mark 7:25–30. Woman with perfume: Matt. 26:6; Mark 14:3; Luke 7:38; John 11:2; 12:3.
12. Mark 2:19 LB.

Chapter 3

1. It is important to make a distinction here between what is implied by the 'deeps' in contrast with the 'lows'. 'Lows' are about depression, perhaps even clinical depression, and do *not* relate to the parasympathetic 'deeps'. Depression in fact consumes a great deal of energy, it is draining and exhausting, quite the opposite to the relaxing and re-invigorating state of the 'deeps'.
2. For a diagrammatic chart of this whole process see Wanda E. Nash, *People Need Stillness*, pp. 6–7 (London, DLT, 1992).
3. See Aryeh Kaplan, *Jewish Meditation* (New York, Schocken Books, 1985).
4. In addition to the references applying to the above times of physical withdrawal, some of those relating specifically to this time spent alone in the remote desert or mountain spaces are: Matt. 14:23. Mark 1:35; 6:46; 13:3. Luke 4:42; 5:16; 6:12; 9:18; 9:28; 11:1; 21:37. John 6:15; 12:36. Plus, of course, the withdrawal of Jesus in the garden of Gethsemane.
5. See Further Reading for a book-list.
6. This quotation is taken from the AV; the others in this section are NJB.

Chapter 4

1. Job 12:10; 33:4; 4:9.
2. Psalms 146:4; 104:29; 150:6 REB.
3. Ezek. 37:5, 9, 10 NRSV.
4. It may be worth noting here, in relation to the descriptions of the polarising power of God's breath, the number of references to the beneficence of God's breath is about equal to the number of references to the destructiveness of God's breath, depending upon how He chooses to use it. The beneficent breath is mentioned as above plus Dan. 5:23; Ps. 33:6; and the destructive ones include the 2 above, plus Ps. 27:12; 2 Sam. 22:16; Isa. 11:4; 30:28; 30:33.
5. Acts 2:2; 1 Kings 19:11.
6. Relevant reading includes:
   Fried, Robert, *The Psychology and Physiology of Breathing* (NY & London, Plenum Press, 1993)
   Nixon, Peter: e.g. 'An appraisal of Thomas Lewis' Effort Syndrome' in *Quarterly J. Med.* 88: 741–7 (1995)
   Timmons, Beverley H. and Ley, Ronald (eds.) *Behavioural and Psychological Approaches to Breathing Disorders* (NY & London, Plenum Press, 1994)
   van Dixhoorn, Jan, 'The Significance of Breathing Awareness (etc.)' in J. G. Carlson et al (eds.), *Clinical Applied Psychophysiology*, (NY & London, Plenum Press, 1994)
7. Each rib moves against seven interfaces with the vertebra and the sternum; there are twelve ribs on each side of the chest. In addition to these are all the joints of the shoulders and pectoral girdle. A wonder of moving mechanics.

Chapter 5

1. For instance: Mark 4:10, 34; 6:31; 9:28; 10:10; 13:3.

Chapter 6

1. See Further Reading, and in particular W. Nash, *Turning the Downside Up* (London, HarperCollins, 1995).
2. P. Brand, and P. Yancy, *Pain: the Gift that Nobody wants* (London, Marshall Pickering, 1994).
3. Matt. 26:53.
4. 'Am I not to drink the cup that the Father has given me?' (John 18:11). Jesus to Pilate, 'You would have no power over me at all if it had not been given you from above' (John 19:11).

Chapter 7

1. He explained to them the passages throughout the Scriptures that were about himself' (e.g. in Luke 4:17–21; 18:31; 20:17; 21:22; 24:27, 32).
2. Quoted from John 2:24–5. See also Matt. 12:25; 16:8; 26:10 etc.
3. Matt. 8:2, 3; Mark 1:40, 41; Luke 5:12, 13 (JB).
4. E.g. Matt. 12:6: 'Now here, I tell you, is something greater than the Temple.' Matt. 12:8: 'For the Son of man is master of the Sabbath.'
5. Matt. 22:15–22 and Luke 20:20–6.
6. See also:
   Matt. 21:27, 'Their reply to Jesus was, "We do not know." And he retorted to them, "Nor will I tell you." '
   Matt. 12:1–8, concerning the picking of corn on the Sabbath, and David eating the disallowed sacred bread.
   Matt. 22:41–6, the passage about David calling the Messiah 'Lord', and Jesus' logical answer, 'How then can he be his son?'; similarly in Luke 20:41–4.
   John 7:21–4, re circumcision on the Sabbath, contrasted with healing on the Sabbath: don't rely on the conventions, but 'let your judgement be according to what is right'.
   John 18:36, Jesus answering Pilot: 'If my kingdom were of this world, my men would have fought to prevent my being surrendered . . .'
7. Quoted from Mark 12:24–5 (LB). See also Matt. 22:29–30.
8. See Matt. 10:16; Luke 16:8–12; Luke 14:28–32 (LB).
9. See Matt. 6:25–34; Luke 12:4, 7, 22–32.
10. Some examples of organisation are to be found in Matt. 8:18; Matt. 5:1; John 6:3; Mark 6:39; Luke 9:14.
11. See Matt. 10:5–42; Mark 6:7; Luke 9:1–6; Luke 10:1–12.
    Matt. 21:2–6; Mark 11:1–7; Luke 19:28–32; John 12:14.
    Matt. 26:18–19; Mark 14:13–16; Luke 22:10–13.
12. Matt. 5:29–30 and 18:8, 9; also Mark 9:43, 45, 47.
13. See Mark 12:28, 32; Luke 20:39 (LB).

Chapter 8

1. The construct known as the locus of control has been fully described by Rotter, among others, see Further Reading.
2. Matt. 4:1–13; Mark 1:12–13; Luke 4:1–13.
3. Matt. 8:2; Mark 1:40; Luke 5:12.
4. Luke 13:31–3.
5. John 7:1 (my emphasis).
6. This incident has strong resonances with the story of the farmer hiring labour in Matt. 20:1–16. When, as he pays out an equal sum to each of the men he has hired, he is accosted by the first workers of the day with the complaint that they have been paid the same as the last, the employer replies, 'Have I no right to do what I like with my own?'
7. John 21:22.

8. Matt. 27:34.
9. Matt. 20:32; Mark 10:51; Luke 18:40.
10. Matt. 20:21; Mark 10:36.
11. John 5:6.
12. John 6:66–7.
13. John 6:70; 13:18; 15:16.
14. See Matt. 9:15; Mark 2:18; Luke 5:33; 18:12.
15. See Matt. 26:11; Mark 14:7; Luke 7:47; John 12:7.
16. See Luke 10:41–2. Further descriptions of Jesus' love for Martha, and Mary, are to be found in John 11:1, 5, 20, 27, 32, 35, 40.
17. Jesus washing feet, John 13:4–10. Parable of the returning landlord, Luke 12:37–8 GNB.
18. Amongst very many other texts, see Matt. 26:39, and Mark 14:36.

Chapter 9

1. From Collins' *Dictionary of Derivations*. These definitions are substantially supported by the *Oxford Dictionary of Etymology* and the *Dictionary of Word Origins* (Columbia, 1990).
2. Matt. 16:13–17; Mark 8:27; Luke 9:18–20.
3. Matt. 10:24; 26:29; Luke 6:40; John 13:13–16; 15:14, 15, 16. The phrase 'I have called you friends' has been variously interpreted as being synonymous with 'companion', 'guest', and 'ally'.

Chapter 10

1. See Matt. 10:37–8; 8:21; Luke 14:26; 8:21.
2. Matt. 22:37; 5:44–7; Mark 12:28–34; Luke 6:27–38.
   The commonly accepted version of the second half of the great commandment is: Love your neighbour as you love yourself. The English language is peculiar in the emphasis it puts on the order of words in the sentence – those stated first assume greater importance. This does not apply to the languages in which the Gospels were written; in both Greek and Aramaic word order is less significant. It has been suggested that it would be equally valid, and as close to the meaning intended by Jesus, if the early translators of the Gospels had simply put the end phrase in front of the first. We would then have been brought up on, '*as you love yourself, love your neighbour*', and our personal histories might have been very different.
3. Matt. 5:47, Luke 6:32.
4. See Matt. 9:12; Mark 2:17; Luke 5:31.
5. A favourite theme in the Gospels. See for instance: Matt. 7:17,20; 12:33; 13:23. Luke 6:43. John 15:2, 4, 8, 16.
6. For instance, the dumb person in Mark 7:33: 'and Jesus led him away from the crowd'; and Mark 8:23: 'Jesus took the blind man by the hand and led

him outside the village.' At the pool of Bethesda, where there were 'crowds
of sick people, blind, lame, paralysed', he only healed *one* person (John 5:3).

7. For instance, healing from a distance: the servant of the centurion – Matt.
8:13, Luke 7:10; the Syrophoenician woman's daughter – Mark 7:25–9.

8. See Jesus' instructions to his disciples in their first mission – Matt. 10:14;
Mark 6:11; Luke 9:5. Jesus left his home town of Nazareth abruptly when
they demonstrated their disbelief – Matt. 13:57; Mark 6:5–6; Luke 4:30.

9. See Matt. 24:16–18; Mark 13:15–16; Luke 21:21–2.

10. For the healing of the man with a paralysed hand in a synagogue on the
Sabbath, see Matt. 12:9–14, Mark 3:1–6, Luke 6:6–10, where the teachers
of the law and some Pharisees 'watched him closely . . . but Jesus knew their
thoughts . . . and was grieved at their obstinacy . . . and he said to the man,
"Stretch out your hand" . . . and he became well again.'

   For the healing of the crippled woman in a synagogue on the Sabbath,
see Luke 13:10–16 where the religious official was angry, until the action of
Jesus in setting the woman free from her infirmity 'made him ashamed, and
the people rejoiced over all the wonderful things'.

11. John 2:4.

12. John 11:1–45; 12:1.

13. See Matt. 13:2–3; 14:22–3; Mark 3:9; 4:1; Luke 5:1–3; 8:4.

   Typical is Mark 3:7 – 'Jesus withdrew with his disciples to the lakeside,
and great crowds from Galilee followed him. [Six regions mentioned.] And
he asked his disciples to have a boat ready for him because of the crowd, to
keep him from being crushed. For he had cured so many that all who were
afflicted in any way were crowding forward to touch him.'

14. See Matt. 14:19; Mark 6:39–40; Luke 9:14; John 6:10.

15. See Matt. 10:5–15; Mark 6:7–13; Luke 9:1–6; 10:1–11.

16. See Matt. 21:1–9; Mark 11:1–10; Luke 19:28–38; John 12:12–14.

17. See Matt. 26:17–20; Mark 14:12–17; Luke 22:8–14; John 13:2.

18. For instance, Matt. 10:5–25; 17:16; Mark 6:7–13; 9:18; Luke 9:1–6; 9:40;
10:1–17.

19. E.g. Matt. 21:1–2 and 26:18.

20. Examples of the way Jesus asked the disciples to 'mediate' for him are: as
they handed out the bread and fish to the crowds of thousands upon
thousands, Matt. 14:19, Luke 9:16; as they went to collect the blind man
from the edge of the road, Mark 10:49, Luke 18:40; and as they baptised in
his name, John 4:2.

21. See Mark 1:44; Luke 17:14; 5:14; John 9:7.

22. See Matt. 12:39; 16:4; Mark 8:11.

23. Luke 9:51; 13:22.

Chapter 11

1. Perhaps those professionally employed in hospitals should be exempt from this
rarity. They have to maintain their work boundaries.

2. This extended list of references has been selected from various biblical renditions. Attributions with exactness would have been tedious here.

Chapter 12

1. For instance – and there are many others – see Matt. 17:22–3; 20:18–19; 26:2; 27:63. Mark 8:31; 10:33–4; 26. Luke 9:22. John 12:31–2; 13:33; 16:4,5.
2. See Luke 21:5,6 and 19:44.
3. Matt. 24:6–51; Mark 13:7–37; Luke 21:9–28.
4. See Matt. 9:15; John 12:35; 14:28; 16:4,16.
5. See Matt. 7:15; 24:42,44. Mark 13:5,9,23,33,37. Luke 21:34.
6. See Matt. 3:15: Jesus says, 'It is fitting that we should . . . do all that righteousness demands'. Luke 3:18, 'If you are repentant produce the appropriate fruits'. Luke 23:41, The thief being crucified says, 'we are paying appropriately for what we did'. All these are from JB.
7. Luke 2:19, 51; Mark 9:10.
8. Obviously contrition and reparation are part of this process, but not the immediate subject of this chapter.
9. For instance his references to the Queen of Sheba in Matt. 6:29 and 12:42; to Solomon in Matt. 6:29 and Luke 12:27; to Chorazin in Matt. 11:21; and to Sodom and Gomorrah in Matt. 10:15, Luke 17:29.
10. Mark 2:27; Luke 6:5.
11. Matt. 15:2–10; Luke 13:15; Luke 14:1–5; Matt. 12:10–13; and Mark 3:1–5 respectively.
12. Mark 9:23 – curing the epileptic; 10:27 – rich man to be saved; and John 11:40 – with Martha.

Chapter 13

1. The reader may like to refer back to the 'highs' and 'deeps' section in chapter 3 (pp. 20ff.).

Chapter 14

1. See Mark 9:42; Luke 17:2.
2. Luke 17:4 and Matt. 18:22; Luke 17:6; and Luke 17:17 respectively.
3. See, for example, Mark 3:5: 'Then he [Jesus] looked angrily round at them, grieved to find them [the watching "religious" people in the synagogue] so obstinate'.
4. The exception to this was the long discourse on the woes to the Pharisees, see Matt. 23:13–36. There is considerable academic difficulty around the original sources of these blasts of fury, and as they do not directly concern Jesus' behavioural management of stress, further comment on them has been omitted here.

5. See Matt. 21:12; Mark 11:15; Luke 19:45; John 2:15.
6. Matt. 12:31, 32; Mark 3:29; Luke 12:10.
7. Matt. 26:66.
8. The theological significance of this fact, that 'guilty' is used in conjunction solely with the one man who has lived without sin, and the Spirit who can commit no sin must be left for others to explore.
9. From the *Dictionary of Word Origins*, Columbia, London, (Ayto, 1990).
10. *The Oxford Dictionary of Etymology* (OUP, 1974).
11. For instance the paralytic in Matt. 9:2–7; Mark 2:3–12; Luke 5:18–25.

Chapter 15

1. See John 1:42; Matt. 16:17–18 REB.
2. See Preliminary Discussion, pp. ixff.
3. To the 'hypocrites', Luke 12:57 REB.
4. Mark 9:32; Luke 9:45; 18:34; John 12:16.
5. See Matt. 18:3,4; 19:14; 21:15; Mark 9:37; 10:14; Luke 9:48; 18:16,17.
6. For instance, Matt. 17:25 to Peter; 18:12 to the disciples; 20:21 to the mother of the sons of thunder; 21:28 to the chief priests and elders; Mark 10:36 to James and John; Mark 10:51 to the blind man, even though Jesus knew the thoughts of each of them (Luke 11:17).
7. Matt. 5:11; Luke 6:22.
8. See John 13:4–17; also Luke 22:27, 'For who is the greater: the one at table or the one who serves? The one at table surely? Yet here am I among you as one who serves!' Also Luke 12:37, 'Happy are those servants whom the master finds awake when he comes. Truly I tell you: he will hitch up his robe, seat them at table, and come and wait on them' (REB).

Chapter 16

1. It is still unclear to me how much Mary of Bethany can be identified with Mary Magdalene. Was Mary who was forgiven much (Luke 7:47 and 8:2), who followed Jesus from Galilee and ministered to him (Matt. 27:56; Mark 15:41), who wiped Jesus' feet with her tears at the home of the Pharisee (Luke 7:37–50), who poured perfumed oil on them while he was dining at her house (John 11:2; 12:3), and on his head when he was dining at the house in Bethany of Simon the leper (Matt. 26:6–13; Mark 14:3–9), who sat at his feet while her sister was overly concerned with domesticity (Luke 10:38–42), who stayed in the house with her private grief at the death of her brother (John 11:28), who watched the crucifixion from a distance (Mark 15:40), who stood at the foot of the cross (John 19:25), who took spices to the tomb (Mark 16:1), the same as Mary in the garden of the sepulchre (Matt. 27:61 and 28:1; Mark 16:1; Luke 24:10; John 20:1)? The detail of these references is ambiguous. All these are apart from the references to the sister of Jesus' mother, also called Mary (NRSV and NJB John 19:25).

2. See John 13:23,25; 19:26; 21:22–3.
3. See John 11:1–46; 12:1–2; Matt. 21:17; Luke 10:38.
4. See Matt. 12:46–50; Mark 3:31–5; Luke 8:19–21.
5. See Matt. 19:29; Mark 10:29–30; and Matt. 19:5; Mark 10:7;
6. For the widow of Nain: Luke 7:11–17.
   Jairus' daughter: Matt. 9:18–19,23–6; Mark 5:22–4, 35–42; Luke 8:41–2,49–56.
   The releasing of Legion: Mark 5:18–19; Luke 8:38–9.
   The disappointed young ruler: Matt. 19:21; Mark 10:21; Luke 18:22.
7. I am indebted to a prayer by Jim Cotter for these three concepts:

Spirit of Wisdom:
    Take from us all Fuss,
        the clattering of noise,
            the temptation to dominate by the power of words,
    the craving for certainty;

Lead us through the narrow gate of not knowing
that we may listen and obey
and come to a place of silence and stillness,
of true conversation and wisdom.

Spirit of Love:
    Take from us all Lust,
        the battering of force,
            the temptation to dominate by physical power,
    the craving for control;

Lead us through the narrow gate of aloneness,
that we may let others be,
and come to a place of solitude and intimacy,
of deep communion and love.

Spirit of Freedom:
    Take from us all Rust,
        the cluttering of things,
            the temptation to dominate by the power of money,
    the craving for comfort;

Lead us through the narrow gate of limitation,
that we may let go of possessions
and come to a place of simplicity and spaciousness,
of glad conviviality and freedom.

Jim Cotter, 'Prayer in the Morning' (Cairns Publications, 1989), p. 51.

Jim Cotter has kindly allowed the use of the words 'aloneness' (line 15) and 'limitation' (line 24) in place of his originals, respectively 'loneliness' and 'constriction', which were felt to be inappropriate in this context.

Chapter 17

1. We are all familiar with the reported saying of Jesus, 'Be ye perfect even as your Father in Heaven is perfect'. The word is derived from the Latin, *perfacere*, and literally means 'to work through', to 'work thoroughly'. The sense of perfect as something that is flawless and without blemish only entered our language around 150 years ago. Modern translation has replaced the word in Matt. 5:48 with 'there must be no limit to your goodness . . . ' REB.
2. John 4:7–30 and Matt. 15:22–8 respectively.
3. *The Independent*, 27 July 1995.
4. Mark 10:17–18; also Matt. 19:16–17; Luke 18:18–19.
5. Mark 2:2–12; Matt. 9:2–7; Luke 5:18–25.
6. Matt. 9:18–25; Mark 5:22–43; Luke 8:41–56.
7. See also Matt. 22:16; Mark 12:14; Luke 20:20 – the Pharisees acknowledge Jesus is unaffected by people's approving opinion; and Matt. 6:2, where Jesus tells us our good works should not be for others' approval.
8. Matt. 8:9; Luke 7:8.
9. See Matt. 7:29; Mark 1:22. Also, for instance, Matt. 12:6–8; and 21:23; Luke 4:36; and 9:1.

Chapter 18

1. Donald Coggan, *The God of Hope* (SPCK, London, 1995) p. 75.
2. Matt. 5:3–12, Luke 6:20–3.
3. *Centuries, the Way to Felicity*, c.1672 (printed in this century by Mowbrays).
4. Initiated by the Revd Roly Bain, this movement is now spread around Great Britain. Holy Fools visit market-places, schools, hospitals, prisons and anywhere where human heaviness and pomposity needs to be lifted and the topsy-turvy values of God rediscovered.
5. See Further Reading for books by Norman Cousins, Robert Holden, Liz Hodgkinson, for a start.
6. Matt. 14:29–31; see also Matt. 8:26. Other texts refer to Jesus' remark which seems to be 'chiding' the people for their anxieties about their growth, clothing and food – Matt. 6:30; Luke 12:28. Is it likely that in those circumstances of anxiety he was ready to pull them down still further? Or was this affectionate good humour?
7. Harry Williams, *Tensions* (London, Michael Beazley Publishers, 1976), p. 111.
8. Osho (place of text unrecorded).
9. Quote from Meister Eckhart (thirteenth century). Printed on a poster.

Chapter 19

1. Luke 13:34; also Matt. 23:37.
2. Contraction of quotation by Jesus in Matt. 13:15 of Isa. 6:9–10. This passage resonates with Isa. 43:8: 'Bring forth the people who are deaf, yet have ears!'

Jer. 5:21: 'Listen to this, stupid, brainless people . . . who have ears and do not hear! Have you no fear of me?'

Ezek. 12:2: 'You are living among a tribe of rebels who . . . have ears and never hear'.

Rom. 11:8: They are 'infused with a spirit of lethargy . . . they have not eyes to see or ears to hear.'

2 Cor. 3:14, 17: 'Their minds were closed . . . and this veil will not be taken away until they turn to the Lord . . . Now this Lord is the Spirit, and where the Spirit of the Lord is, there is freedom.'

3. Mark 8:17–18.
4. Mark 4:9 and Matt. 11:15: 'He that hath ears to hear, let him hear.'
5. Psalm 131 NRSV.
6. See Matt. 5:13 and Mark 9:50 – Jesus is saying we should *all* be 'salted with fire' because salt is a good thing; but if salt becomes insipid, what will make it salty again? It will be good for nothing, and be thrown out to be trampled under people's feet. He says, 'You are salt *for* the earth . . . ' 'Have salt in yourselves, and be at peace with one another.'
7. According to the DLT *Modern Concordance to the New Testament* (1986) there are at least ten root words in the Greek which are commonly translated into English using the one word 'sick'. 'In a wretched condition' is the phrase which most appropriately translates the word in these specific texts, Matt. 9:12 and Luke 5:31.

Chapter 20

1. Lest this extrapolation should appear too facile, this passage (taken from the REB) continues: 'If I do judge, my judgement is valid because it is not I alone who judge, but I and He who sent me' (John 8:16). The earlier passage from John 3:19 continues: 'This is the judgement: the light has come into the world, but people preferred darkness to light because their deeds were evil.' And the following passage from John 12:47 continues: 'There is a judge for anyone who rejects me and does not accept my words; the word I have spoken will be his judge on the last day . . . What the Father has said to me – that is what I speak' (John 12:48,50). The points made in the main text are unaffected by these extensions.
2. Also Luke 6:37,38.
3. Letter to the Galatians 6:1,2,4 REB.
4. (With all its various connotations!)
5. See Matt. 6:5,7.
6. Matt. 23:5; Mark 12:38, 40; Luke 11:43. See also Matt. 6:2, 16; Luke 18: 11.
7. John 12:42 as worded in the Living Bible.
8. John 6:29. It is worth mulling over the origins of this word. By various routes it has come from 'lief' – love, allegiance, trust – and 'leave' – permission. Some have noted the relationship of 'Believe' and 'leave Be'! Note also that the original Hebrew idea behind the word 'faith' is to lie down on the ground, in a position of total inactivity and dependence.

9. See Matt. 4:23; Mark 1:21; Luke 4:15, 16, 31, 44.

10. For instance, before choosing the Twelve, Luke 6:12-18; before the last Passover John 11:54; and before his passion John 12:36.

11. Matt. 7:12; Luke 6:31.

12. From *Jewish Meditation* by Aryeh Kaplan, p. 45 (see Further Reading). Also, 'There is ample evidence that meditative practices were widespread among Jews throughout Jewish history. References to meditation are found in major Jewish texts in every period from the biblical to the premodern era . . . Until the rise of the Jewish Enlightenment, mysticism and intellectualism had equal status within Judaism . . . the first values to fall by the wayside [in the path of Reason and scientific method in the nineteenth century] were Jewish mysticism in general and meditation in particular.' p. 40. In the modern era both Kabbalistic and Chasidic types of meditation and mysticism are enjoying renewed research and practice.

Chapter 21

1. The classic authors who, in their various ways, put words around something that is wordless – being still with God – include St John of the Cross, Dame Julian of Norwich, the anonymous author of *The Cloud of Unknowing*, St Teresa; and in more recent years Evelyn Underhill, Thomas Merton, Arthur Slade, Bede Griffiths, Carlo Carretto, Robert Coulsdon, John Main and Laurence Freeman among others. Details are to be found in Further Reading.

2. Compare this with the virile truth of the young prisoner who said, 'I go to church to see what I can get out of it, don't I?' He was speaking for us all with devastating accuracy. Is it what God does *for* me that most interests me, or what God does *with* me?

3. Matt. 6:9–13; Luke 11:1–4. Some experts point out that in the original the Paternoster was unlikely to have been in the form of a list of imperatives as we have it today; Jesus would have used the continuing present tense in his native tongue, which emphasises the activity of God in *this* here and now. For instance, 'Our Father, you are in heaven, your name is being hallowed, you are giving us our daily bread, you are leading us away from temptation, you are delivering us from evil . . .' etc. This closely approaches mindful meditation.

4. See Luke 11:9,13; 18:1.

5. See Matt. 6:6, 18.

6. See also John 6:15. As the delighted crowds pressed towards Jesus he realised they were wanting to make him king by force; so he 'departed again into a mountain himself alone' (AV).

7. For addresses and more information, see Appendix 10.

8. This is the word used by Jesus. When we are exhausted or driven or distressed he offers us not more power or strength or vitality, but *rest*. 'Come ye apart and *rest* awhile'. We have expanded that simple concept into polysyllabic and high-sounding words like relaxation, meditation, contemplation. Jesus asks us to rest.

9. These are all variants of the one word found in different modern translations of the same saying, e.g. John 15:4. See also 1 John 2:6, 'He that saith he abideth in him, ought himself also so to walk, even as he walked' (AV).

10. In some cases this can get the closest humans arrive at to hibernation. It is nothing to do with being in a 'trance', or being 'hypnotised'; the consciousness is fully awake and totally in charge of what is happening. I don't hand my self over in any way. Consciousness is only lost if I go to sleep, and although this may be useful it is not the goal of meditation.

11. Tapes of relaxation/meditation exercises similar to this one can be obtained from the author.

Chapter 22

1. Luke 12:51–3 NRSV; Matt. 10:21, 35.
2. John 16:33 REB.
3. Matt. 10:34 REB.
4. Matt. 11:12; Luke 16:16 JB.
5. Matt. 10:16; Luke 10:3.
6. This is the translation suggested by the *Modern Concordance to the New Testament* (DLT, 1986), which is specific to the word used here for 'sick'. It occurs in this context in each of the synoptic Gospels – Matt. 9:12; Mark 2:17; Luke 5:31. See also note 7, Chapter 19.
7. Matt. 26:38; Mark 14:34.
8. John 12:20–8.
9. John 18:37.
10. Mark 14:62; see also Matt. 16:27; 25:31; 26:53, 64; Mark 8:38; Luke 9:26.
11. Luke 22:40, 46.
12. Matt. 16:22–3.
13. Matt. 26:52–3.
14. 'What has come into being in him was life, life that was the light of men; and light shines in darkness, and darkness could not overpower it' (John 1:4–5).
    'It is sown in weakness; it is raised in power' (1 Cor. 15:43 AV).
    ' "Power is at full stretch in weakness." It is, then, about my weaknesses that I am happiest of all to boast, so that the power of Christ may rest upon me; and that is why I am glad of weaknesses . . . and distress for Christ's sake. For it is when I am weak that I am strong' (2 Cor. 12:9–10).
15. This is a compilation of Mark 5:34 and Luke 8:48.
16. Luke 7:50.

Chapter 23

1. Heather Ward, *The Gift of Self*, p. 14 (slightly re-arranged phrases).
2. Mark 8:36; Luke 9:23; from the Living Bible – 'put aside his own desires

and conveniences and carry his cross with him every day and keep close to me'.

3. It has sometimes been put bluntly: it is much easier to deny myself than to know my Self.

4. See Matt. 16:26; Mark 8:36; Luke 9:25. The New Living Translation (1996) reads: 'If you try to cling to your life/keep life for yourself, you will lose it; but if you give up your life for me (and for the sake of the Good News) you will find true life. And how do you benefit if you gain the whole world but lose your life/soul in the process? Is anything worth more than your soul?'

5. Luke 21:19, and 28. Notice also how firmly Jesus stood before Pilate when he refused to answer false accusations (Luke 23:9); and how he admired the man who built his house 'firmly' on a rock (Matt. 7:25; Luke 6:48).

6. 'Wannas' and 'gottas' can be developed further with reference to head-knowing, heart-knowing, and gut-knowing. For expansion of this theme, see W. Nash, *Turning the Downside Up*, (HarperCollins, 1995).

7. Matt. 8:2–4; Mark 1:40–2; Luke 5:12–14.

8. Heather Ward, op.cit.

9. Luke 12:37; 22:27.

10. Matt. 25:14–30; compare with Mark 13:34–7.

11. This is a favourite theme of Dame Julian of Norwich in her *Revelations of Divine Love* (fourteenth century).

Selected Further Reading

The following is a list of books that have particularly influenced the content of *Christ, Stress and Glory*, with one area deliberately omitted. The present work is not a theological study, so scholastic input of this sort is not included here.

References given in full in the Notes are not repeated here.

The following partitions are arbitrary. Like the four areas of the personality, they all overlap.

General Reading – underpinning the theory of stress:

Bond, Meg, *Stress and Self-Awareness: A Guide for Nurses*, London, Heinemann Medical Books, 1986

Fontana, David, *Managing Stress*, London, BPS and Routledge, 1990

Greener, M., *WHICH? Guide to Managing Stress*, London, Consumers' Association, 1996

Handbook of the Core Content of Stress Management Training, International Stress Management Association, South Bank University (LPSS, 103 Borough Rd, London SE1 0AA), 1996

Harding, Geoffrey, *Lying Down in Church*, Worthing, Churchman Publishing, 1990

Horsman, Sarah, *Living with Stress*, Cambridge, Lutterworth Press, 1989

Jacobs, Michael (ed.), *The Care Guide*, London, Cassell, 1995

Looker, Dr Terry and Gregson, Dr Olga, *Stresswise*, London, Hodder & Stoughton, 1989

Nash, Wanda E., *At Ease With Stress*, London, Darton, Longman & Todd Ltd, 1988

Sapolski, Robert M., *Why Zebras Don't Get Ulcers*, New York, W.H. Freeman & Co., 1994

Warren E. and Toll C., *The Stress Work Book*, London, Nicholas Breasley Publishing Ltd, 1993

and – *Modern Concordance to the New Testament*, London, Darton, Longman & Todd Ltd, 1986

Titles Enlarging on Part 1 – to do with the body:

Benson, Herbert, *Beyond the Relaxation Response*, London, Collins Fount, 1985

Fried, Robert, *The Psychology and Physiology of Breathing*, New York, Plenum Press, 1993

Magdalen, Margaret, *A Spiritual Check-up*, Crowborough, Highland Books, 1990

Timmons, Beverly and Ley, Ronald (eds.), *Behavioural and Psychological Approaches to Breathing Disorders*, London, Plenum Press, 1994

Yancey, Philip and Brand, Paul, *Fearfully and Wonderfully Made*, London, Marshall Pickering, 1993

Titles specific to pain:

Brand, Paul with Yancy, Philip, *Pain – the Gift that Nobody Wants*, London, Marshall Pickering, 1994

Cotter, Jim, *Healing – More or Less*, Sheffield, Cairns Publications, 1990

Francis, Jenny, *Belief Beyond Pain*, London, Triangle SPCK, 1992

Mayne, Michael, *A Year Lost, A Year Found*, London, Darton, Longman & Todd Ltd, 1991

Nash, Dr Poppy, *Living with Disfigurement*, Aldershot, Avebury, 1995

Spufford, Margaret, *Celebration*, London, Fount Paperbacks, 1989

Working Party on Hospice Experience, *Mud and Stars*, Oxford, Sobell Publications, 1991

Titles Enlarging on Part 2 – to do with the mind:

Breakwell, Glynis, *The Quiet Rebel*, London, Century Publishing, 1985

Fontana, David, *Social Skills at Work*, London, BPS and Routledge, 1992

Grey, Mary, *Wisdom of Fools*, London, SPCK, 1993

Handy, Charles, *Inside Organisations – 21 Ideas for Managers*, London, BBC Books, 1990

Harris, Paul, *Christian Meditation*, New Jersey, Dimension Books, 1993

Kriegel, Robert and Marilyn, *The 'C' Zone – Peak Performance Under Pressure*, London, William Heinemann, 1992

Montefiore, Hugh (ed.), *The Gospel and Contemporary Culture*, London, Mowbray, 1992

Nelson, John (ed.), *Management and Ministry*, Norwich, Canterbury Press, 1996

Palmer, Stephen and Dryden, Windy, *Counselling for Stress Problems*, Sage Publications Ltd, 1995

Ross, Maggie, *The Fire of Your Life*, London, Darton, Longman & Todd Ltd, 1996

Rotter, J.B., 'Generalised expectancies for internal versus external control of reinforcement' in *Psychological Monographs*, 80:1 (1966).

Taylor, John V., *The Christlike God*, London, SCM Press Ltd, 1992

Williams, S., *Managing Pressure for Peak Performance*, London, Kogan Page, 1994

Titles Enlarging on Part 3 – to do with the emotions:

Campbell, Alistair, *The Gospel of Anger*, London, SPCK, 1989
Dainow and Bailey, *Developing Skills with People*, London, John Wiley, 1988.
Holden, Robert, *Living Wonderfully*, London, HarperCollins, 1994
Jeffers, Susan, *Feel the Fear and Do It Anyway*, London, Arrow, 1991
Long, Anne, *Listening*, London, Darton, Longman & Todd Ltd, 1990
Magdalen, Margaret, *The Hidden Face of Christ*, London, Darton, Longman & Todd Ltd, 1994
McGreal, Wilfrid, *Guilt and Healing*, London, Geoffrey Chapman, 1994
Mountney, John M., *Sin Shall be a Glory*, London, Darton, Longman & Todd Ltd, 1990
Sheppard, Grace, *An Aspect of Fear*, London, Darton, Longman & Todd Ltd, 1989
Tournier, Paul, *The Meaning of Gifts*, SCM Press Ltd, 1964
Walls, Roland, *From Loneliness to Solitude*, Oxford, Fairacres Publication, 1992
Williams, Harry, *Tensions – Necessary Conflicts in Life and Love*, London, Mitchell Beazley Publishers Ltd, 1976

Titles specific to laughter:

Bain, Revd Roly, *Fools Rush In*, London, Marshall Pickering, 1993
Cousins, Norman, *Head First – the Biology of Hope*, New York, E.P. Dutton, Penguin Books, 1989
Hodgkinson, Liz, *Smile Therapy*, London, Macdonald Optima, 1987
Holden, Robert, *Laughter, the Best Medicine*, London, Thorsens, 1993
Kuschel, Karl-Josef, *Laughter, a Theological Reflection*, London, SCM Press, 1994
Trueblood, Elton, *The Humour of Christ*, London, Darton, Longman & Todd Ltd, 1965

Titles Enlarging on Part 4 – to do with the spirit:

Carretto, Carlo, *Letters from the Desert*, New York, Orbis Books, 1972
Coggan, Donald, *The Servant-Son*, London, Triangle SPCK, 1995
Cotter, Jim, *Prayer in the Morning*, Sheffield, Cairns Publications, 1990
Hay, David, *Exploring Inner Space*, Middlesex, Penguin, 1987
Jeff, Gordon, *Spiritual Direction for Every Christian*, London, SPCK, 1987
Kaplan, Aryeh, *Jewish Meditation, a practical guide*, New York, Schocken Books Inc., 1995
Kabat-zinn, John, *Mindfulness Meditation for Everyday Life*, London, Judy Piatikus Ltd, 1994
Kelsey, Morton K., *The Other Side of Silence – a Guide to Christian Meditation*, London, SPCK, 1977
John-Julian OJN, *A Lesson of Love – the Revelations of Julian of Norwich*, London, Darton, Longman & Todd Ltd, 1988
Julian, Dame, *Revelations of Divine Love*, edited by Dom Hudleston, London, Burns Oates, 1952

Main, John, *Word Into Silence*, London, Darton, Longman & Todd Ltd, 1980

de Mello, Anthony, *Sadhana – a Way to God*, India, Gujarat Sahitya Prakash Anand, 1983

Nash, Wanda E., *People Need Stillness*, London, Darton, Longman & Todd Ltd, 1992

Pennington, Basil, *Centering Prayer*, New York, Image Books, 1982

St Teresa of Avila, *Interior Castle*, London, Sheed & Ward, 1974

Traherne, Thomas, *Centuries*, London, Mowbray, 1995

Way, Robert (ed.), *The Cloud of Unknowing*, Wheathamstead Herts, Anthony Clarke, 1986

Titles Enlarging on Part 5 – recognising my self:

Duncan, Bruce, *Pray Your Way – Personality and Myers-Briggs*, London, Darton, Longman & Todd Ltd, 1993

Johnson, Robert, *Inner Work*, San Francisco, Harper & Row, 1986

McGrath, Joanna and Alistair, *The Dilemma of Self-Esteem*, Cambridge, Crossway Books, 1992

Nash, Wanda E., *Turning the Downside Up*, London, HarperCollins, 1995

Nouwen, Henri, *Life of the Beloved*, New York, Crossroad Publishing Co., 1993

Smith, Martin, *A Season for the Spirit*, London, HarperCollins, 1991

Valles, Carlos, *Unencumbered by Baggage*, India, Gujarat Sahitya Prakash Anand, 1987

Vasey, Michael, *Strangers and Friends*, London, Hodder & Stoughton, 1995

Ward, Heather, *The Gift of Self*, London, Darton, Longman & Todd Ltd, 1990
Giving Your Self Away, Grove Booklets No. 26, Nottingham 1988